MacArthur's Escape

MacArthur's Escape

John "Wild Man" Bulkeley and the Rescue of an American Hero

George W. Smith

ZENITH
PRESS

This edition published by Zenith Press, an imprint of MBI Publishing Company, Galtier Plaza, Suite 200, 380 Jackson Street, St. Paul, MN, 55101-3885 USA.

MBI Publishing Company Books are also available at discounts for in bulk quantities for industrial or sale-promotional use. For details write to Special Sales Manager at MBI Publishing Company, Galtier Plaza, Suite 200, 380 Jackson Street, St. Paul, MN, 55101-3885 USA

Cover and Layout by Tom Heffron

ISBN: 0-7603-2176-0

Printed in the United States

As aide to Admiral [Francis W.] Rockwell, I saw John Bulkeley many times, almost daily. Bulkeley was a wild man. Daring, courageous and admirable in many ways but still a wild man. He reminded one, on first glance, of a swashbuckling pirate in modern dress. He wore a long, unruly beard and carried two ominous looking pistols at his side. His eyes were bloodshot and red-rimmed from constant night patrols and lack of sleep, but his nervous energy was tremendous and never seemed to give out. He walked with a cocksure gait, and one could always count on him to raise particular hell with any Jap he met. High-strung, temperamental, brave, and gallant, John Bulkeley was one of the most colorful figures in the Philippine campaign.

——Captain M. M. Champlin

Contents

Preface

The fall of the Philippines in the spring of 1942 was a debacle of the first order. As far as anyone can be sure, about 76,000 men—some 12,000 Americans and almost 64,000 Filipinos—surrendered on Bataan on April 9. It was the greatest capitulation in U.S. military history. A month later, on May 6, another 12,000 troops, most of them Americans, would be forced to surrender the nearby island fortress of Corregidor.

The ensuing Bataan Death March to notorious prison camps some seventy miles north of Manila would become one of the major atrocities of World War II as the Japanese committed a multitude of wanton acts of cruelty and murder on the helpless prisoners.

Of the approximately 70,000 men who started the march, about 54,000 reached Camp O'Donnell, one of the most brutal prison camps in history. No one will ever know the exact death toll, because many of those unaccounted for escaped en route, only to die in another place. Historians believe that 7,000 to 10,000 men died on the march from malaria, exhaustion, starvation, beatings, or execution. Of those dead, about 2,330 were Americans. Thousands more would die at the hands of the Japanese over the next three and a half years in squalid prison camps and as slave labor throughout the Far East.

The Japanese military code forbade surrender under any circumstances, so the enemy regarded prisoners of war (POWs) as disgraced, cowardly criminals, scarcely human. In the Japanese mind, guarding these prisoners was almost as dishonorable as being one. Consequently, the Japanese tended to assign misfits, troublemakers, alcoholics, and even the insane as guards and prison administrators.

The accounts of Japanese cruelty are difficult to comprehend, but they did happen. "[The Japanese] were worse than beasts," according to one survivor. "A beast is an animal, and animals kill only to eat. The Japs killed for fun."

To this day, the Japanese government has not admitted any cruelty, tendered any apologies, or offered any reparations for those who were forced to work as slave labor.

The Japanese actually treated the Filipinos worse than they did the Americans. The propaganda slogan of the Japanese sweep through the Philippines and other areas in the Far East had been one of racial nationalism, but the invaders came on so heavy-handedly that the appeal to ethnic unity didn't work. So they resorted to their old tactics from China—terror, torture, and a horrible death for all in their path.

Word of the savage treatment of the Bataan and Corregidor captives reached the United States in the summer of 1943, when several Americans escaped from a Mindanao prison compound. After making their way to Australia, they reported the atrocities they had endured and witnessed to General Douglas MacArthur and his horrified staff. For a time, Washington delayed publishing their report for fear of Japanese reprisals against American POWs. But by early 1944 newspapers were given the go-ahead to publish the whole dark and dirty story of the death march.

Media coverage west of the Hawaiian Islands, particularly in the Philippines, was almost nonexistent during the first six months of the war. The American press was occupied by the disaster of Pearl Harbor, the mobilization of men and equipment on the home front, and the war in Europe. America's "neglect" of the situation in the Philippines so angered Philippine president Manuel Quezon that he called President Franklin Roosevelt a "scoundrel."

"For thirty years I have worked and hoped for my people. Now they burn and die for a flag that could not protect them," Quezon said to anyone who would listen. "I cannot stand this constant reference to Europe. I am here and my people are here under the heels of a conqueror. Where are the planes that they boast of? America writhes in anguish at the fate of a distant cousin, Europe, while a daughter, the Philippines, is being raped in the back room."

Historian William Manchester, a marine veteran who went ashore on Guadalcanal in the summer of 1942, implied that America didn't try hard enough to rescue the doomed Philippine defenders, writing that the country devoted most of its energies to saving Europe first.

"Hitler was still the prime target," wrote Manchester. "Since the beginning of the stand on Corregidor, German U-boats had sunk 206 ships off the East Coast of the United States, yet convoys were leaving daily for Egypt and England; a bridge of bombers was being thrown across the Atlantic; American GIs had begun landing in Northern Ireland on January 26; and despite the loss of sixty-nine vessels on the Murmansk run, the grim effort to supply the Soviet Union with tanks and munitions was accelerating."

Japan's aggression throughout the Pacific had been swift since its attack on Pearl Harbor on December 7, 1941. Wake Island and Guam fell in a matter of weeks, with Singapore and the Dutch East Indies not far behind. The Japanese met little resistance except in the Philippines, where the outnumbered Allies held out for almost five months without any air or naval support. Lack of food and medicine contributed as much to their eventual surrender as enemy firepower and fresh troops.

Some historians believe that the five-month holdout in the Philippines may have given America the time it needed to repair its shattered fleet at Hawaii, move men and equipment to Australia, and strike back—first in the Battle of the Coral Sea on May 8, then at Midway in early June, and finally the invasion of Guadalcanal by the U.S. Marines on August 7. Additionally, while the Japanese were bogged down in the Philippines, Lieutenant Colonel Jimmy Doolittle was able to lead sixteen B-25 bombers off the deck of the *Hornet* on a surprise raid over Japan in mid April. The raid turned out to be more symbolic than destructive, but the psychological harm to Japan was enormous. It proved that the Japanese homeland was not invulnerable, and it forced the enemy to divert more planes and ships to the home islands to ensure that such a raid would not happen again.

It was clear on the first day of the war that the Philippines was not adequately prepared or properly equipped to counter and then repel a Japanese invasion. Although the U.S. Air Force had learned nine hours earlier of the bombing of Pearl Harbor, practically all of General MacArthur's air force was wiped out on the first day—on the ground.

The reaction to the Japanese attack was slow and confused; a strange paralysis seemed to grip MacArthur's headquarters in Manila. MacArthur had often said he believed that Japan wouldn't be ready to attack the Philippines until April 1942.

Within hours of the Japanese air attack on Clark Field, some sixty miles north of Manila, on December 8, the Allied air commander, General Lewis H. Brereton, offered a plan to fly his B-17s north to bomb Japanese staging areas on Formosa. Brereton was told that MacArthur was in conference and that he (Brereton) was "not to undertake any offensive action until ordered." MacArthur was under orders not to make the first "overt act."

On the eve of war, MacArthur had 35 B-17s (17 of them at Clark); 107 P-40s, some of them early B models; and a handful of obsolete P-35s (35) and P-26s (16) that were assigned to the Philippine Air Corps. For hours following the alert from Pearl Harbor, many of the planes shunted about in confusion. Fighters and bombers were sent aloft on false alarms, hunting mythical Japanese ships and aircraft.

When the Japanese attack on Clark Field came shortly after noon, the enemy caught seventeen B-17s and dozens of fighter planes on the ground, lined up like sitting ducks waiting to be refueled. In one stroke, the Japanese destroyed almost all of MacArthur's air force and won control of the air in the Philippines.

Manchester called the destruction of MacArthur's air force on the ground "one of the strangest episodes in American military history. [MacArthur] was a gifted leader and his failure in this emergency is bewildering. His critics have cited the catastrophe as evidence that he was flawed. They are right; he was."

MacArthur and Brereton share the blame for the disaster. Brereton failed to provide air cover during the lunch hour, with all of his planes lined up and bunched together on the ground. MacArthur, on the other hand, waited too long before ordering Brereton to launch an air strike on Formosa, where the Japanese air attack originated.

With his beleaguered troops six thousand miles away from the nearest supply depot and with much of the American fleet destroyed at Pearl Harbor, MacArthur knew that it was next to impossible to receive reinforcements in the next few weeks. Ever the optimist, however, he naively clung to the remote hope of a relief effort—that is, until he was ordered to Australia by President Roosevelt in early March.

The man who took MacArthur and his family and staff off Corregidor on the first leg of their journey to Australia was navy lieutenant John D. Bulkeley, the hyper-aggressive commander of a worn-out "fleet" of four motor torpedo boats (a PT boat, in navy parlance; a "mosquito" boat, in journalese). The emblem of a mosquito riding a torpedo, which was affixed to all the early PT boats coming off the assembly line, was designed by Walt Disney and was as famous as any military symbol in the war. (See Appendix One.)

MacArthur had great respect for Bulkeley's derring-do reputation during the first three months of the war. MacArthur greatly admired the skill and daring of the man and his powerful little speedboats—so much so that he did not hesitate to trust him with the lives of his wife, Jean, and their four-year-old son, Arthur, on a two-day, 560-mile dash through enemy-patrolled waters to the island of Mindanao. There they would board B-17 bombers for the flight to Australia.

MacArthur was impressed by Bulkeley's toughness and can-do attitude, and the two spent many hours together planning the escape. At a time when the army and navy were often bitter rivals, the close relationship between a legendary sixty-two-year-old army general and a blunt thirty-year-old navy lieutenant was unusual, to say the least.

In the two decades after World War I, the army and navy had clashed repeatedly over the meager funds available for national defense. The army didn't trust the navy, the navy didn't trust the army, and everybody, it seems, was suspicious of MacArthur. When Admiral Thomas C. Hart, commander of the tiny U.S. Asiatic Fleet, stationed in Manila, received a radio message about the bombing of Pearl Harbor, he felt no urgent need to pass the information on to MacArthur.

"It was characteristic of relations between the services that Hart neglected to share this vital information with MacArthur or any other Army officer," Manchester wrote.

The army would get its revenge. When MacArthur decided to declare Manila an "open city" and move his headquarters to Corregidor on Christmas Eve, he conveniently neglected to notify Hart that he was leaving.

"This turn of events was indicative of the less-than-cordial relations between the Army and Navy commanders in the Far East," wrote historian W. G. Winslow. "MacArthur, openly disdainful of Hart and his little

Asiatic Fleet, operated mostly on his own and apparently had no interest in cooperating with his naval counterpart."

One of MacArthur's last acts before leaving the Philippines was to recommend to the War Department that all units on Bataan and Corregidor, with the exception of the marines and the navy, be awarded unit citations. When questioned about leaving out the naval units, MacArthur reaffirmed his directive, reportedly telling one of his aides that he felt that "the marines had won enough glory in World War I."

Indignant Marine Corps and navy officers thought at first that it was an oversight, but they were bluntly told it was not. This was just part of the bitter internecine squabbles that had originated in the Philippines with the personality clash between General MacArthur and Admiral Hart in the prewar days. It was to prove a source of bitterness in later years that too often marred army-navy relationships in the conduct of the Pacific war. Later in the campaign on Corregidor, the relationship between the marines and the army—certainly in the command echelons, less so in the field—could best be described as one of mutual irritability.

MacArthur was a controversial figure, to be sure. Much of the animosity toward him, however, was born of envy. He had risen rapidly since graduating number one at West Point at the turn of the twentieth century. He became the youngest general in World War I, the youngest superintendent of West Point, and the youngest Chief of Staff of the Army. In the latter position he ruled supreme over every military matter in the country during the first half of the 1930s. He controlled the purse strings of both services and was responsible for every promotion and nonpromotion in the upper echelons of the army.

So when Bulkeley became a trusted favorite of MacArthur, some of the navy brass howled behind Bulkeley's back. They called him "MacArthur's errand boy," and worse. One of the favorite aphorisms applied to MacArthur by both services was "God's cousin." Nothing stung more, however, than the nickname "Dugout Doug," which the doomed men of Bataan hung on MacArthur for his reluctance to leave his retreat on Corregidor to visit his men on Bataan.

Just as MacArthur was chided for his love of publicity, Bulkeley was accused of being a "self promoter." That both men were heroic figures, however, is unquestioned.

"Criticism of Bulkeley, a genuine war hero, is difficult to fully comprehend," one historian wrote. "Certainly there was some jealousy or envy among his contemporaries, and Bulkeley's friendship and outright adoration of MacArthur was seen as some kind of anti-Navy bias—almost traitorous."

Both MacArthur and Bulkeley would receive the Congressional Medal of Honor, and the latter's exploits would later be turned into W. L. White's best-selling book *They Were Expendable*, and the hit movie of the same name.

It was the third time that MacArthur had been recommended for the Medal of Honor. He had been nominated in 1915 at Veracruz and again on the fields of France in World War I. Both times, technicalities had kept him from receiving it—the first time because war had not been declared against Mexico, and the second time because the war had just ended, and it was decided not to make the award to any general officer. MacArthur's receipt of the award in 1942 matched a feat achieved by his father, Arthur, who had won the medal for leading a charge of Sheridan's division up Missionary Ridge in the Civil War.

Historians have argued that the junior MacArthur received the medal more as a political gesture than for any heroic action. Furthermore, they assert that the presentation of the medal was arranged to partly counteract negative publicity coming from the Axis powers that labeled him a "deserter" and a "coward" for leaving his troops for the safety of Australia.

Bulkeley would achieve undying glory for a feat that, when written up in the American press, gave the PT boat a glamour somewhat akin to that of a Spitfire in the Battle of Britain, bravely confronting superior odds at a dark moment in the war. Upon his return to the United States in May

1942, Bulkeley was greeted by adoring crowds and a crush of media attention in his native New York City.

MacArthur had been lionized by the media six weeks earlier after his arrival in Australia. An eight-column headline in the March 18 edition of the *New York Times* proclaimed:

> *M'Arthur In Australia As Allied Commander;*
> *Move Hailed As Foreshadowing Turn of Tide*

Washington had hoped to keep MacArthur's arrival secret, but the man couldn't resist the glare of fame. His first-person proclamation of "I Shall Return" became a rallying cry throughout the Far East over the next three years.

The first details of his daring escape (MacArthur preferred calling it an "ordered evacuation") were noted two days later by the same newspaper in a six-inch wire story on page five. Bearing a London dateline, the story read:

> *General Douglas MacArthur's escape by speedboat and plane from the Philippines to take supreme command in Australia will make any story of the war hitherto written look pale by comparison, the News Chronicle's correspondent with the United States troops reported today.*
>
> *The correspondent said that the General, accompanied by his wife, son and staff members, dashed through the Japanese blockade around Bataan Peninsula by speedboat, then flew across a sea of islands patrolled by enemy planes and dotted with warships for more than 2,000 miles.*
>
> *General MacArthur and his party, the dispatch said, assembled on Bataan's dark beach the night of March 11 and cautiously boarded fast motor torpedo boats.*

"These small craft slipped silently out to sea, swung southward and maneuvered into formation," the dispatch said. "Their throttles were opened up, and they tore away."

Their speed was their protection against submarines and before dawn the boats, now far beyond Luzon Island, crept into an inlet where the jungle hid them from view during the daylight.

The next night the dash southward was resumed. Two days later the rendezvous was reached and there began a wait for three days until the planes arrived. The planes came, the party was transferred aboard them, and on March 17 they landed in Australia.

The day the *Times* story ran, President Roosevelt, obviously much relieved that MacArthur had made it through to Australia, regaled the press with his own version of MacArthur's heroic adventure. The president revealed to the media that he had told an unidentified lady dinner guest at the White House the night before that MacArthur "had taken a rowboat, disguised himself as a Filipino fisherman and had passed by lots of Japanese warships, destroyers and submarines, whose personnel never suspected that he was General MacArthur until he had reached the open sea.

"And then," the president continued after pausing for effect, "General MacArthur rowed the 2,500 miles to Australia.

"The lady and some other dinner guests really believed me," the president said with a broad grin as the media broke out in laughter.

This is the true story of that flight to safety.

Chapter One

Back to the Rock

Buster, has this place changed!
——John D. Bulkeley

Approaching the twilight of his distinguished fifty-nine-year navy career, Rear Admiral John D. Bulkeley had come full circle in the summer of 1977 when he set foot on the island fortress of Corregidor for the first time in thirty-five years. During his previous visit to Corregidor, on March 11, 1942, Bulkeley led a group of four PT boats that rescued General Douglas MacArthur, his wife and their four-year-old son, and his staff from the "jaws of death" to win everlasting glory and a chest full of medals.

Bulkeley's career would later take him to Utah Beach during the Normandy invasion and to Cuba in the mid 1960s, when he would outfox Fidel Castro in the latter's attempt to shut down the American base at Guantanamo. But his shining moment came during the dark days of 1942 with the rescue of MacArthur.

In 1977, Bulkeley was midway in his twenty-one-year term as president of the Board of Inspection and Survey (INSURV), a powerful committee that determined whether a ship was "fit for war." Bulkeley's no-nonsense,

tell-it-like-it-is reports ruffled the feathers of more than a few senior officials when he refused to compromise any of his principles that might risk
the safety and security of the navy. Bulkeley was accountable only to the secretary of the navy and the chief of naval operations, and his inspection
reports had ruined many promising naval careers. Any officer who deliberately avoided his team of inspectors did so at his own peril.

Still a "wild man," Bulkeley had become more of a curmudgeon in his
later years. "Rough as a cob" was the way some of his contemporaries
described him. He spoke his mind and didn't care who was listening. One
of America's most decorated warriors, he was both respected and feared
throughout the navy.

Bulkeley traveled to the Philippines several times in his capacity as
president of INSURV, but he had never found the time to revisit
Corregidor. In August 1977, just short of his sixty-sixth birthday, Bulkeley
made another inspection tour of ships based in the Philippines, and this
time he made sure it included a side trip to "the Rock."

Corregidor. Just the name evokes a chilling memory to all who fought
there in the bitter winter and spring of 1942. Trapped without any hope
of escape or reinforcement, the American and Filipino defenders of this
mighty island fortress were doomed to die or be captured in one of the
bloodiest sieges of World War II. Capture, in many cases, would prove to
be a fate worse than death.

Called the "Gibraltar of the East," Corregidor sits just two miles off the
coast of Bataan and about twenty-five miles due west across the bay from
Manila. It is one of some 7,000 islands in the Philippine archipelago, most
of them too small to have names.

The Philippines, with eighteen different dialects, was ceded to the
United States for a fee of $20 million following the Spanish-American War
in 1898. Also becoming U.S. property at the same time were the islands of
Guam and Puerto Rico.

Heavily fortified, Corregidor was the largest of four island forts (Fort

Mills) that guarded the entrance to Manila Bay. Built before the age of air-power, it was believed to be invulnerable.

Three and a half miles in length and one and a half miles at its widest point, the Rock was shaped like a tadpole, its head pointed toward the west and its tail stretched eastward. At the junction of its head and tail, it was only six hundred yards wide. This narrow, sandy, low area—called Bottomside—contained a small village, docks, shops, warehouses, the power plant, and the cold-storage plant. To the west of Bottomside, the promontory rose to a small plateau known, appropriately enough, as Middleside. Here were the hospital and barracks.

Topside was the name of another plateau, the highest point on the island, some 628 feet in elevation. It had a parade ground with officers' quarters, headquarters, and barracks grouped around it. From Topside the cliffs, cut by two ravines, dropped to the sea.

The largest part of the tail end of the island was Malinta Hill, and under it was the most extensive construction on the island—Malinta Tunnel. It was built for storage, not human habitation. Its main tunnel, connecting Bottomside with the tail end of the island, was fourteen hundred feet long, twelve feet high, and thirty-five feet across at its widest point. It had twenty-five laterals, each about four hundred feet long, branching out at regular intervals. Malinta ran almost due east and west. A hospital was housed in its own set of laterals and had an entrance facing north.

The tunnel, which served as General MacArthur's headquarters from Christmas Day 1941 until he left on March 11, 1942, was a dark and gloomy excavation, rife with aromas of unwashed bodies, substandard sanitation, and poor ventilation. Engineers had rigged neon lights; the bluish glow they cast throughout the laterals added to the air of unreality. Naked bulbs created shadows on the stone cave of men working at their desks like bewitched beings. It was a macabre scene.

The air in the tunnels was thick with dampness. Everywhere was the smell of wet rock, like a graveyard. Even in the dry season, the tunnel was hot and foul, and the walls constantly dripped moisture. Ordinary breathing became a chore and coughing could be heard throughout the complex. Many, to include MacArthur, himself, gladly risked leaving the tunnel to enjoy some fresh air and perhaps a smoke, even during enemy air raids.

Each small lateral tunnel was crammed with twenty-eight people, who shared a communal toilet and washbasin. The tunnel housed a crucial communication center, the only place in the Philippines that allowed MacArthur radio contact with both Washington and units scattered throughout the islands.

Corregidor had sixty-five miles of roads and an electric railroad with thirteen and a half miles of track.

Before the war, the island was one of the most beautiful spots in the Philippines. Its roads wound in and out and up and down through luxuriant tropical tangles. Birds were everywhere. The island's high cliffs commanded gorgeous views of deep blue water in every direction. To the east across the wide sweep of Manila Bay lies the capital city, with its gleaming white buildings, starkly visible on a clear day. To the north rise the beautiful green-clad slopes of Mount Mariveles, on the Bataan peninsula, less than three miles across a heavily mined channel.

The westerly winds blowing in from the South China Sea act as a kind of air conditioning, a relief from the stifling tropical heat of the mainland. Corregidor is one of the few places in the Philippines where one can sleep without mosquito netting.

On paper, the armament of Corregidor was awesome. Fifty-six coastal guns ranging in diameter from 3 to 12 inches ringed the island. Two of the 12-inch guns had a range of fifteen miles; there were six 12-inch guns with a range of eight and a half miles and ten mortars of the same caliber. Nineteen other 155mm guns could also reach out to more than nine miles. In the antiaircraft department there were twenty-four 3-inch guns, forty-eight .50-caliber machine guns, and five 60-inch searchlights.

Although there was plenty of ammunition, little of it was of the type suitable for attacking land targets. Still, whoever held Corregidor controlled Manila Bay, for it stuck in its throat like a bone. Corregidor was the gateway to a lovely port of call.

Time-Life correspondent Melville Jacoby wrote that from Bataan the island looked like "a huge, quiescent whale rising from the water's surface."

During a four-week siege of the fortress, from April 10 to May 6, 1942, hardly a square inch of the island was spared from enemy bombs or artillery.

When the Allies returned in February 1945, they faced an enemy determined to die rather than surrender. The battle for Manila, where more than 100,000 civilians were killed in a murderous rampage by the Japanese, was one of the most destructive battles of the entire war. United States airborne forces parachuted onto Corregidor to rout out the Japanese, who fought to the last man.

It was a typically hot and sultry August day in 1977 when John Bulkeley and a dozen members of his staff arrived by helicopter on Corregidor after a thirty-minute flight from Subic Bay. Bulkeley was sweating and his heart was pounding as he stepped from the aircraft onto familiar soil. He felt as though he was in a time warp.

Bulkeley had asked his aide, Bruce Bachman, to bring a wreath along on the visit so he could place it at the foot of a monument to honor the gallant defenders of Corregidor. The Philippine government had erected the monument in 1949.

"For long moments [Bulkeley] stood there, motionless. Tears had welled up in his eyes," Bachman later wrote. "No doubt his thoughts had harkened back to the death, destruction and suffering that had ravaged Corregidor and nearby Bataan."

Bulkeley was oblivious to those around him as he scanned the scene. Bataan, less than three miles in the distance, could be seen clearly. The waters where Bulkeley's PT boats had scurried back and forth through deadly minefields to the mainland were calm, as if they, too, were paying their respects to this hallowed battlefield.

A blue and white passenger bus arrived, according to Bachman's narrative, and took the party to Malinta Tunnel, where MacArthur and others had sought refuge from the daily bombings and shelling some thirty-five years earlier. Absent were the wails of air-raid sirens, the cries of dying men, and the smells of unwashed bodies and raw sewage. Everything seemed to be in slow motion. There was no sense of urgency. One could almost sense the presence of ghosts who were there to welcome the little admiral.

Bulkeley strolled up to the tunnel entrance and, putting his hands on his hips, told an aide: "Buster, has this place changed! General MacArthur and his boys would call this a palace if they could see it today!"

Corregidor had become a tourist attraction for both U.S. and Japanese veterans. Many were quietly roaming the island taking pictures and noting points of interest. Some swore they could hear the ghosts of the island crying out in anguish.

Once inside the tunnel, Bulkeley gestured to where MacArthur's quarters and the hospital had been.

"The entrance was made of concrete, much the same as it is now, but the inside of the tunnel was nothing but rocks in those days," he said.

Quietly, Bulkeley roamed the gloomy tunnels, lost in thought. Several times he stopped and spoke softly to no one in particular.

"Back in through there was where the men with wounds so severe that only miracles could help them were stacked," Bulkeley said, waving his arm. "They'd run out of morphine. There were days when I would come to see General MacArthur and it was nearly impossible to talk for the screaming. You can't forget the screaming. Men, once strong specimens of life, begging for help and something to ease the pain. God, there's nothing worse."

Bulkeley looked quickly away as tears came to his eyes.

"Disheveled, perspiring nurses were constantly at work," Bulkeley said. "Most of them tended patients for seventy-two hours at a stretch. Some nurses keeled over from sheer exhaustion and themselves became patients. [Most] of them were captured."

The last stop was a visit to the pier where MacArthur and his family had boarded Bulkeley's 41 boat for the first leg of his trip to Australia. The pier didn't look anything like it did back in 1942, but Bulkeley recognized it immediately.

"There it is! No question about it! That's where we took off with General MacArthur and his party," Bulkeley said.

Told by a Filipino escort officer that his history book said they left by the South Dock and not the North Dock, Bulkeley quipped: "Your history books are wrong. You'd better have them corrected."

A few moments later, a group of Filipino schoolchildren between the ages of ten and sixteen gathered around Bulkeley, shouting, "Admiral, admiral," obviously excited about meeting the naval hero.

Wrote Bachman, "Visibly moved, Admiral Bulkeley opened his arms and the children encircled him and touched his uniform and body. He had returned, this hero who was part of each Filipino child's history. They had read about this fearless and dashing American naval officer who had waged an unbelievable battle with his wooden boats of lightning, against all odds, in their fathers' and grandfathers' time."

One youngster found in his history book a picture of Bulkeley taken during World War II and excitedly showed it to him. The admiral stared at the photo, then broke into a grin. "I've changed a little," he said.

Continued Bachman, "One at a time, the admiral began autographing the youngsters' books, asking each child his or her name and taking the time to personalize each inscription. After each book was autographed, the youngster shook hands with the admiral, stepped back, and saluted. The admiral returned the salute.

"As we headed back to the bus, Admiral Bulkeley was quiet and thoughtful," Bachman wrote. "Then the man who had been showered with decorations and honors by America, who had walked with presidents, kings and princes, said of his encounter with the Filipino children: 'This is one of my proudest moments.'"

Chapter Two
The Beginning

I learned how to take a punch. We all need to learn that, you know.
———John D. Bulkeley

John Duncan Bulkeley was born in New York City on August 19, 1911. He came from a long line of seafarers. One of his ancestors, Lieutenant Charles Bulkeley, had been second in command of the *Bonhomme Richard*, flagship of Captain John Paul Jones in 1779 during the Revolutionary War. Yet another forebear, Richard Bulkeley, had served as a midshipman aboard British lord Horatio Nelson's HMS *Victory* at Trafalgar in 1805.

Bulkeley's father, Frederick, had served a hitch in the U.S. Navy before the turn of the twentieth century and contracted a severe case of typhoid fever during a port of call in Panama. While hospitalized in New York City, he met and fell in love with one of the attending nurses, Mary "Elizabeth" MacCuaig, a recent immigrant from Scotland. They married on September 1, 1908.

Young John grew up with a fascination for the sea. He would sit spellbound as his father told him of his ancestry, of exotic ports, and navigating by the stars. Often he would fall asleep holding pictures of sailing ships, lost in dreams of high adventure and world travel. Little did he know that all these dreams would someday come true.

By the time he was eleven, John Bulkeley knew for certain that he wanted to attend the United States Naval Academy and spend his life on the sea. Later that summer, Frederick accommodated his son's desires by signing him up for a summer tour as an ordinary seaman aboard the SS *Baracoa*, of the Colombian Steamship Line. He was paid a dollar a day in wages and gained a priceless education in the ways of the sea by sailing throughout the Caribbean.

For three successive summers in the mid 1920s, Bulkeley sailed with a crew that rarely consisted of "red-blooded" Americans. Amid a racially and internationally mixed crew, Bulkeley's white skin and his relatively high level of education made him a standout, whether he liked it or not. Just a teenager, Bulkeley had to grow up in a hurry. To make matters worse, the vessel's captain was a raving alcoholic. The first mate was a former alcoholic, as was the engineer. Luckily, Bulkeley fell under the influence of a master German sailor, who taught him many facets of shipboard life and operation.

"Had this excellent craftsman of the sea not been aboard," Bulkeley said many years later, "only the gods would have seen us arrive at our scheduled ports of call. The captain stayed drunk from departure to arrival and never knew if we were carrying cattle, bananas, or manure for cargo."

Meanwhile, the family had moved out of New York City to Hackettstown, New Jersey. John—powerfully built from summers of hard work aboard cargo ships— excelled as a halfback on the high school football team while remaining focused on a career in the navy. Asked by a teacher what he would like to do after high school, Bulkeley reportedly answered: "United States Naval Academy—and I'll make it!"

Bulkeley had taken the entrance examination for the naval academy during his senior year in high school, but he did only well enough to be designated as "first alternate." That meant he would get in only if the principal designee decided to forgo his appointment. Bulkeley wasn't about to sit around and wait for that to happen.

Still only seventeen, Bulkeley went to Washington, D.C., in the summer of 1928 looking for a legislator to sponsor him to the academy. Finally, he got the ear of Texas congressman Morgan G. Sanders, who had a vacancy because one of his candidates had flunked the entrance examination. Sanders became intrigued when Bulkeley told him that his father owned some land in the congressman's district.

Sanders was impressed by Bulkeley's initiative and determination. He took great delight in telling Bulkeley that he had openings for both Annapolis and West Point.

"Take your pick, Bulkeley, and I'll see what I can do," Sanders said in a slow Texan drawl.

Bulkeley passed the examination and reported to Annapolis the next summer as a plebe and an "instant Texan."

Although Bulkeley was fascinated by the history and architecture of the naval academy, he rebelled against one of its old traditions, hazing, which he found to be unnecessary and cruel.

"We plebes were beaten severely, often with broom handles, for failure to pronounce flawlessly the passages in Reef Points, a large collection of Navy lore and tales," Bulkeley said. "Often the pain was nearly unbearable. Most of this savagery, which had no relation whatsoever to producing top-notch and dedicated Navy officers, was inflicted by a small percentage of first-classmen [seniors]. Three of the first-classmen in the class of 1930 stand out in my mind even today as the cruelest of the whole lot, and they later attained flag rank [admiral]. I do not begrudge their career success, but I damned well hate the manner in which they obtained their personal goals. No doubt, in advancing to the top levels of their profession, these three bastards had often directed their sadistic streaks against junior officers and enlisted men."

There was little that a lowly plebe could do but take it. To object or resist, which rarely happened, would result in the plebe being "bilged" from the academy and sent home in shame. Although the plebe was entitled to appeal, his reporting an upperclassman for such "traditional" behavior would label the accuser as a "squealer" and someone who should be kicked out.

During his first year, Bulkeley was selected at random for a "senseless and brutal" hazing ritual. He endured a beating of more than a hundred blows from a broom handle and fell unconscious. He would remember it for the rest of his life, refusing to attend any of his class reunions in protest.

Other than the hazing incidents, Bulkeley appears to have had a thoroughly good time at the academy. During his four years he answered to several nicknames—"Jack," "Buck," and "Bull" being the most common. Said a passage about him in a book of naval heroes:

> Bull Bulkeley was a Texan and had all the reckless rebellious courage that the word implies, but absolutely no desire to ride a horse. The sea was Bulkeley's choice from the moment he was old enough to decide between ice cream and a chocolate for dessert. He started out in the Merchant Marine and had learned many things most plebes don't know before he came to Annapolis. He was big and handsome and very tough.
>
> You couldn't say that he took his career at the Academy seriously. According to the Lucky Bag [the academy yearbook] he was a versatile and talented disciple of the doctrine of leave and liberty and the pursuits of Cupid and Morpheus. Besides these paramount interests, studies and athletics were strictly non-essential. As a result Bull was graduated so far down the line that he was promptly retired by a Navy that didn't have ships enough to go around.

Required to participate in organized sports, Bulkeley ran cross-country, played a little tennis, and tried out for the boxing team. The latter sport seemed to appeal to his natural instincts.

"I probably didn't have the best left jab in the world, but I sure as hell learned how to connect with a right hook," Bulkeley said. "Never had the reach, but I sure learned the advantages of footwork. But, best of all, I learned how to take a punch. We all need to learn that, you know."

Bulkeley was only five feet eight inches tall and had a stocky, muscular frame. His black hair was already thinning. He had penetrating blue-gray eyes that seemed to mask a fire burning behind them. Though tough on the outside, he was praised by his peers for his fun-loving qualities.

"Bull has little in the way of outward prowess with which to bid for fame," the editor of his yearbook wrote, "yet behind his whimsical smile and steady eyes are the requisites of a seagoing salt and good humor that make delightful company in any society. Friends find him human; enemies can't find him at all; and we find him just right."

In the early 1930s, favoritism was rampant at the naval academy. Midshipmen who were the sons of career men and politicians were "looked after." Being part of the "in group" ensured favorable treatment, the best billeting, and choice assignments. That does a lot to explain Bulkeley's graduation number.

Bulkeley's standing in the class of 1933 was 394 of 431 graduates. He walked up on the stage to get his diploma and a handshake from President Roosevelt. But because of the small navy at the time, only the top 50 percent received commissions. Bulkeley was, in fact, a civilian with a naval academy diploma.

Not one to lie around and feel sorry for himself, Bulkeley applied for and was accepted as a flying cadet by the Army Air Corps. He reported to Randolph Field, in San Antonio, Texas, in the fall of 1933—and was quickly disillusioned. Though he was paid seventy-five dollars a month, he had to endure more senseless hazing. It affected his concentration and almost cost him his life.

"John Bulkeley cracked up an airplane or two at Randolph, and that brought an end to his career as an Army pilot," academy classmate Stanley Barnes said. "Even in those days, John seemed to lead a charmed life, for he walked away from the accidents. Years later he told me that he had gotten a real hard blow on the head in his last crack-up, and felt that ever after he had become a different person."

In March 1934, President Roosevelt recalled to active duty those naval academy graduates who hadn't received a commission. Even though the commissions were "probationary," Bulkeley was elated to be back in his beloved navy. He hoped that he would be assigned to the navy's flight program in Pensacola, Florida. But instead he was ordered to duty aboard the cruiser *Indianapolis* at Provincetown, Massachusetts, in June 1934.

Two years later, Bulkeley would make a name for himself throughout the navy in a most daring—and unusual—way while demonstrating an aptitude for foreign intrigue. Reacting to what he believed was a suspicious situation, he managed to pilfer a briefcase belonging to the Japanese ambassador to the United States while they were both aboard a coastal steamer en route from Norfolk, Virginia, to Washington, D.C.

While the *Indianapolis* was docked in Norfolk, Bulkeley decided to spend a weekend in Washington. Attired in his dress white uniform, he boarded the small steamer and noticed four Japanese men seated at a nearby table. One of them was dressed in formal civilian attire. Even though Bulkeley was told that one of the men was the Japanese ambassador, he thought the four of them might be spies.

Bulkeley asked to be seated next to the men in the hopes of overhearing any conversation. But they spoke only in Japanese. While observing the men, Bulkeley noticed an official-looking briefcase propped against the ambassador's chair. Bulkeley convinced himself that it was his duty to take possession of the briefcase and get it into the hands of the American intelligence community.

"I saw that the Japs at the table had drunk enough tea at dinner to float a battleship. So they would have to use the head during the night, I concluded," Bulkeley said. "The tiny cabins did not have their own heads, so passengers had to use a communal one on deck.

"I did a quick recon to locate the Jap ambassador's cabin, then [for] four or five hours hid in the darkness outside, waiting for him to go to the sandbox. Not long before dawn, it must have been about oh-four-hundred [0400 hours] the ambassador came out and walked down the deck toward the sandbox to heed the call of nature.

"Moments later, I scrambled through the hatch of the Jap's cabin, grabbed his briefcase, and barreled back through the hatch. I slipped along the deck to the stern, and then all hell broke loose. The chief Nip had returned to his cabin and found his briefcase gone. He began screaming and hollering and raising holy hell. Then the other Japs joined in the screaming. The racket was so loud, they no doubt heard it in Tokyo."

While this was going on, Bulkeley quietly slid over the side of the steamer into the chilly Potomac River and, holding the briefcase over his head and out of the water, began to sidestroke toward the Maryland shore. Dripping wet and still attired in his dress whites, he hitchhiked to Washington, where he hid out until Monday morning when the Office of Naval Intelligence would be open.

First thing Monday morning, he put on his now dry dress whites and went to the main navy building. After being directed to an unmarked office, he banged on the door for a full minute until somebody answered.

"Some old gent—he must have been a hundred and six years old and going down for the third time—cautiously opened the door. He was stone-faced, and wearing civilian clothes. I found out later that he was a captain in naval intelligence. He never invited me inside. Merely said 'Yes?' and stood there while I told him of events on the Norfolk-Washington steamer. Then I proudly held up the Jap ambassador's briefcase. The old bastard turned ashen—I thought he was going to faint. Finally, he asked my name, rank, and duty station, then slammed the door shut in my face.

"I was mad as hell and frustrated. Suddenly the door opened again, and the same gent snatched the briefcase out of my hand, told me to report back to the *Indianapolis* immediately, and again slammed the door."

Returning to the *Indianapolis*, Bulkeley was told to report to the captain. He expected to be congratulated for his daring deed. Instead, his skipper gave him a stern look and told him that he didn't want to know any of the particulars of the heist. Bulkeley was told to keep his mouth shut about the incident.

Then, in the next breath, the captain told Bulkeley that he was to settle up his personal affairs and report to the transport USS *Chaumont*, which was docked at Norfolk. It was Tuesday, and the *Chaumont* was to sail for Shanghai, China, on Thursday.

Bulkeley, who hadn't thought to look inside the briefcase, would never learn of its contents.

Chapter Three
Slow Boat to China

On our first meeting, I saw a rather boyish young man
with a zest for life and terrific drive.
——Alice Wood Bulkeley

Bulkeley had a lot of time to think of his daring adventure with the Japanese ambassador on the six-week trip to Shanghai. Though word of his exploit had spread throughout the navy, no one had said anything officially to him, or was anything entered on his record. The navy appeared to have forgotten the incident, and Bulkeley decided to let sleeping dogs lie so he could concentrate on the present.

Though technically assigned as a "passenger" on this slow boat to China, Bulkeley made himself available for as many deck watches as possible, honing his ship-handling and navigation skills to a fine edge. The *Chaumont* skipper grew to depend on Bulkeley's seamanship, assuring the younger man that if he kept his nose clean during his next tour of duty, all would probably be forgotten.

Bulkeley was greatly relieved, and he took the older man's advice to heart.

Arriving in the international city of Shanghai in December 1936, Bulkeley was assigned to the coastal gunboat *Sacramento*, a coal-burning relic from another time. The ship, which could have been the model for the one depicted in the movie *The Sand Pebbles*, was affectionately referred to by navy personnel as the "Galloping Ghost of the China Coast." These were tense times, because China was in the midst of a war with Japan. Keeping in character, the irrepressible Bulkeley didn't sit around and watch all the intrigue going on around him. Perhaps thinking of his exploit with the Japanese ambassador a few months earlier, Bulkeley let it be known that he was amenable to any surreptitious duty the navy saw fit. It would prove to be a life-altering experience for the young ensign.

In February 1937, Bulkeley eagerly accepted an undercover assignment ashore, which in essence made him a spy. He was to dress in civilian clothes, pose as a foreign sightseer or shopper, and disguise a small camera on his person and snap photographs of Japanese armor, artillery, troop concentrations, and warships in the Yangtze River.

Apparently the navy hadn't completely forgotten about Bulkeley's first attempt at espionage on the Potomac.

The Japanese, of course, were on the lookout for suspicious foreigners and made every attempt to thwart them. They put up large signs at their boundaries telling all foreigners that they must "realize that the sentry on duty represented his Imperial Majesty the Emperor of Japan and must bow to him and wish him good morning or good evening."

Bulkeley, refusing to kowtow to anyone, would always cross into the Japanese sector with a wave and a "hi" to the sentry.

"As an American, I was not about to stop and take a deep bow before anyone, especially a Japanese son of a bitch," Bulkeley said. "The guards got used to seeing me, and paid no attention. But one day there was a new boy on the block. This one thought he was truly a Son of Heaven. I gave him my customary wave and 'hi' and he responded angrily by lowering his rifle, pointing it directly at me, and gesturing wildly toward the sign.

"In Pidgin English, he ordered me to bow to him. I said no way. We had a hell of an argument in Japanese and English, and finally a few other Japs showed up and I was hustled off to the Nip jug. There I was defiant as hell. I identified myself as an American naval officer, and told the Nips that we didn't bow to anyone.

"I could not explain away why I had a camera concealed on me, so I was taken to Japanese naval headquarters in Hongkew. There I was confronted by an Admiral Hasgawa, who spoke fluent English and asked me how was 'Tommy Hart.' Hasgawa was an Annapolis graduate as an exchange student, and had been a classmate of my big boss, Admiral Thomas Hart."

Hasgawa asked Bulkeley to get back and bow to the sentry and all would be forgiven, but he refused. After spending the night in the brig, Bulkeley was offered another solution to the problem. If he would write out a thousand times, "I must bow before sentries who represent the Imperial Majesty the Emperor of Japan," he could go. He refused.

After a couple more days, Bulkeley became fed up with the terrible food, dirty water, and bug-infested straw bed in his cell. Appearing before the admiral once again, Bulkeley agreed to write out the sentence a hundred times. When he did, he was released.

The experience planted within Bulkeley a seed of deep hatred of the Japanese, and he vowed to himself that he would get his revenge. It wasn't long in coming.

A few weeks later while on watch aboard the *Sacramento*, Bulkeley intentionally failed to sound the alarm when two Chinese torpedo boats roared up the Whangpoo River straight at Admiral Hasgawa's flagship.

"I stood on the platform of the accommodation ladder and cheered on the Chinese torpedo boats with a 'Go, man, go!' When the boats got opposite Hasgawa's flagship, they turned a hundred and eighty degrees and fired four torpedoes, and at least two of them hit the target. After dawn we could see that the Jap admiral's flagship had sunk—right up to the gunwales in the mud of the Whangpoo River. What a joyous sight! That was my revenge.

"Admiral Hasgawa called on his 'old pal' Admiral Tom Hart to complain bitterly about the lack of warning when the Chinese boats struck. I believe that Hart knew the whole story, but he said nothing."

Another defining moment for Bulkeley occurred on December 12, 1937, when Japanese aircraft deliberately bombed and sank the American gunboat *Panay* on the Yangtze River. The planes then machine-gunned the American survivors floundering in the river not far from where the *Sacramento* was tied up.

When Bulkeley later saw the riddled bodies of the American sailors, something inside him boiled to the surface. Although the U.S. government would accept Japan's official apology, Bulkeley would never forget or forgive what he saw. His hatred of the Japanese became ingrained in his soul.

He also vowed he would never be taken captive by the Japanese.

It wasn't all work and no play for Ensign Bulkeley in China. He took great delight in bedeviling the Japanese at every opportunity. As boarding officer of the *Sacramento*, Bulkeley would often pay surprise courtesy visits to newly arrived Japanese ships, trying to catch them off guard and cause maximum embarrassment and loss of face.

In his later years, Bulkeley loved to tell the story of his greatest triumph, one involving a Japanese warship.

"I headed downstream with all pretense of not boarding this heavy cruiser," Bulkeley said. "I then deftly and quickly headed toward the accommodation ladder. The Japanese always placed two sailors at the foot of the accommodation ladder, and most of their seamen did not wear shoes. But shoes were put on when a 'foreigner' came aboard.

"With the gig made fast, I ran up the accommodation ladder before the officer of the deck could get his side boys together, with their shoes on.

"This situation, much to the embarrassment of the Japanese commanding officer, was intolerable. I entered the commanding officer's receiving area, paid my due respects, and headed for the bow of the ship.

"When I appeared on the quarterdeck, suddenly (to surprise the officer of the deck again!) I was flabbergasted to see the deck officer busy belting all of his side boys with his long glass. To cap the hilarious situation, the mighty Japanese commanding officer of the mighty heavy cruiser gave his flailing officer of the deck a hearty kick in the seat of his pants.

"I beat it down the accommodation ladder before I got a kick in the pants myself. Mission accomplished."

Bulkeley came to know many of the sights in Shanghai very well, from the singles hangout called the Chocolate Shop to the seedy cabarets and bars run by both the Chinese and Japanese. The Chocolate Shop, according to Bulkeley, was a hangout for unmarried women looking for romance, as well as good candy. Many years later, Bulkeley told an audience that just the mention of the place still produces a surge of adrenaline in his body.

"I often catch myself smiling (before Mrs. 'B' catches me, of course!) whenever I pass a candy store today," he said.

One of the most famous places in Shanghai was a strip called Blood Alley, complete with "bars, brawls, booze and broads." The American hangout was the Frisco Bar, a place that Bulkeley had visited a time or two, both on duty and off.

One memorable evening, according to Bulkeley, an American sailor from the *Sacramento* walked into a French bar, picked up an unescorted White Russian woman, and walked across the street to the Frisco Bar. Right behind them came most of the males from the French cafe.

"The American sailors, true to their unspoken vow of free enterprise and the rights to 'true love,' greeted the unwelcomed French counterparts with gusto!" Bulkeley said. "A bloody brawl ensued, and the 'Frenchies' were getting their romantic tails whipped. They called to their fellow Marines for assistance, and all hell broke loose. Shots were fired, and one of the French bastards threw a hand grenade behind the bar! Men and women alike were wounded, but the fight continued.

"As I was the shore patrol officer on duty that night in Shanghai and had been provided with but four enlisted 'patrolmen' to accompany me, I did just what any red-blooded American shore patrol officer would do: my men and I provided emergency assistance to the injured women and let the 'international' sailors fight it out!"

In the fall of 1937, Bulkeley met his wife-to-be, Hilda Alice Wood, called Alice by her family and friends, at a farewell reception aboard the British warship HMS *Diana*, which was to sail for England in a few days. The *Diana* and the *Sacramento* were anchored near each other at Swatow (now called Shantou), a seaport city 180 miles northeast of Hong Kong.

While waiting to board the *Diana*, Bulkeley noticed a group of British civilian guests arriving, particularly one very attractive young woman.

"She caught my eye immediately," Bulkeley said. "Funny, she was the last 'boarder' in her group, as I had been only minutes earlier. I stationed myself as one would at the end of the receiving line, appearing 'official' and involved. Right handily, I captured this beautiful young lady for conversation and the passing of time. Little did either of us know at the time that Miss Alice Wood would soon capture my romantic fancy."

Miss Wood was a British subject who had been born in Swatow, where her father, Cecil, was a port pilot in the employ of Lloyd's of London. He was responsible for escorting merchant ships and later warships through the complex Swatow harbor. The family was surrounded by, and moved within, an entire community of expatriates, many but not all of whom were British. Interestingly, Alice's mother, Emily, was of Japanese-German ancestry. These two nations would become America's most hated enemies.

The Wood household, which included two sisters and a brother, employed some thirty-two Chinese servants, to include a cook and helpers, boatmen, gardeners, upstairs and downstairs maids, houseboys, rickshaw coolies, and nannies, called amahs. The family also had a summer home and a large yacht. An accomplished athlete, Alice excelled in the classroom, too, studying law at a university in Hong Kong.

The attraction between John and Alice was mutual from the beginning, as Alice would later write.

"On our first meeting, I saw a rather boyish young man with a zest for life and terrific drive, with the Navy blue and gold running through his veins," she said. "We talked for hours on our first dates, and I felt he was draining me of all my thoughts and experiences. His courage and strength were very evident to me, and I felt that if ever I was in trouble he would come through for me, or for that matter anyone who called upon him for help. And beneath that rough exterior I came to see a sensitive and compassionate man, one who had been hurt deeply, and one who did not intend to be hurt again. This made for the complexity of the man I came to know, admire, and love."

The course of true love ran into some choppy water several months later when Bulkeley went to ask Alice's father for her hand in marriage. Much to Bulkeley's shock, the old man would not give him his blessing, stating that he would not permit his daughter to marry an American naval officer.

That situation changed over the course of time, according to the Bulkeley's oldest daughter, Joan Bulkeley Stade, who wrote lovingly of her parents in a book published in 2001.

"The Woods were just as fond of John as he was of Alice," Stade wrote. "Cecil could get lost in conversation about the sea as John recounted tales of his Caribbean travels aboard a Colombian freighter when he was only twelve. Cecil knew John could be Alice's way out of this tumultuous situation, which was deteriorating quickly."

John and Alice often took bike rides through Swatow, photographing some of the destruction and atrocities being committed by the Japanese. The situation in Swatow and other Chinese cities along the coast was tense and getting tenser.

Wood offered to give the couple a formal wedding dinner, but Alice explained that as a navy wife she could not go to a war zone while her husband's ship was on duty there; thus a trip for her and her husband together to Swatow was out of the question. Cecil consoled his daughter in a letter, saying he thought it was "positively an utterly absurd idea of an antediluvian American Admiralty to discipline naval wives." He was clearly concerned that his daughter would become just another woman enjoyed by a sailor and left alone in a hotel room with promises of married life.

After a year's courtship, the pair was married on November 10, 1938, by a judge at the American consulate in Shanghai. No one from either family was able to attend the wedding, but John did send his new father-in-law a cable to confirm that he and Cecil's daughter had been legally married.

"If the ceremony was not what Alice had expected, the honeymoon was to be an even greater surprise and shock," Stade wrote. "After the ceremony, the Bulkeleys caught a launch from the former Standard Oil dock along with several young Marines to the *Sacramento.* They boarded the ship just as dinner was being served and dined in the wardroom with the other officers. The meal was simple. Wedding cake and champagne were not on the menu for the evening."

More surprises were to come. After dinner John told her that he was unable to switch assignments that night and would have to stay aboard as duty officer. Alice took the news stoically. Their "first night together" would actually be spent apart.

John and a few of his shipmates escorted Alice ashore to a large abandoned house that was formerly the residence of the Shanghai manager of Standard Oil. Marines were patrolling the area. They walked around to the back of the house and went down some stairs to a basement apartment.

Alice remembered the room as being fairly clean, with cement floors, a small cot, and one light. It had a tiny washroom. The cot, she said, had clean sheets on it.

"It looked kind of bleak and cold and I shivered," Alice recalled many years later. She also noticed that none of the officers was joking around as they had through dinner.

Alice stood in the middle of the room wearing the suit she had been married in and holding her pocketbook. The other officers quietly filed out of the room and walked up the stairs. Her husband of just a few hours hung back to say good night.

John gave his new bride a big hug and a kiss, then handed her his .45-caliber service pistol. As he put the gun into her hand, Bulkeley casually said to her: "You may need this." She put it under her pillow and tried to go to sleep. Never before had she held or shot a pistol.

Early the next morning John showed up and took her to the ship for breakfast. That afternoon the two went on a brief honeymoon in Shanghai that had its share of excitement. According to Alice, John brought a BB gun with him and took great delight in shooting Japanese soldiers in the backside from the window of their hotel room, then watching them look around to see where the shot had come from.

Shortly after the wedding, Alice's father wrote her a warm letter offering his heartfelt congratulations.

"It is true the manner of your marriage gave us somewhat of a shock—our misfortune, of course, of being old-fashioned—still, if you have found happiness it doesn't matter greatly one way or another that something of dignity, solemnity and sanctity was missing from it."

Chapter Four
The Mosquito Fleet

I couldn't wait to sink my heart and soul into the program.
——John D. Bulkeley

On December 26, the *Sacramento*, badly in need of a complete over-haul, was ordered back to the United States. Dependents were not allowed to follow the ship but had to return directly to their American homes. Alice, still a British citizen, had no American home and had to remain behind temporarily until John reached the States and could send for her. She stayed with a married sister in Hong Kong. She would also have an opportunity to say good-bye to her parents before the Japanese closed in on Swatow. As it turned out, she would never see her father again.

The *Sacramento*'s journey westward would take five months and cover some 18,000 miles. There were fourteen stops, which provided Bulkeley with a wealth of worldly experience. The ship visited Hong Kong, Manila, Singapore, Malay, Ceylon, Bombay, Arabia, Egypt, Naples, Marseilles, Gibraltar, the Azores, and Bermuda before finally docking at the Brooklyn Navy Yard on May 27, 1939.

Bulkeley received an official commendation for his performance of duty as engineer officer on the trip home, as well as a promotion to lieutenant, junior grade. His experience and leadership abilities were noted. Throughout the arduous voyage, only three officers had been permitted to stand as officer of the deck during any of the special operations, such as entering and leaving port and traversing uncharted waters: the skipper, the executive officer, and Bulkeley.

While war raged on in Europe, the Bulkeleys set up a residence in Long Island City, New York. John marked time with engineering duties until January 1940, when he was reassigned to the carrier *Saratoga*, which was undergoing repairs at the Bremerton (Washington) Navy Yard. The assignment would rekindle his love of flying and a need for action.

Fate then stepped in and changed his life. On his way to his assignment to flight school at Pensacola, Florida, in February 1941, he made a brief stopover in Washington, D.C., where he heard about the navy's new motor torpedo boat program that was looking for bright, aggressive junior officers. It would be an opportunity to command.

Bulkeley had been in the navy long enough to know that you don't turn down such offers if you wish to be promoted and have a long career. Besides, Bulkeley loved the sales pitch. The PT boats, as they were called, were the navy's hot-rodders, dashing and swerving and attacking at high speed. They required the physical strength and devil-may-care attitude of very junior officers. Nobody else could handle them.

Bulkeley was hooked. Within a week he was reassigned to the Brooklyn Navy Yard, where he would begin testing the navy's newest weapon.

"Whatever in the hell these PTs were, [they] captured my imagination. I couldn't wait to sink my heart and soul into the program," Bulkeley said.

On February 20, 1941, Bulkeley took command of Motor Boat Submarine Chaser Squadron 1. The unit consisted of six experimental PT boats that were specially equipped to detect then sink enemy submarines with gunfire or depth charges. These prototype boats were seventy feet long and twenty-five feet wide. Powered by three twelve-cylinder Packard marine engines that burned high-octane aviation fuel, with each engine rated at 1,200 horsepower, the boats were designed to make better than forty knots at full war load if properly maintained. Because of the wear and tear of the powerful engines, overhauls were recommended every 600 hours.

Each boat could carry 3,000 gallons of 100-octane gas. Weaponry on the early boats included four 18-inch (diameter) torpedo tubes, which were used in World War I, and a pair of twin .50-caliber machine-gun turrets. There was no armor plate, and the gunners stood in the open to fire their weapons.

Bulkeley quickly saw the glamour of these little boats, and he also saw the danger. They were highly vulnerable to air attack and were, in effect, designed for nocturnal hunting. He knew that on a PT boat there was very little room for error. One false move could lead to total destruction. The boat's effectiveness was more reminiscent of the close-action skirmishers in the age of sail than long-range engagements in the age of steam.

The U.S. Navy had been shopping around for a rugged, dependable PT model since the late 1930s and finally settled on a seventy-foot British model designed by Hubert Scott-Paine that was partially constructed of plywood. It was powered by three Rolls-Royce Merlin aero engines totaling 3,000 horsepower. Initial armament of the British-built boat consisted of two 21-inch or four 18-inch torpedo tubes plus two 20mm antiaircraft guns and one 25mm gun in power-operated turrets. Its biggest strength was its rugged construction and maneuverability in heavy seas.

The prototype boat arrived in New York as deck cargo on September 5, 1939, and was designated as PT-9 by the Electric Boat Company (Elco), the boat's licensee in the United States. Testing in Long Island Sound failed to impress the U.S. Coast Guard, but the navy was thoroughly sold on the craft. It was at this point that Charles Edison—the interim secretary of the navy since Claude Swanson's death in July and the son of the famed inventor—made the single most controversial decision in the entire PT development saga. Instead of merely building one or two boats based on Scott-Paine's design, to test alongside the other eight experimental boats then undergoing construction, he hoped to build enough boats for two squadrons. By doing so, he sought, with one swift stroke, to take the PT program beyond the experimental to the operational, to the point where a single proven type suitable for operations with the forces afloat would be mass produced.

Edison had $5 million to spend—enough, said Elco, to build sixteen boats. The navy wanted twenty-four boats to form two squadrons: twelve submarine chasers (PTCs number 1 through 12) and twelve PTs (number 10 through 20, with the twelfth boat to be PT-9).

Elco agreed to build twenty-three boats and, with hopes for future business, earmarked $700,000 to expand its plant in Bayonne, New Jersey. All twenty-three boats would be identical to PT-9, except 1,200-horsepower Packard engines would be substituted for the original Rolls-Royce engines. The navy officially awarded Elco the contract on December 7, 1939.

The deal set off a firestorm of protest from the American boat-building industry, which understandably felt that its prestige had been dealt a severe blow. Many were outraged by the deal, not only because a British-designed boat instead of an American one was being mass produced but because no competitive bidding had taken place.

Meanwhile, the program ran into unexpected delays. Elco engineers found the Scott-Paine blueprints to be inadequate, which forced them to rely on PT-9 as a working model. By the time the first of the new 70-footers joined the fleet in November 1940, they were already obsolete. These boats were originally designed to carry four 18-inch torpedo tubes, to take advantage of a surplus of World War I 18-inch torpedoes. It was decided to upgrade the torpedoes to 21 inches, which meant that future boats would have to be bigger, 77 feet instead of 70 feet. The newer boats would also have four .50-caliber machine guns in two twin turrets. These latter boats began arriving in the fleet in June and July 1941; most of the 70-footers, including the original PT-9, were sold to the British under the Lend-Lease program in the spring of 1941.

One of the most interesting aspects of the PT's construction was the use of plywood surrounding the wheel and bridge area. The hull consisted of two layers of one-inch mahogany planking laid over laminated wood frames, which were fastened with thousands of Monel screws. A layer of airplane fabric, impregnated with marine glue, was ironed on between the two layers of planking. The result was a light, strong hull—one that was resilient enough to stand up in heavy seas. The hulls were built upside down on an assembly line, which made it easier to fasten the screws.

The new and improved 77-footers that came off the assembly line early in the summer of 1941 weighed forty-six tons and drew five and a half feet of water. Operating at full power, they were a sight to see, throwing a huge wake to each side and a huge rooster tail aft, which looked like a giant scarf blowing in a strong wind. In the coming war, the Japanese would come to call them "devil boats." Other members of the U.S. Navy and the public would come to affectionately call them the "Mosquito Fleet" or "Stinger Fleet." The press would also come up with some colorful names for these doughty warriors, the best of which were "Spit Kids," "Water Wasps," and "Jap Slappers."

In typical fashion, Bulkeley dove into his new assignment with all the gusto he had. His orders were to see what these new boats could do and what sorts of men were needed to handle them. A war was under way in Europe, and he felt it was only a matter of time before America would have to deal with the Japanese in the Pacific.

Commented Robert R. Green, who joined Bulkeley's outfit in the spring of 1941, "Things were very confused in the new PT-boat service. No one really knew what he was doing. Bulkeley was always hopped up on security. To some extent, there was good reason for concern about sabotage to the PT-boats, for there were plenty of pro-Nazi types around New York harbor. He often got us out on the dock and gave us demonstrations and lectures on how to approach a suspected saboteur or spy. We held anti-sabotage drills, and Bulkeley would go out at night and try to creep up on guards without being detected. I'm sure other people at the Brooklyn Navy Yard thought we were nuts."

In early March, Bulkeley took four of the prototype 70-footers on a shakedown run to Key West and back. The boats were equipped with sonar devices attached to their hulls. By the time they reached their destination, all four of the devices had been torn from the hull by pounding waves, disappearing forever into the choppy sea. Even when operational, however, the sonar devices didn't work. When the boat was under way, the noise of its engines drowned out the echoes of the sound equipment. If the engines were shut off and the boat was laying to in anything but a dead calm, it developed such a short, sharp roll that it could not pick up the echoes. These boats were also to be sent to the British under the Lend-Lease agreement.

Bulkeley decided to give the boats and men a hard test run on the 1,300-mile trip north, operating under full throttle much of the way. Typical of a Bulkeley operation, the trip was not without adventure.

Pulling into Norfolk, Virginia, to refuel, the boats were unwittingly moored by their crews in front of Admiral Ernest J. King's quarters. The crews, exhausted after a full day of fighting heavy seas, were lounging on deck eating cold sandwiches and drinking warm Cokes. They were wet, dirty, and unshaven, and most were dressed in dungarees and oil-stained T-shirts.

The sight didn't go unnoticed. King's flag lieutenant marched down to the dock and, adjusting the high collar of his dress whites, told Bulkeley: "Admiral King wants you to report to him immediately—in the uniform of the day." That meant dress whites.

Bulkeley knew that his crews looked like a band of pirates, and he knew of King's famous temper. In addition, he hadn't brought a dress white uniform with him on the trip. What to do? Because the aide had neglected to get his name, Bulkeley decided to make a run for it, telling his men: "To hell with that old bastard King."

A year later, King, then the commander in chief of the U.S. fleet, would nominate Bulkeley for the Medal of Honor.

Shortly after the remaining 70-foot prototype boats were shipped to England, Bulkeley was given another command with the brand-new 77-foot PT boats. He set out to stock his unit with the best men he could find. Thanks to the test runs made to the Caribbean, Bulkeley realized that he needed a special kind of sailor, one who could take the punishment of riding heavy seas as well as think fast and sail even faster.

Related Henry J. Brantingham, "After the subchaser squadron was dissolved in New York, Bulkeley went to its officers and men, seeking volunteers for a new PT-boat squadron that was to be deployed in 'an exciting secret place.' This approach produced sufficient eager volunteers, including myself," said Brantingham.

Bulkeley was full of enthusiasm and needed little encouragement to accept his new assignment. He had fallen in love with the little speedboats. He loved the power of the boats as they rode high atop the waves at full throttle, smashing through the whitecaps. He later said he felt like a jockey hanging on to a bucking bronco. One of the crew members described the boats as usually running like nervous horses with a trembling all over and the muscles seeming to bulge out into you as you rode it. Bulkeley told his new volunteers that serving in a PT-boat unit was a very personal experience, one that was filled with danger.

There were only three squadrons of PT boats in the U.S. Navy in the late summer of 1941. Squadron 1, with twelve boats (numbers 20 to 30 and 42), were shipped out for duty at Pearl Harbor on August 13; Squadron 2 (boat numbers 36 to 40 and 43 to 48) continued training in the New York area preparing for assignment to Panama after the war began.

In early August, the navy created Squadron 3 (actually a half squadron of six boats (31 to 35 and 41) from the remaining 77-footers for a rapid deployment to the Philippines. Bulkeley, not yet a full lieutenant, was given command. He had been conducting intensive rough-water training for several weeks off the tip of Long Island. The boats came equipped with four 21-inch torpedo launchers and two pairs of .50-caliber machine guns in power turrets. Later, two .30-caliber automatic weapons on fixed mounts were installed on the forward deck, giving the boats the hardest punch per ton of any ship in any navy.

It was Bulkeley's job to see what each of the boats could take. He had to train six crews and get them ready for a combat deployment overseas. In late July, a test speed run by ten boats, including two (boats 31 and 33) that would become part of Squadron 3, was conducted in the open Atlantic off Long Island. The course began off Groton, Connecticut, then ran around the east end of Block Island and around the Fire Island lightship to a finish line at Montauk Point's whistling buoy. Two of the boats finished with best average speeds of 39.72 and 37.01 knots. Over a measured mile, the boats averaged 45.3 knots with a light load and 44.1 knots with a heavy load.

A second so-called "plywood derby" was held on August 11 and 12, when the PTs raced against the destroyer *Wilkes*. With seas running at eight to fifteen feet, the little boats took a pounding. Most of the time they were out of sight in the trough of the huge waves or hidden by flying spray. The destroyer won the race, but the navy board had been impressed by the sea-worthiness of the tough little PT boats and decided to proceed with their construction and deploy them as soon as possible.

What Bulkeley didn't know was that the destination of his six boats had already been decided.

General MacArthur had become a big fan of the PT boat. He believed that a relatively small fleet of such vessels, manned by crews thoroughly familiar with every foot of the Philippine coastline and surrounding waters and carrying—in the form of a torpedo—a definite threat against large ships, would be a compelling reason for any hostile force to proceed cautiously and think twice about employing small detachments.

When MacArthur heard that the United States was sending this type of boat to Great Britain as part of the Lend-Lease program, he pleaded with the navy to send some of them to the Philippines. The navy agreed to send six boats as soon as they could and another six in a few months when they had completed testing.

By August, Bulkeley said his crews were ready for deployment. Each crew consisted of two officers and ten to twelve enlisted men. They had grown close in a short time and built a fine esprit de corps, according to Bulkeley.

All of the officers and most of the senior enlisted crew were hand picked by Bulkeley. Five of the twelve officers of Squadron 3 were graduates of the United States Naval Academy, and three others had attended the school but dropped out. Besides Bulkeley (class of 1933), the other Annapolis graduates were the executive officer, Lieutenant Robert B. Kelly (1935), as well as Lieutenant (j.g.) Edward G. DeLong (1937), Lieutenant (j.g.) Vincent E. Schumacher (1938), and Ensign Henry J. Brantingham (1939). All five would serve stints as a boat captain along with Ensigns Barron W. Chandler, Anthony B. Akers, and George E. Cox, Jr. The other officers included Ensigns Bond Murray, William Plant, Cone Johnson, and Iliff Richardson.

Bulkeley was promoted to full lieutenant on September 2, 1941, retroactive to May 1, 1941. Kelly was promoted to the same rank that fall.

Kelly, a tall, sandy-haired native of New York City, was a lot like Bulkeley in temperament and toughness. A hard worker and aggressive on the water, he had commanded a subchaser squadron before Bulkeley appeared on the scene. Kelly would prove to be an excellent choice as second in command.

In high school in New Britain, Connecticut, Kelly had run track and loved the stage, appearing in several plays. During his junior year he was awarded the Harvard Book Prize, given to the outstanding student in each class. He was certified for acceptance to Annapolis in his senior year.

"His heart is like the sea," proclaimed the caption of his 1931 high school graduation picture, which ended with a rather grim farewell that read: "Goodbye, Commodore. See you at the bottom of the ocean, some day."

Kelly made a name for himself at the naval academy as a member of the boxing team and for his sociable qualities.

"And in this corner, ladies and gentlemen, we have Battling Bob, the Behemoth of the Bronx," his yearbook noted. "As a disciple of [coach] Spike Webb, Bob has become a hard man to put down (with fist, bull or bottle)—Bob's a ladies' man, the women may be the ruin of him yet."

Kelly was to have a flirtatious interlude with a nurse in the Philippines that was innocently depicted in W. L. White's *They Were Expendable*.

Several of the non-academy graduates, including Cox and Richardson, were selected by Bulkeley because of their experience and maturity. Cox, called "Bud" by his friends, had served in the American Volunteer Ambulance Corps in France in 1940 and received the Croix de Guerre. A good-looking, yellow-haired youngster, he grew up in Watertown, New York, where he learned to race speedboats on the Saint Lawrence River.

Richardson, who had dropped out of college in California, had an urge to travel and see the world. He toured extensively in Europe and the Middle East as war erupted in that part of the world. He returned home and immediately joined the navy, graduating from officer candidate school in early 1941.

Richardson would distinguish himself as a guerrilla fighter, helping pave the way for MacArthur's return to the Philippines in late 1944.

On August 16, 1941, Bulkeley watched as his six little boats were loaded aboard the oil tanker *Guadalupe* at the Brooklyn Navy Yard, along with nine extra engines and all the spare parts he could get his hands on.

The tanker steamed out of New York harbor three days later, heading south toward the Panama Canal. Then they would head straight to Hawaii, where, after a few days' rest, the ship would resume its westward track.

Just before reaching the Panama Canal, Bulkeley called the men together and gave a stirring talk about where they were going and what to expect.

"We were sure we were going to be in the war, but he called us together and told us we were going on a suicide mission," remembered Machinist's Mate First Class John Tuggle, who was later assigned to Bulkeley's 41-boat. "He warned us that some might not come back, so anyone who wants to back out now go ahead. No one backed out, not a single man."

Tuggle was one of the tough old veterans of the squadron, quiet by nature but an expert on the Packard engines. He had grown up in Lynchburg, Virginia, a shoe-factory town in the central part of the state, and quit school in the sixth grade after his parents died. He was one of seven children. After a couple of years working in the Civilian Conservation Corps, he joined the navy in 1936 when he was twenty years old. His friends told him that the navy would never take him because of his lack of education. They were wrong.

"I guess they wanted some nutty guys, so they took me," Tuggle said in a 2003 interview. "I had been doing crazy things all my life. I didn't [worry much] danger in those days. I was raised near bootleggers and moonshiners and as a kid I used to swing across rivers on vines—like I was Tarzan."

Tuggle left the navy when his first hitch was up in 1940, but his leave-taking lasted only two months. He knew that war was coming, so he reenlisted; in early 1941 the navy sent him to school at Elco in Bayonne, New Jersey, to learn about PT boats and the Packard engine. When Bulkeley's squadron was formed in the summer of 1941, Tuggle volunteered.

The Pacific crossing was uneventful, according to Tuggle. There were no movies. Some of the men played cards or read. Some wrote letters. There were a few drills; the men were ever mindful that they were riding a tanker carrying a million gallons of gasoline.

Bulkeley conducted "skull sessions" every day with the men aboard the *Guadalupe* on PT-boat strategy and tactics. There was no book to read on the subject. These men would be the first to deploy PT boats in combat and would, in effect, write the book.

By the time the boats arrived in Manila on September 28, Bulkeley and his crews were itching for action.

Chapter Five

Pearl of the Orient

Oh, the monkeys have no tails in Zamboanga,
Oh, the monkeys have no tails in Zamboanga,
Oh, the monkeys have no tails,
They were bitten off by whales,
Oh, the monkeys have no tails in Zamboanga.

Life was good in Manila in the early 1940s—so good, in fact, that there was a waiting list for duty there. For many, an assignment to the "Pearl of the Orient" was a two-year vacation with pay in a tropical playground.

For the Americans who lived and worked in the Philippines, that island archipelago was like India to the British: a hot and enervating land rich in servants and other amenities of colonial life. It was a land where living was opulent yet cheap.

Many of the soldiers and sailors employed servants. A captain and his wife could hire a staff of four, and even a lowly private, on his pay of $21 a month, could employ a Filipino to polish his boots, buff his brass, and make his bed for only $1.50 a month. For an extra dollar a month, the Filipinos would do all the KP duties that an enlisted man might draw.

"It took us no time at all to find that life was impossible without a battery of servants to wash our clothes, make our bunks, keep our shoes polished, and fetch tall cool drinks at our beck and call. All these services were available to us for a few cents a day," wrote Lieutenant Edgar Whitcomb, a B-17 navigator who arrived at Clark Field on Luzon in early November 1941.

Manila was a major, bustling port of call, with a population of some 625,000 people. Located on Luzon, the largest island in the Philippines, it was a city of ancient nunneries and chrome-fronted nightclubs, of skyscrapers towering over nipa shacks, of antiquity and modernity. Lovely acacia trees shaded broad Dewey Boulevard, which ran along the bay.

Filled with ships from all over the world, Manila's deep, clean harbor made it a popular cruise stop. One could find an unlimited variety of merchandise at prices so low that it was a shopper's paradise, even for the poorly paid American soldier.

The city was a curious and thrilling blend of the old and the new, of the East and the West. There were modern buildings and wide boulevards crowded with automobiles cheek by jowl with Filipino tribesmen in native dress and farmers with ox-drawn carts. There was even an exotic smell to the place, at once refreshing and nauseating, a pungent mixture of jasmine, burning incense, garbage, and sewage.

There were more horse-drawn carriages (called *carromatas*) than automobiles on the crowded, dirty streets, and the thousands of undersize taxis seemed literally to pump themselves along with their horns. Wrote Lieutenant Whitcomb, the horn seemed to be by far the most important part of the vehicle as the taxi driver pushed madly across town, "honk! honk! honking! his way along the old part of the city."

On the streets in the early hours of the morning, the pride of Uncle Sam's navy could frequently be seen sitting in the driver's seat of a *carromata* racing down the boulevard, the Filipino driver holding on for dear life in the passenger seat.

Many of the local businesses catered to American tastes. Frozen beef was shipped in from Australia and sold for an affordable seventeen cents a pound. All the latest American movies played at theaters throughout the city.

Though it had a strict Catholic culture, Manila offered a variety of exotic nightlife and beautiful women to rival those of any city in the Orient. Although fraternization was discouraged, it flourished throughout the islands. One of the popular refrains of the day went like this:

> *Roses are red and violets are blue,*
> *My girl's brown, what's it to you?*

Prostitution was a family business, aided and supported by the hordes of taxi drivers.

"You want a very beautiful girl, Joe?" they would ask over and over. "She is very beautiful and very clean. Only two pesos [one dollar]."

But the girls were neither beautiful nor clean. The houses of prostitution were nothing more than Filipino homes with mother, father, and all the rest of the relatives sitting around the living rooms where the bargain was made for girls as young as fourteen to fifteen years of age.

Wrote Whitcomb, "It was rumored about Manila that the V.D. rate for the men on a two-year tour reached 130 percent, which meant that the average soldier should expect to have the 'scourge' one and one-third times during his stay in the islands."

There were even American nurses stationed in the islands, about a hundred of them. All were volunteers who dreamed of adventure and romance—and weren't disappointed.

It was a halcyon life: cocktails and bridge at sunset, white jackets and long gowns at dinner, good gin and Gershwin under the stars. At Fort McKinley, seven miles south of Manila, a streetcar ferried people between the post pool, the bowling alley, the movie theater, and the golf course. Life was so easy that some of the officers joked about "fighting a war and a hangover at the same time."

The only disadvantage to duty in the Philippines was the climate. Only fourteen degrees above the equator, Manila was steamy and humid most of the year. Between July and October, more than 150 inches of rain fell. The moisture permeated everything, causing short circuits, fungus, mildew, flash flooding, and disease. Because of these conditions, a tour of duty in the Philippines was generally limited to two years.

Only one American combat unit was stationed in the islands. The 31st Infantry Regiment was known as the Polar Bears for its distinctive patch, which displays a white polar bear. The regiment was also referred to as the "Thirsty First" for its reputation as heavy drinkers, with its members called *dhobie* soldiers, a Tagalog word meaning they had "gone native" and were a little "wacky." The 31st was a curious mixture of the best and worst of the U.S. Army, as was the large American adviser cadre that was assigned to the Philippine units. Many of the American career officers and noncommissioned officers (NCOs) had grown soft between the wars. And because Manila was the farthest duty post from the States, the Philippines often became a kind of dumping ground for the army's misfits, troublemakers, and short-timers.

The workday began at 7 a.m. and ended at noon for both officers and enlisted men. The afternoon sun was thought to be much too hot for any military activity. Instead, the soldiers went swimming, played some golf, or took naps.

The cocktail hour, or "calling hour," began at 5 p.m. and lasted until 7 p.m. Scotch was the favorite beverage. Another favorite was "rum-gum-and-lime," a concoction of rum, lime juice, and sugar syrup. These were happy times to relax among good friends.

After the calling hour and dinner, it was time for the parties. There were many—often held at NCO and officers' clubs on post or at the Army-Navy Club in downtown Manila, which overlooked the bay and its gorgeous sunset. These were gala events, with live bands, dress uniforms, yards and yards of taffeta, and a great deal of booze. Some of the bachelor officers ended the evening on "drunkard's row," a long row of cots on the second-floor veranda of the club.

These were golden days—these days of empire in the winter of 1940–41—days in which the poorly paid professional army lived a life of ease, luxury, glamour, and fun. It wasn't to last, however.

The first big change came when the army sent the dependents home starting in the spring of 1941. The end of family life brought a sense of crisis to the Philippine garrison, a feeling that time was rapidly running out. A spirit of urgency was in the air, and the mood turned serious. Workdays no longer ended at noon, and the men found themselves conducting training exercises even in the heat of the midday sun.

"The sparkle went out of Manila in the spring of 1941," wrote General Jonathan Wainwright. "War was coming and we all knew it."

Dan Crowley was typical of many army recruits who wound up in the Philippines in the spring of 1941. He and a couple of his buddies from Greenwich, Connecticut, all high school dropouts, were looking for adventure. "How about the Philippines?" a recruiting sergeant asked them. "Why not?" they answered.

"We were told that it would be a two-year enlistment and if we didn't like it after one year, we could buy our way out of the Army and return home," Crowley said. "We looked upon it as kind of a cruise vacation."

Crowley had a terrible feeling when his ship, the USS *Grant*, left New York harbor and headed out past the Statue of Liberty. "I knew right away that I had made an awful mistake and that there was nothing I could do about it," said Crowley, who would spend almost three and a half years in Japanese prison camps.

The ship stopped in North Carolina to pick up some National Guard troops, then made its way to Panama, where the men had a short but enlightening liberty.

"The Military Police all wore pistols strapped to their hips like western gunslingers and were selected for their ignorance, size, and brutality,"

Crowley said. "They looked like they had a license to kill. The ranking sergeant was like the character Fatso in the movie *From Here to Eternity*."

The ship next visited San Francisco, but the recruits on board were allowed to debark only on nearby Angel Island. In Hawaii, they spent ten days in tents pitched around Hickham Field and never did get to sample the delights of Honolulu or Pearl City. The next stop was Guam, an island renowned for its brothels and rum factory. A much-needed liberty was enjoyed by all.

When the ship finally arrived in Manila in early March 1941, Crowley found out he had been assigned to the 17th Pursuit Squadron. The men were trucked to nearby Nichols Field, where they set up camp in tents.

"The heat was overbearing and bugs crawled over everything," Crowley remembered. "It was a low point. I wasn't a very happy camper."

Crowley and his mates never had any boot camp. They didn't know how to salute, march, or fire a weapon. And none of them knew anything about pursuit planes. "We were a bunch of incompetent, ill-trained warm bodies," Crowley said.

That wasn't the case with the pilots and NCOs, according to Crowley. The commanding officer of Crowley's 200-man squadron was Lieutenant Boyd "Buzz" Wagner, who became the war's first ace, shooting down five Japanese planes in the first week.

Asked what his duties were for his first few months in the Philippines, Crowley said he spent a couple of hours every day "wiping the wings of the planes."

With war looking more and more inevitable, President Roosevelt recalled Douglas MacArthur to active duty on July 26, 1941. MacArthur, who had retired as Chief of Staff of the Army in 1935, had gone to the Philippines the following year to become a military adviser, with the rank of field marshal, in President Manuel Quezon's new government. Congress had given the Philippines Commonwealth status in 1934 with the promise of complete independence in 1946.

Roosevelt, among others, openly encouraged MacArthur to take the job, partly as a means of distancing him from the American political scene. During MacArthur's long term as Chief of Staff of the Army (1930–35), he had fought hard for more money and materiel for the armed forces, bucking heads with the politicians almost on a daily basis. He had become a thorn in Roosevelt's side, and angered many career officers over the slow rate of promotion. Roosevelt and other Democrats, who saw MacArthur as a possible political rival in the 1940 elections, did their best to encourage him to accept a new assignment in far-off Manila.

"MacArthur," according to historian Robert H. Ferrell, "had worn out his welcome with the president, who felt that the Philippines was a suitable distance for the man whom Roosevelt privately had denominated as one of the two most dangerous men in the United States, the other being Senator Huey Long, who was felled by an assassin's bullet the same year that MacArthur went to the Philippines. And the United States Army's leaders after MacArthur were just as pleased as President Roosevelt to get MacArthur a good distance away from the State, War and Navy buildings in Washington."

MacArthur was to receive his regular salary, about $8,000, plus an additional allowance of between $18,000 and $30,000 from the Philippine government. His critics claimed that the latter figure was closer to $50,000 annually, which MacArthur denied by saying he "would not sell my sword."

Furthermore, the Philippine government agreed to furnish quarters for MacArthur and his staff. MacArthur was installed in a six-room air-conditioned penthouse apartment atop the newly rebuilt government-owned Manila Hotel. The place took on a woman's touch in the spring of 1937 when MacArthur, then fifty-seven, married the former Jean Faircloth, whom he had met aboard ship en route to the Philippines in late 1935. Jean, thirty-eight when she married, was a daughter of the South from Murfreesboro, Tennessee. A son, Arthur, was born to the couple in

Manila on February 21, 1938. President Quezon and his wife were the boy's godparents.

The penthouse was a spacious monument befitting a man with the title of field marshal. It had a large reception room done in the Spanish style, a den filled with rare books collected by MacArthur and his father, and a formal drawing room that opened to MacArthur's sitting room, complete with bath. Beyond his room was Mrs. MacArthur's room. Farther beyond, on the end, was a little breakfast room and the dining room. There were terraces at either end, one looking over the city, the other looking out across the bay and at the spectacular sunsets behind the profiles of Corregidor and Bataan.

To be invited to dinner or a social gathering at the penthouse was a treasured experience. As author John Hersey later wrote, such gatherings were "always full of splendid rhetoric."

Hersey, like many other writers and artists, was highly impressed with MacArthur's coolness and sense of history, particularly his place in it. "[MacArthur] always looked healthy and trim, never tired, never worried, never angry," Hersey wrote. "He always looked as if he was enjoying what Mark Twain once called 'the calm confidence of a Christian with four aces.'"

All in all, the Manila Hotel was a focal point for the city's more conservative social and semistate activities. It was the residence of many high United States and Commonwealth officials, and visiting foreign dignitaries invariably made it their temporary home. All the "regulars" had their own tables in the hotel pavilion, where there was excellent cuisine and music by two orchestras. Until the end of 1939, a table adjoining General MacArthur's was always reserved for a popular young couple known to almost everybody as Ike and Mamie—Lieutenant Colonel and Mrs. Dwight D. Eisenhower.

Eisenhower had been with MacArthur for seven years, until he was reassigned back to the United States in December 1939. Nobody in the army knew MacArthur better. Eisenhower was later to remark that during his career he learned "tactics" from General Fox Conner and "theatrics" from General MacArthur.

MacArthur's life in the Philippines was one of aloofness—from both the Americans and the Filipinos. His life was led almost in seclusion, in hotel suites in Manila or in carefully managed offices, apart from the heat and sticky inconvenience endured by the American officers. The latter worked away, day after day, month after month, with their conscript Filipino army, which was supposed to stand up to the Japanese if war ever came.

The Philippine government had promised MacArthur that it would appropriate approximately $10 million per year for the new army and defense plan, an amount that proved entirely too optimistic. The sum appropriated for 1940, for example, was only $1 million.

MacArthur was officially made a field marshal by the Philippine Republic on August 24, 1936. Many of his contemporaries, including Eisenhower, snickered at the vanity of the man, who accepted his new rank—symbolized by a gold-encrusted baton—dressed in a custom-made uniform of black sharkskin pants and a white tunic, with splashy medals and gold cord draping his chest.

MacArthur's critics asked themselves whether an American general should accept a rank higher than his own country has to offer. In accepting the gold baton from President Quezon, MacArthur was placed in an embarrassing position. If he had refused the baton, he would have hurt the pride of the Philippine people; in accepting it, he left himself wide open for attacks by his critics. But MacArthur had grown used to the bitterness, jealousy, and intrigue, which seemed to dog his every step; he accepted it.

There were some who believed that MacArthur not only designed his new uniform but had suggested the title of field marshal as well.

One historian summed up the difficulties MacArthur had in cultivating friendships: "The worst thing that can happen to an Army man is to be promoted over the heads of senior officers, for this was precisely what happened to General MacArthur, and accounts greatly for the enmity and indeed hatred he had borne all his life."

Chapter Six

War in the Air

The situation is tense out here—and no fooling!
——John D. Bulkeley

War in the Far East kept growing closer and closer. By late September 1940, the Japanese army had moved into northern French Indochina and signed a Tripartite Pact with Germany and Italy. Roosevelt responded by putting an embargo on the sale of scrap iron and steel to Japan. The following month, FDR signed the Selective Service and Training Act, under which 16 million Americans would register for military duty.

Admiral Thomas Hart, commander of the small and antiquated U.S. Asiatic Fleet, moved his headquarters to Manila on October 21, 1940. From that time on, no ships of the fleet other than the gunboats in China and an occasional navy transport operated north of Philippine waters. In addition, when replacements for the marine detachments at Tientsin and Peking arrived in the Philippines, they were not sent forward. Later, this practice was applied to the 4th Marines, stationed at Shanghai, so that as the size of all marine detachments in China decreased, the number of marines in the Philippines increased.

Some 2,000 naval dependents were evacuated to the United States by the end of the year, and the army did the same the following spring.

Hart's fleet, which consisted of one heavy cruiser (USS *Houston*) and one light cruiser (USS *Boise*), thirteen World War I–era destroyers, twenty-nine submarines, thirty-eight seaplanes, six minesweepers, five gunboats, two tankers, and one oceangoing tugboat, engaged in extensive training in the southern Philippines in the spring of 1941.

By May of that year, the restrictions on oil and essential raw materials were making Japan's situation desperate. Like a cornered rat, it would have to move quickly if it was to keep its war machine and economy from floundering. When Japan took control of all French Indochina on July 24, FDR ordered all Japanese assets in the United States frozen, and he placed an embargo on oil to Japan.

The fuse of war was lit. Only a diplomatic miracle could snuff it out.

When MacArthur was recalled to active service, he had about 20,000 Filipino regulars and some 125,000 native reserves. The latter had received hardly any basic training. There were no live-fire exercises because of a severe shortage of ammunition. Placed under his command were about 19,000 U.S. Army troops, which included the highly trained Philippine Scouts

In addition, there were about 5,000 Army Air Corps personnel equipped with a mixture of some 200 planes, including 35 B-17 Flying Fortresses, 107 P-40s (some of them early B models), and obsolete P-35s (35) and P-26s (16), the latter two fighters assigned to the Philippine Air Corps. The Japanese Zero was designed from the P-35 but was greatly modified before the outbreak of war. Initially, the P-35s had been intended for Sweden, together with a hundred Curtiss P-40B Tomahawks. Even the hard-pressed British had turned down the Tomahawks because they were inferior to the Messerschmitt 109s, whereas the air force in the States was equipped with the newer, faster, and more heavily armed P-40E Kittyhawks. So some of the Tomahawks were sent to the Flying Tigers in

Burma, and the 17th Pursuit Squadron in Manila got the outdated P-35s and P-26s. All the dials on the instrument panel of these aircraft were metric, including the air-speed indicator, which showed kilometers.

More bombers and pursuit planes were promised in the coming months. The Pensacola convoy was scheduled to arrive on January 4. Its seven transports, which were diverted to Australia after war broke out, carried fifty-two dive-bombers as well as two regiments of artillery and large amounts of badly needed ammunition and supplies. In addition, thirty Flying Fortresses, which would almost double the current bomber force, were due to arrive in early December. Twelve had already taken off from California and were scheduled to land in Hawaii on December 7.

The first Kittyhawks, armed with their six .50-caliber machine guns, arrived on October 24, but they were without special engine coolant needed to fly at altitudes above 20,000 feet. Some overzealous quartermaster at San Francisco had obviously decided that antifreeze was not a priority cargo for the tropics; as a result, the planes were grounded for another month until the coolant arrived.

Admiral Hart was led to believe that he might get an aircraft carrier, four heavy cruisers, nine destroyers, and four fast minelayers. None of it happened. Hart would have to make do with a fleet he said was "old enough to vote," referring to the fact that most of his destroyers were built in 1917 and 1918.

When MacArthur returned to active duty and assumed command, no reinforcement of the Philippine garrison had been contemplated. After five days of badgering, MacArthur got the army's new Chief of Staff, General George Marshall to reverse his stand and declare that it was "the policy of the United States to defend the Philippines" and that MacArthur's requirements would enjoy "the highest priority."

On September 26, the troopship *President Coolidge* tied up at the Manila dock, and fourteen companies of American soldiers swung down the gangplank. Two days later, Bulkeley's six PT boats arrived, to mixed reviews. MacArthur was thrilled to have the little mosquito boats, but the navy was clearly disappointed. What Admiral Hart really needed, he told his staff, were more cruisers, destroyers, and submarines, something more substantial than a handful of untested speedboats with wooden hulls.

Hart expressed concern over the lack of spare parts, maintenance personnel, an adequate tender, and supplies of 100-octane gas. Hart was also aware that Pacific Fleet commander Admiral Husband Kimmel was less than pleased with the performance of the dozen PT boats (Squadron 2) sent to him in Hawaii.

"The 12 PTs which you sent to us I fear will be of very little use in this area," Kimmel wrote navy chief Admiral Harold Stark in October. "We sent them on an average day to make a trip from Oahu to Molokai. . . . They were practically useless in this sea and could not make more than 10 knots. Several of them had to turn back and a few personnel were quite seriously injured from being thrown about. We need something much more substantial to be of any use out here."

Stark responded immediately to Hart, admitting that the PTs had some serious deficiencies but he hoped they could be worked out.

"These boats have shown weakness when pounded into heavy seas," he said. "I might add that we know the weaknesses of these PTs. We gave them some grueling tests in fairly heavy weather from New London up around Block Island, down around Fire Island and back. They made a destroyer hump to stay with them, but all the boats which made the race suffered severe structural damage. We deliberately pounded them to see what they would stand and to develop their weaknesses. Profiting by what we learned, we hope to develop a much sturdier craft. Meanwhile, we sent out what we had, hoping they would be of some use."

The Philippine navy had three smaller torpedo boats of its own. Two were built in Great Britain and shipped to the islands in 1939; the third was constructed locally in 1941. They were called Q boats, in honor of President Quezon.

Two shipments of tanks arrived in the Philippines in October and November, each carrying a battalion of the M-3 Stuart light tank. Featuring a 37mm cannon, the little tanks were described as "overworked, high revving, superheated sweat boxes." Another deficiency duly noted by the crews was the fact that the machine guns spewed burning hot shell casings all over the men inside the tank, causing burns and blisters. Still, the tanks were welcomed with a parade through downtown Manila.

Also joining MacArthur's command were assorted quartermaster and ordnance units and the 4th Marines. The latter unit consisted of two thin battalions of about eight hundred troops, which were enjoying garrison duty in Shanghai. (They were known as the "Shanghai Millionaires" because of their luxurious duty in China. In Shanghai the exchange rate was forty Chinese dollars for one American dollar. The average marine could easily afford comfortable lodging, several servants, and all the women he desired. It was almost impossible for a marine to spend his pay no matter how hard he tried.) The men arrived at Subic Bay on Bataan in early December, their footlockers bursting with treasured souvenirs of Shanghai—ivory, jade, silk robes, and photographs of the best duty in the Marine Corps. A couple of weeks later, after the start of hostilities, the marines were relocated to Corregidor to become "MacArthur's bodyguards." They were told to burn everything behind them, including, sadly, a warehouse that stored all of their footlockers.

Attempts to evacuate other American military personnel in China would come too late.

MacArthur's best-trained unit was the Philippines Division, which included the American 31st Infantry Regiment and two Filipino Scout regiments, the 45th and 57th. Attached was the 26th Cavalry, the last horse unit in the U.S. Army. The rest of his infantry consisted of newly conscripted native forces with American advisers.

MacArthur had returned to active duty as a two-star general and was quickly promoted the next day to lieutenant general, which still made him junior to Admiral Hart, who reported directly to Washington. (MacArthur would get his fourth star in February 1942, returning to the rank he held when he retired as Chief of Staff of the Army.) One of his first moves was to relieve Major General George Grunert as the senior field commander and replace him with Major General Jonathan Wainwright. Grunert, who had been the U.S. Army garrison commander until MacArthur's activation, was sent back to the States.

Meanwhile, the War Department assured MacArthur that 50,000 more men would land in February 1942, with ammunition for them to follow shortly. But between the establishment of MacArthur's new command in late July and the following December 7, his strength was increased by just 6,083 American regulars. Moreover, only half his Filipino soldiers were stationed on Luzon. The rest of them would prove to be useless, because the scarcity of inter-island shipping was appalling. To protect the sea lanes Admiral Hart commanded a pitifully weak force that included only one modern ship, the heavy cruiser *Houston*. The rest of the so-called surface fleet consisted of one light cruiser, thirteen World War I–era destroyers, and six minesweepers.

In addition, much of the ammunition to reach the Philippines in those last months of peace, including 70 percent of the mortar shells, proved to be duds. The mortars themselves were twenty-five years old; like the obsolete Enfield rifles and the shiny pith helmets, they were symbolic of the pacifism and isolationism that MacArthur had fought so hard, and so unsuccessfully, during his years as Chief of Staff of the Army.

There were six airfields within an eighty-mile radius of Manila, but only one of them, Clark Field, was big enough to handle B-17s. Though there were seven radar sets in the islands, only two had been set up by the first week of December.

Bulkeley's half squadron, which consisted of six boats and a crew of twelve officers and sixty-eight enlisted men, was initially assigned to moorings at the Manila Yacht Club while boat sheds were being constructed for them at the more spacious Cavite Navy Yard on Manila Bay, some ten miles south of the city. Bulkeley reported in to Rear Admiral Francis W. Rockwell, who was one of Admiral Hart's subordinates in charge of the 16th Naval District.

Cavite, the old Spanish naval base that Admiral George Dewey had captured in 1898, had a beautiful *comandancia*, where the Spanish naval commanders had lived and Admiral Rockwell made his headquarters. The United States had poured millions of dollars into Cavite over the years to make it a great modern naval base with repair shops, ammunition stores, and oil supplies.

While the little boats were put in the water, the nine extra engines and assorted spare parts that Bulkeley had brought along on the trip were unloaded and stored in secret areas.

"We immediately commenced maneuvering exercises in an effort to 'shake down' my boats and crews," Bulkeley said. "Additionally, it was necessary for skippers to learn to work with one another, as well as with me. I'm sure they each thought during the first two weeks of exercises that I was a 'flaming nut.' I demanded precision and excellence at maneuvers and meticulous maintenance once we docked."

The American boats also held a few joint maneuvers with the three Philippine Q boats.

Bulkeley's first meeting with the "peppery" Hart was similar to the one he had with Admiral King's aide in Norfolk a few months earlier. Returning to Cavite after a long, hard day of maneuvers in the pouring rain, Bulkeley spotted Admiral Hart watching from some cover as the boats backed into their slips. Because of the heat and humidity, many of the men, including Bulkeley, were shirtless.

"Crooking his finger, Admiral Hart summoned me. I jumped from my boat and jogged to his position, saluted, and recited my name, rank, and serial number," Bulkeley said.

"What are you doing here, Bulkeley?" Hart asked with those piercing eyes that subordinates said could drill a hole in the armor of a battleship.

"I am commander, Motor Torpedo Boat Squadron Three and captain of PT-41, sir," said Bulkeley.

"Hart then expressed astonishment that a 'squad dog' [nickname for navy squadron commanders] would be not only working in the rain, but handling his own boat—risking his health, as well," said Bulkeley. "Hart emphasized that 'with war around the corner, it is very, very important that our Navy live, eat, and sleep as well as possible.' What in hell was he talking about, war around the corner?

"In no uncertain terms," Bulkeley continued, "Hart then directed that my officers and men were not to sleep on the boats, but would be berthed in hotels and eat hot meals prepared by the hotel staff. The Navy would pay the tab. Lastly, Hart clearly instructed that I was no longer to conduct operations in the rain at the risk of health."

Bulkeley's opinion of Hart, which was cool at the start, grew more frigid as the weeks passed, until the admiral fled the area just after Christmas. Hart, an old-line navy man, never warmed to the PT boat and doubted its effectiveness in modern war. He had made up his mind that the boat's contributions could best be made as patrol vessels. Bulkeley saw his boats as "fleet weapons," not "offshore patrol" vehicles.

After getting nowhere with Hart's staff, whom he privately called a "band of novices," Bulkeley formally requested a meeting with Hart, in which he got him to agree to a test under warlike conditions. The PT boats, according to Bulkeley, managed to slip undetected past a screen of six destroyers and close on the light cruiser *Marblehead*, using flare guns to simulate a torpedo attack.

"Luck was with us as the night was clear, with but a shade of overcast. We found the formation (by luck also) and commenced our devised and prescribed attack plan," Bulkeley said. "We were without radar, and our eyes and ears would have to suffice. We knew that the sound of our thundering engines would give us away and that the task force would be 'keen' on hearing our approach.

"We drifted right through the screen, undetected. When the *Marblehead* came to within 300 yards of our position, we opened fire with our Very pistols. Victory was ours! We had 'sunk' a great light cruiser and had penetrated a screen of warships. After 'firing' had ceased, my squadron [re-formed] on my command. We gave the unbelieving onlookers a taste of our maneuverability and headed home."

There were some hitches, however. The 34-boat hit a small buoy; it punched a hole in her bottom, and she had to limp into port for repairs. Also there was too much confusing radio chatter as the boats jockeyed into position. Hart and the navy remained skeptical.

Bulkeley wrote home in early November and told Alice that war with Japan could happen at any time. Three weeks later he wrote again, this time leaving no doubt about his feelings.

"Boats are OK—but plagued with engine troubles. . . . The situation is tense out here—and no fooling! Our decks are cleared. If Japan wants war, we are ready. It sure seems to me very close. We are all saving our strength for when it hits."

Bulkeley was also told that his other six PT boats had left the States and were to reach him by the end of the year. When war broke out, the six boats were at Pearl Harbor and in the process of being loaded aboard the oiler *Ramapo* for the trip to the Philippines. Boats 27, 29, 30, and 42 were in cradles resting on the *Ramapo*'s deck; PT-26 and -28 were in cradles on the dock near a huge crane that was about to lift them aboard.

A few of these boats managed to pour out more than 4,000 rounds of .50-caliber fire at the diving Japanese planes, but none of the boats made it into the water. To reduce a possible fire hazard during shipment, the gasoline tanks of all six PTs had been blanketed with carbon dioxide. Consequently the crews could not start the gasoline engines to compress the air, which in turn forced oil through cylinders to move the power turrets.

The boat crews quickly cut the hydraulic lines, freeing the turrets to be moved by hand.

Several enemy planes in the area were knocked down, but there was so much firing that it was impossible to assign individual credit for the kills.

By the time the smoke cleared and word of a similar attack on the Philippines had reached Hawaii, it was decided to keep the boats (which were undamaged) where they were rather than risk sending a convoy to Manila Bay.

Bulkeley and Squadron 3 would have to do the best it could with only six boats.

MacArthur received an "alert" warning from the War Department on November 28 saying that negotiations with Japan appeared to be terminated. "Japanese future action unpredictable," it said, "but hostile action possible at any moment. If hostilities cannot be avoided the United States desires that Japan commit the first overt act."

Despite the knowledge that war with Japan was probable, there was no panic. On the contrary, there was an air of confidence, and even arrogance, among the American fighting men in the Philippines.

"The feeling of American superiority had a strong hold on each of us," wrote Lieutenant Whitcomb. "Since childhood we had been taught that American machines, American planes, American equipment, and American men were superior in quality to all others on the face of the earth. With few exceptions our autos traveled faster, our planes flew higher and faster, and our athletes excelled in more sports than those of any other country in the world. Why, then, should any of us doubt that we would be able to crush the Japanese in a very short time if they were foolish enough to attack us?

"We had been told that the Japs, by the very nature of their physical makeup, were poor pilots. Their vision and balance were poor and their aircraft were vastly inferior to our own. On the other hand, our B-17s could fly so high that they were beyond the reach of the Jap's antiaircraft and planes, and with our secret bombsights we could pinpoint targets and destroy them with miraculous accuracy."

As the Americans would find out, that was not the case.

Even if the Japanese got ashore, the Americans had a well-rehearsed plan to turn defeat into victory. The grand strategy, as simple as it was naive, called for the U.S. Navy to come to the rescue, sallying forth from their sanctuary at Pearl Harbor to "succor" the Philippines. There would be a grand victory somewhere in the South China Sea. In the unlikely event that the fleet should be delayed, the garrison—made up of American troops and Philippine Scouts—would retreat into the mountain fastness of Bataan and onto the island forts until the navy arrived to save the day. America, after all, was an optimistic nation that had never known defeat.

Chapter Seven

Disaster

It sounded like a billion hornets.
——Private Dan Crowley

The teletype machine at Admiral Hart's headquarters in Manila clattered into action at about 0320 hours on December 8 (0820 hours on December 7 in Hawaii). The message, sent in the clear by Morse code, announced that Pearl Harbor was under attack from Japanese aircraft, and the Philippines could be next. The message was sent twice.

Hart was quickly notified, and navy units throughout the islands were put on alert. Hart, who had been feuding with MacArthur ever since the latter was recalled to duty, neglected to inform his army counterpart of the war news. What happened next was a comedy of errors and indecision.

When the army eventually got the word on the Pearl Harbor attack—from a commercial broadcast—MacArthur quickly went into meetings with his staff. Meanwhile, his air officer, Major General Lewis Brereton, was pacing the floor in Major General Richard Sutherland's office, fretting at the delay in seeing MacArthur, who was at the time talking with Admiral

Hart. Sutherland, MacArthur's chief of staff, had not the slightest intention of interrupting their conference.

Brereton wanted permission to launch a raid by his B-17 bombers on the Japanese naval and air facilities in southern Formosa, some 600 miles north of Luzon. Unable to wait much longer and yet unwilling to interrupt his chief, Sutherland ordered Brereton to prepare for the raid. As Brereton hurried away, Sutherland stressed that his was an order to stand by only. MacArthur would have to give his personal approval.

An hour later, Brereton returned and confronted Sutherland. (There was little love lost between them in the best of times.) Now Sutherland agreed to ask the general.

After a few minutes, Sutherland came out of the general's office, shut the door quietly behind him, and turned toward Brereton. "The general says no. We must not make the first overt act."

Brereton argued in vain. "For Chrissake, what do you call Pearl Harbor?" he asked. "Hell, nothing could be more overt than that!"

Failing to convince Sutherland or gain access to MacArthur, Brereton returned to his headquarters at Nielson Field, on the outskirts of Manila.

Warned by a telephone call from General Henry H. "Hap" Arnold in the United States not to be caught with his aircraft on the ground and suffer the same fate as the anchored ships in Pearl Harbor, Brereton sent the B-17s on patrol, but without bombs, at 0800 hours. At 1045 hours, the bombers were given permission to attack airfields on southern Formosa "at the earliest daylight hour that visibility will permit." (The airfields had been fogged in all morning.) The patrolling bombers were brought back to Clark Field to bomb up and refuel.

While the bomber pilots and those of the 20th Pursuit Squadron were having lunch, their planes were lined up on Clark Field to be armed and refueled. At that precise moment, a Japanese force of 108 bombers, escorted by 84 fighters, arrived over Clark Field, achieving complete tactical surprise. What they saw below them was a virtual shooting gallery.

The Japanese turned Clark Field and surrounding areas into a mass of flame, smoke, and destruction, destroying planes, hangars, barracks, and warehouses before they left an hour later. The same thing occurred at the Iba Field fighter base, a few miles to the west. Japanese Zeros came up behind eighteen P-40s of the 3d Pursuit Squadron that were almost out of gas and circling to land, and shot down sixteen of them.

In little more than an hour, at the loss of seven Zeros, the Japanese had destroyed seventeen B-17s, fifty-six P-40 fighters, and some thirty miscellaneous aircraft and damaged many others. Total casualties were 80 killed and 150 wounded. The attack had been so one sided that Japanese officials in Formosa found the statistics hard to believe. Yet as more and more pilots reported in, it was clear that the Japanese had achieved complete surprise. It was a second Pearl Harbor.

MacArthur's air force was virtually wiped out, despite the nine-hour heads-up following the attack on Pearl Harbor.

Said Private First Class John Falconer of the 194th Tank Battalion, "Around chow time I walked over to Clark Field, which is right next to Fort Stotsenburg, and when I looked up in the sky I saw all those nice beautiful planes coming over. They started dropping something. To me it looked like pepper coming from the planes."

Machine gunners on the ground barely had a chance to answer back. They had no idea how much to lead the fighters and shot wildly into the sky. They eventually learned to concentrate their fire on a single plane instead of randomly selecting their own targets. Some of the men sought refuge under gas trucks and met instant death. It was total chaos.

General Wainwright had just left his quarters en route to his office at Fort Stotsenburg when he heard a menacing hum, one that grew louder and louder.

"Suddenly the thunder of a flight of approaching planes hit my ears," he wrote. "I ran down on the lawn just as they roared over the backdrop of the Zambales Mountains. There were about eighty of them, bombers mainly, but also dive bombers and fighters. They swept over Stotsenburg, shaking the ground, and let their bombs go on Clark Field—most of whose bombers were on the ground.

"The Jap came to Clark Field with his biggest bombs. The very air of Stotsenburg rattled with concussion. In the midst of the almost uncontested raid, my Filipino boy, Felemon San Pedro, ran startled from the house, his eyes like big black marbles. In his frenzy he had put on my steel helmet.

" 'Mother of God, General, what shall I do?' he shouted.

" 'Go get me a bottle of beer,' I yelled. It seemed to help him. I know the beer helped me. I drained it, handed him the bottle, and walked over to my headquarters."

A short while later, Wainwright's aide, Captain Tom Dooley, came racing up the road in an automobile. He screeched to a halt, jumped out, and reported for duty.

"Tom, you damned fool, you didn't drive past Clark during this bombing, did you?" Wainwright shouted at him angrily.

"Sure, sir," he said. "You sent me orders to report to you as fast as I could, and I was worse afraid of you than I was of those bombs."

"I stalked inside my headquarters, with Tom at my heels, and quickly wrote out the order which gave him and a young gunner Silver Stars," continued Wainwright. "I guess they were the first decorations of the Pacific war."

A lot of personnel were a bit hung over that morning after attending a gala party at the Winter Garden Ballroom and pavilion of the Manila Hotel. Sponsored by the 1,200 airmen of the 27th Bombardment Group, the party had lasted into the wee hours of the morning. For many, the attack on Clark Field was like the jolting screech of an alarm clock.

The enemy bombers dropped their loads first, walking their ordnance straight across the runway. Then, after a brief lull, the pursuits came in to finish the job.

Wrote antiaircraft gunner Sergeant Joe Smith in *Life* magazine:

> *Those pursuits kept diving right over us. They had come in from every direction at once in a sort of crisscross formation. They did a beautiful job, but once we started firing we felt fine. They got very close before they felt our fire. At first we all just aimed at any plane we saw. Then we calmed down and every gun would pick on the same plane at once.*
>
> *He'd stay in the dive maybe to within 22 yards and then seem to be afraid to come into our fire, especially into the 37-mm. They came so close we could have reached up and slapped them. I saw the pilots clearly but couldn't tell what they looked like because they had goggles and helmets on. I never had any harsh feelings toward Japanese before, but I learned to hate them right then.*

Lieutenant Moore, commanding the 20th Pursuit Squadron, was among the first to react. Hurling the remains of a hot dog from the cockpit, he gunned his motor into life and taxied into position for takeoff. As the bombs first straddled and then obliterated the mess halls, he raced his Kittyhawk along the runway, closely followed by eight more fighters. Moore's plane zoomed away in a desperate bid to gain the height it needed to give battle to the enemy.

Two more fighters gathered the necessary speed to achieve liftoff. Tails up, they inched off the ground—but flew straight into a stack of incendiary bombs neatly piled at the end of the runway. The planes, transformed into fireballs, spewed into a line of parked P-26s, a low-wing open-cockpit fighter used for training Filipino pilots. The conflagration engulfed man and machine alike.

John White, a crew chief on one of the P-26s, was in the cockpit running a preflight check. He killed the engine, jumped out of the plane, and raced for a nearby slit trench as the flames devoured his machine. He was lucky to make that ditch; many didn't.

Lieutenant Edgar Whitcomb, who was on duty at group headquarters at the south end of Clark Field, heard someone yell, "Here they come," and he instinctively looked for somewhere to take cover. He described what happened next:

> I rushed to the back steps and made a wild dive for the trench about twenty feet away. The air was charged with a loud crackling sound like that of dry boards being broken. Then, as I hit the bottom of the trench, there was a terrible explosion followed by another, another and another. The earth rocked and rolled, and huge weights fell on me, one after another, until I felt I was crushed. Everything went black but the rumbling and roaring continued for a long time. I struggled to move, to get my gas mask on, but it was no use. I twisted and squirmed until I realized my face was buried in the dirty Luzon sand. It was in my mouth, nose and ears.
>
> After a long time the roaring and rumbling subsided, and I found that I was on the bottom of the trench and that a large number of other persons had tried to get into the same trench. . . . There, across the field, we could see our beautiful silver Flying Fortresses burning and exploding right before our eyes as we stood completely powerless to do anything about it.

The entire raid took about fifty-three minutes. As at Pearl Harbor, the enemy had achieved complete tactical surprise. The antiaircraft gunners of the New Mexico National Guard manned museum pieces they had never before fired, even in practice. The ammunition, some dating back to World War I, was heavily corroded and unable to be used. Shells burst at least 5,000 feet beneath the Japanese bombers.

"When we limped back to our barracks, our clothes were hanging from the rafters. There was a big hole where the Japs dropped one right through the roof," said Private First Class Victor Mapes, of the 14th Bombardment Squadron. "We couldn't find anyone from our unit so we wandered away. We saw a man in his '38 Ford lying there, shot. Looked like he was trying to get off the base. When we got to the edge of the jungle there was firing and yelling. Everyone was trigger-happy. It was dangerous to be moving. We spent the night at the edge of the jungle behind two logs."

Understandably, there was a good deal of panic that first day. No one seemed to know what the score was. After Clark and Iba were hit, the order came down to get the remaining planes at the other airfields off the ground.

Said Technical Sergeant William "Cowboy" Wright, of the 17th Pursuit Squadron, "Sometime between 4:00 and 5:00 p.m. on the 8th, our fighters on Nichols Field took off for another airstrip. All the aircraft got off. One came back, however, and landed. My line chief told me to go over and see what was wrong. As soon as I got up on the wing I knew what the trouble was. The pilot was shaking like a leaf."

Another pilot from the 17th Pursuit Squadron, 2d Lieutenant John Posten, took off from Nichols Field, outside Manila, and landed a short while later that night at Clark Field.

"The hangars were still burning and every once in a while a lot of ammunition would go off that had been stored there," Lieutenant Posten said. "Automobiles, trucks, and planes were wrecked and burning all over the place. All the wounded had been taken away, but the dead were still lying where they fell. There was a whole B-17 crew lying dead next to their burning ship. They had been hit by a bomb before they could reach cover."

At daylight, Mapes and his buddies awoke to the sound of a P-40 revving its engine for takeoff. The men rushed to the airfield, only to see the P-40 crash and explode as it ran into a crippled B-17. Mapes walked down what was left of the flight line, assessing the damage and being careful of the ammunition lying around.

"I noticed from the bullet holes that the Jap fighters had strafed our planes both ways. First they strafed the length of the fuselages, then they turned around in a figure eight and came down the wings. That's how neat a job it was," Mapes said.

Many years later, some of the survivors could make light of the disaster. The attack actually saved one man a lot of money. The night before at the NCO club, he had treated his buddies to a party celebrating his promotion. "I signed a chit for seventy-five dollars, but before I could pay it the Japs blew up the club," he said.

Another man had spent a quiet night at the movies watching the first half of *Gone with the Wind*. "I didn't get to see the second half until four years later," he said.

Most of the PT-boat crews weren't surprised at the attack. In fact, they had been expecting one for weeks. What they did find surprising was that the first target was Hawaii.

"I was prepared for war," Lieutenant Kelly said. "I'd heard about the secret operations orders—what the fleet would do under any of three eventualities, so the night before I'd gone over to the Army and Navy Club at Manila and put aboard the thickest charcoal-broiled filet mignon I could buy there. Plus I had French fries and a big tomato with Roquefort dressing, finishing off with brandy and a cigar. I figured I'd at least have them to remember."

While one of the PT boats patrolled the bay that first day of war, the other five dispersed along the shoreline at Cavite and scrounged up all the canned food they could find. No bombers flew over Manila that first day, and only a reconnaissance flight appeared the next.

Bulkeley's boats spent those first two days running messages, patrolling, and preparing the boats for combat by arming the torpedoes and loading machine-gun ammo. Just before dark, Lieutenant Kelly led three boats (numbers 32, 33, and 34) to the southern tip of Bataan as an advance party to scout out a new location, should it become necessary. Everyone knew that the Japanese would be back, with a vengeance.

"Remain on the alert and attack anything I order you to attack," Bulkeley told Kelly before his three boats shoved off. Then Bulkeley went over to navy headquarters to meet with Admiral Rockwell.

According to Torpedoman First Class Charles DiMaio:

> *When John Bulkeley came back from Admiral Rockwell's office, he began issuing orders, calmly as though this was just another practice run. He saw to it that we began immediately to put warheads on our torpedoes at Cavite. It was a good thing, for this was slow and tedious work. It took us from early Monday morning to Wednesday morning to put warheads on twenty-four torpedoes and get them ready to be fired.*
>
> *If Bulkeley hadn't insisted that we rapidly fit out our PT-boats, we would have been out of luck—and out of the war—as far as torpedoes went. For when we had put the last armed torpedo on the last boat, all hell broke loose at Cavite.*

Kelly's three boats, meanwhile, had surprised some jumpy Filipino soldiers with their reconnaissance to Bataan that first night. The roar of the PT engines, which echoed against the mountains, convinced some Filipinos that they were Japanese planes. Searchlights winked on and off and drew some fire, fortunately toward the sky.

The following morning, Kelly's boats cruised along the tip of Bataan and set up shop at a small native fishing village on Sisiman Cove.

Just after noon on the third day, Wednesday, December 10, the enemy returned, this time hunting for targets around Manila Bay. Nearby Nichols Field, the Army Air Corps' major base in the Philippines, and Cavite Navy Yard, the only U.S. sea base in the Far East, were the two prime targets. This time, the defenders got some advance warning.

Private Dan Crowley ran to his defensive position at the Nichols airfield that morning and waited for the attack to come. He was part of a crew that operated a weapon consisting of three ancient Lewis guns in tandem. The piece was set up in the open behind a wall of sandbags. There were no foxholes or trenches to crawl into.

At noon, a mess truck came out on the airfield to offer the men some lunch. The men at Crowley's position decided to send one man at a time to the truck. Crowley went first.

"Just as I got to the truck and got a canteen cup of boiling water and a hardboiled egg I heard the noise. It sounded like a billion hornets," Crowley said.

He looked back at his machine-gun position and it was blown to bits. He ran for the nearest cover he could find.

Dive-bombers wheeled over nearby rice paddies, searching out and strafing everything in sight with their chattering machine guns. Men were hunted down like wild animals as they desperately sought refuge. Many, unable to find a place to hide, just sat down and cried.

"The air attack seemed to last forever, back and forth, back and forth they came. The fighters sprayed everything on the way out," Crowley said. "The Japs didn't have to come back because they had destroyed everything, including our brand-new barracks."

The action stopped as quickly as it had begun. The rest of the afternoon was spent digging through rubble, helping the wounded, and burying the dead. By sundown the survivors were exhausted but not ready to go to sleep.

"I showered at the YMCA in Manila that night," Crowley remembered. "And then I went out on the town."

Bulkeley ordered his three boats (numbers 31, 35, and 41) out in the bay, where they could maneuver against the Japanese planes, which numbered about 125. Twenty-five miles to the west, Kelly also ordered his three boats into the bay, to be ready for any action coming his way.

"The Japs passed on out of sight over the mountains, and then we began hearing the rumble of bombs—only first we felt the vibrations on our feet, even out there in the water, and we knew something was catching hell," Kelly said.

The dull roar of the Japanese bombers and fighters was like the rumble before a storm. The aircraft circled the doomed navy base at Cavite leisurely; there were no antiaircraft guns to break them up. At 20,000 feet they were well out of range.

About a dozen Kittyhawks of the 17th Pursuit Squadron were scrambled late from Nichols Field. They climbed straight into the waiting ranks of Zeros, which had both height and the sun in their favor. A Japanese pilot in modulated English welcomed the American pilots by name into combat. Forty Zeros blocked the route to the bombers, and within seconds the sky over Manila was full of screaming, twisting planes. Though the Americans with three squadrons airborne had mounted their biggest air operation to date, the pilots were overwhelmed by the numbers and superior combat skill of the Japanese.

The pattern set two days earlier at Clark Field was now repeated at Nichols Field. High-level bombers maintained their formation and bombed with precision. Hangars and mess halls, workshops, and the administration block disappeared behind the blast and debris of high explosives. A second formation wheeled in behind and rained incendiaries. Fires broke out everywhere. Meanwhile, with the air defenses brushed aside, the Zeros came in low and completed the devastation.

The first planes started bombing Nichols Field at 1247 hours. A few minutes later a wave of some thirty-five bombers started to work over Cavite. Said Bulkeley:

> They kept beautiful formations, all right. The first big V had fifty-four planes in it, and they came in with their fighters on up above to protect them from ours—only ours didn't show! We couldn't figure it.
> First they swung over Manila and began to paste the harbor shipping. It was a beautiful clear day, and I remember the sun made

rainbows on the waterspouts of their bombs. They were from a hundred and fifty to two hundred feet high, and it made a mist screen so dense you could hardly tell what was happening to the ships. It turned out nothing much was—they only hit a few.

That big beautiful V pivoted slowly and moved over Cavite and began circling it like a flock of well-disciplined buzzards.

Five of the bombers peeled off and dove straight at Bulkeley's three PT boats, which began a series of high-speed maneuvers, a kind of snake dance across the water. The boats would wait until the bombers reached their release point before executing a hard turn while opening up with their .50-caliber machine guns and .30-caliber Lewis guns.

Like water bugs, the PTs began the pattern of lightning zigzags that were to become so familiar to Japanese gunners later in the war. Whenever an enemy plane screamed down at a PT boat, the helmsman simply watched for the bomb to sail loose, then jumped out of the way. Angrily, the planes bore in again and again, but each time the little boats darted left or right out of harm's way.

Spray from the bomb bursts and spume from the bow waves lashed the gunners as the boats dodged and turned. Suddenly the lead plane turned from the attack and began to make off down the bay, wobbling. Then it plunged into the water. Gunners Joe Chalker, of Texarkana, Texas, and John Houlihan, of Chicopee Falls, Massachusetts, solemnly reached across and shook hands to celebrate their first kill. Then they targeted another enemy plane and continued to pepper the sky with .50-caliber fire.

The tactic worked to perfection. Not a single Japanese bomb came close, and the PTs claimed to have shot down three enemy planes that day. Two were credited to the 31-boat and one to the 35-boat. There was so much firing going on in the bay, however, that it was difficult to tell who actually shot down the planes.

The first bomb fell on the navy yard at 1314 hours, and the air raid continued for an hour. Three waves of twenty-seven bombers each swept unopposed over Cavite, dropping their deadly cargo at will. Practically every bomb fell within the navy yard limits, with direct hits scored on the power plant, dispensary, torpedo repair shop, supply office, warehouse, signal station, commissary, barracks, and officers' quarters, and several ships, tugs, and barges along the waterfront. The entire yard and one-third of the city of Cavite were ablaze.

The beautiful *comandancia* was burned to the ground as Admiral Rockwell barely escaped with his life.

"They'd flattened it—there isn't any other word to describe it," Bulkeley said after his boats returned to the navy yard.

Bulkeley quickly realized what this meant to his PT boats. The destruction of Cavite virtually eliminated any possibility that his boats could be properly equipped and maintained in the future.

High Commissioner Francis B. Sayre, who viewed the destruction from his residence in Manila, later wrote in a *Life* magazine article that after the first fifteen minutes of bombing, "Cavite was wiped off the map."

"Cavite took a terrible beating," wrote Corporal Paul Sarno, of the 20th Pursuit Squadron. "The bombs just completely demolished it. I'm not ashamed to tell you that I was assigned to go out and bring the dead in. My lieutenant gave me some whiskey first, and then told me what had to be done. We took everyone we could find, and after a bombing many men were just in pieces. We used the Jai Alai Fronton Pavilion as a morgue. They were stacked all over the place. I don't know how I did it. I couldn't do it today, but in 1941 I was a kid and didn't know any better."

The bombers left at around 1500 hours, and an eerie hush fell over Manila Bay. Bulkeley and his three crews slowly entered the harbor, dodging bodies and other flotsam in the water. They couldn't believe the complete destruction.

They had no time to gawk. They were quickly pressed into duty transporting wounded military and civilians to area hospitals for much of the afternoon.

Said Bulkeley, "There was half an inch of blood on the landing platforms—we could hardly keep on our feet, for blood is as slippery as crude oil—and the aprons of the hospital attendants were so blood-splattered they looked like butchers."

Ensign Cox remembered hospital personnel wandering around the rubble collecting heads, arms, and legs and putting them into bomb craters, then quickly shoveling dirt over them to mask the awful smell of rotting bodies.

The nearby Canaco Hospital, the largest and most beautiful medical facility in the Far East, was totally destroyed.

Said Machinist's Mate First Class John Tuggle, "That was a shame. You should have seen the beautiful floors in the hospital. They used to polish them with oil from the coconuts, and the floors were this thick," Tuggle said, holding his fingers two inches apart. "Those Jap bombs just blew the hell out of that place. It was a real shame, what a shame."

More than a thousand people had been killed on the base and in the adjacent town of Cavite. Many more were buried under rubble. The submarine *Sealion*, tied up for repairs, took a direct hit and sank at its mooring. Also, a store of some 233 torpedoes and thousands of gallons of 100-octane fuel was lost. Several tugs and barges along the waterfront were destroyed. Also destroyed was the low-frequency radio tower for transmitting to submerged submarines. This meant that submarines could be contacted only on the surface at night.

Fortunately, about forty merchant ships in the bay were unscathed. Many of them were able to escape in the coming days to islands farther south.

December 10 was a bad day elsewhere: a flight of Japanese high-level bombers and torpedo planes sank the British battleship *Prince of Wales* and battle cruiser *Repulse* off the coast of Malaya as they were returning to Singapore. They were the only Allied capital ships west of Hawaii. Also on this busy day, Admiral Hart ordered his tiny fleet of surface ships, save the submarines and smaller vessels, south out of harm's way. Hart would stay in Manila for another two weeks; then he, too, would leave, along with his submarines.

The United States had suffered its second Pearl Harbor within seventy-two hours—this one possibly even more catastrophic than the one in Hawaii. The Philippines were now wide open for invasion.

Back home in the United States, most Americans were completely stunned by the speed and power of Japan's attack on Pearl Harbor and the Philippines. For the most part, Washington officials were in as great a state of shock as the man on the street. The smashing of the Pacific Fleet and the destruction of the heart of MacArthur's air force had altered in a single day the entire concept of war in the Pacific. The most immediate fear of the War Department was another Japanese carrier attack—this time on the locks of the Panama Canal or on aircraft factories on the California coast, or a new attack on Pearl Harbor and its still largely undamaged navy yard.

As the reality of these initial losses swept through Washington, a wave of hysteria gripped many eminent government officials. One even telephoned the White House, shouting that the West Coast was no longer defensible and demanding that battle lines be established in the Rocky Mountains.

Marine general Holland "Howlin' Mad" Smith, looking back on the events of early December 1941, said that America had been virtually helpless to stop a Japanese invasion of the West Coast if the Japanese had chosen to do so.

"Our greatest shortage was ammunition for rifle and artillery practice," Smith said. "The country had allowed its reserve to sink so low that if the Japanese had continued from Pearl Harbor with an amphibious force and landed on the West Coast they would have found that we did not have enough ammunition to fight a day's battle. This is how close the country was to disaster in 1941."

America was frightened and vulnerable those first few weeks after the start of the war. Military guards sprang up at strategic factories, ports, and shipyards. Crowds gathered outside the White House and peered through the gates, watching and waiting for something to happen. On that first night of war, they huddled together and sang "God Bless America." The people were looking to Roosevelt for guidance and support. Roosevelt, for his part, accepted an increase in his security force but would not accede to positioning tanks around the White House, which could be interpreted by some as a sign of panic.

Many citizens were irate at the Japanese treachery. A heavy police guard was required to protect the Japanese Embassy on Massachusetts Avenue. On the first night, someone had vented his animosity toward the Japanese by chopping down four cherry trees along the Tidal Basin near the Jefferson Memorial that had been a gift from the citizens of Tokyo in 1912. A sign on the pen housing the Japanese deer in New York City's Central Park was changed to read "Asiatic Deer."

On the West Coast, where the threat of invasion was thought to be more than just a possibility, antiaircraft batteries were hurried into position on the Hollywood Hills and at Long Beach and Seattle, where large aircraft manufacturing plants were located. Farmers armed with pitchforks and shotguns patrolled the empty beaches of Puget Sound to help ward off expected enemy landings. Miles of barbed wire were rolled into positions along the entire coast. Lights were turned off and families huddled in basements and cellars waiting for the enemy to come ashore.

In Los Angeles, which had a Japanese American population of nearly 50,000, FBI agents and soldiers from Fort MacArthur took "key" Japanese citizens into custody and interned them in a barbed-wire enclosure at the Sixth Street Pier. The police and FBI were inundated with spy and sabotage reports against native Japanese Americans, who then and later proved to be no threat to America's war effort. Still, many Americans expressed their outrage against Japanese Americans by smashing store windows or boycotting their businesses. It was but the first step toward a national program that would intern the entire Japanese American population into camps for the duration of the war. By the late spring of 1942, some 120,000 Japanese Americans in the western United States were driven from their jobs, homes, and businesses on the suspicion that they were spying or plotting some form of sabotage. Not a thread of evidence was found then or ever that they were anything but completely loyal citizens, yet they were herded into camps at gunpoint. Later in the war, a unit of Japanese Americans from the Hawaiian National Guard, the 100th Infantry Battalion, fought with distinction at Monte Cassino in Italy. The unit, called the "Go For Broke" and "Purple Heart" battalion, became one of the most highly decorated outfits in World War II.

Eleanor Roosevelt did her best to stem a flood of prejudice and fear against Japanese Americans, but it was to no avail. The hysteria was so strong that her calls for tolerance were thrown back at her by a media that was hell-bent on crucifying anyone who could be labeled as a "Jap lover."

The humiliating defeats early in the war acted as a spur to the people and awakened a sleeping giant. Instead of creating fear and panic, the defeats filled them with fury and fight and a resolve to exact revenge. They would never forget Pearl Harbor, Wake Island, and the struggle going on in the Philippines.

Had Americans needed a reminder of the danger they were in, it was provided on February 23, 1942, when a Japanese submarine surfaced off the California coast near Santa Barbara and lobbed a couple of shells in the vicinity of a nearby oil field.

Chapter Eight

Withdrawal to Bataan

It was like watching a cat go into a sack.
——Anonymous Japanese officer

When Bulkeley reported in to Admiral Rockwell for orders at dusk on December 10, he was told to take his boats over to Sisiman Cove on Bataan and join the rest of his squadron. He was also told to report daily to him for orders. When Bulkeley asked whether rumors of a Japanese landing on the northern tip of Luzon were true, Rockwell nodded his head and said yes.

Bulkeley offered to take his boats to the north and harass the Japanese landing craft. Rockwell smiled. He appreciated Bulkeley's enthusiasm but said that the Japanese force had already come ashore.

The first Japanese landings were made on the little island of Batan, about halfway across the strait separating Luzon from Formosa, and near the coastal villages of Aparri and Vigan, with a total force of some 2,500 men. The immediate objectives were airfields from which fighters could operate and cover the main landings, which would follow. The enemy also landed some forces farther south on Mindanao.

General Wainwright was inspecting the deployment of one of his Filipino units along Lingayen Gulf when word arrived of the Japanese landings. Both he and MacArthur recognized the landings as feints intended to dissipate American strength. They refused to be drawn into using large reinforcements, though MacArthur ordered the flight of B-17s from Clark to attack the beachhead at Vigan.

During the next two days, more than a hundred enemy bombers and fighters swarmed over Luzon, attacking any suitable target without much fear of retaliation. The Americans could counter with fewer than thirty serviceable aircraft. Seven navy PBY float planes were shadowed as they returned from a patrol and were shot down as they attempted to land off Olongapo Naval Station on Bataan. The next day, Admiral Hart decided to withdraw his remaining floatplanes south; a couple of days later they were followed by all the remaining B-17s that could still fly. The latter, less than a dozen, were sent all the way to Darwin, Australia, after a refueling stop at the Del Monte pineapple plantation airfield, on Mindanao.

The Far East Air Force had ceased to exist as a fighting force. Except for a few patched-up fighters, the army was without air cover, and the navy was forced to rely mainly on submarines and PT boats to protect the thousands of miles of beaches against a massive invasion, which Washington thought was sure to come.

MacArthur, of course, was furious at Admiral Hart for pulling out his surface and air elements. The men hardly spoke to each other. MacArthur was counting on Hart's forces to help keep the sea-lanes open for transports bringing him troops and supplies in the coming months. For his part, Hart was just obeying Navy Department orders issued the previous month stating that, in the event of war, what surface vessels he did have would immediately withdraw to the Malay barrier and await reinforcements from the Pacific Fleet.

MacArthur would later write that he believed that the navy had been "terrorized by Pearl Harbor" and that the admirals had made "no effort to keep open our lines of supply when a westward sally by the Asiatic Fleet might have cut through to relieve our hard-pressed forces."

MacArthur said of Hart in his memoirs, "Apparently he was certain that the islands were doomed and made no effort to keep open our lines of supply. In addition to his refusal to risk his ships in resisting the landings made on Luzon, he made no effort to oppose the Japanese blockade."

Back home, where the nation was reeling from the Pearl Harbor disaster, MacArthur was becoming a lone symbol of defiance. His optimism was contagious as he fought to curtail a panic.

A weary Bulkeley took his three boats across Manila Bay to their new home on Sisiman Cove, just east of Mariveles, on the southern tip of Bataan. His latest orders were to report to Admiral Rockwell daily in Manila and to provide a messenger service to Bataan, Corregidor, and Manila to make up for the loss of the navy's prime radio installation at Cavite. The boats were also to patrol the entrance to Manila Bay and the coastline north along the west coast of Bataan and to the south. The three Philippine Q boats were given the assignment of patrolling Manila Bay and the east coast of Bataan. MacArthur was particularly concerned that the enemy would attempt an end-run amphibious attack on Corregidor.

Bulkeley's men were exhausted from a busy day carrying the dead and wounded to nearby hospitals. The stench of blood and body parts clung to the little boats as pungent reminders of the horror they had witnessed on December 10.

Bulkeley remembered one time during the day when he looked up and saw antiaircraft shells bursting 10,000 feet below the Japanese bombers. "Only then did it begin to dawn on me how completely impotent we were," he said.

Lieutenant Kelly showed Bulkeley their new home after tying up at a rickety old fishing dock at Sisiman Cove. It was a far cry from their luxurious accommodations at Cavite.

The men would live in native nipa huts, a one-room hootch with a thatched roof and sides. The huts were about four feet off the ground, leaving space below to keep pigs and chickens. The floor was split bamboo, with space between the boards so crumbs could be dropped to the animals below. In the corner was a sandbox where the cooking was done. Because the huts had no chimney, the smoke escaped any way it could—out a window opening or through cracks in the floor or roof.

"But for the most part we lived on our boats—had to," said Kelly, "because we never knew when we would have to haul out into the bay in case of a dive-bomber attack."

The men would just have to make the best of it, and they did. On the first day in their new home, someone had put up a sign that read: "Sisiman Bay Yacht Club."

Lieutenant Kelly became the squadron's first casualty when he somehow "snagged" his right index finger on a piece of equipment aboard his boat while on a patrol. The wound became dangerously infected and caused blood poisoning to spread up his arm almost to the shoulder.

"My hand was the size of a catcher's mitt," Kelly said. "I couldn't lie down for any length of time; I had to hold my arm up, else it would drive me nuts. The doctor at Mariveles offered me morphine, but I didn't dare take it because at any time we might have to get the boats to sea quick. The worst thing was the flies that kept buzzing around my hand."

Bulkeley ordered Kelly to report to the hospital on Corregidor. There an army doctor scared the wits out of Kelly by telling him he'd "probably" lose the arm because he had delayed getting to a hospital. The doctor gave Kelly some sulfa pills and packed his arm in hot-water bags before ordering him to bed. Kelly would spend almost a month in the hospital on Corregidor while his arm healed. He was told by doctors that had he waited even one more day before reporting to the hospital, he would have had to have his arm amputated. The hospital stay wasn't a total loss, however. Kelly met and became good friends with a "cute" army nurse, whom he later invited to dinner with his shipmates at the "Sisiman Bay Yacht Club."

The nurse, Lieutenant Beulah "Peggy" Greenwalt, who was played by Donna Reed in the 1945 movie *They Were Expendable*, was later taken prisoner by the Japanese when they overran Corregidor in early May. Interestingly, Greenwalt sued the filmmakers over her portrayal—as innocent as it was—in the movie and was awarded $5,000.

While Bulkeley reported in every morning to Admiral Rockwell or his chief of staff, Captain Harold Ray, the rest of the crews performed maintenance and went on scrounging missions for food, gasoline, and spare parts. The first two were easier to find than the latter.

Barrels of oil and 100-octane gasoline were loaded aboard two barges and towed across Manila Bay to storage areas about a hundred yards off Sisiman Cove. It was safer than storing the highly flammable substance adjacent to the piers, for obvious reasons. The dangerous job of refueling the boats was done by hand, using a small funnel. It was a tricky job that was usually performed by the officers.

"No use to ask men to take risks when officers should lead," Kelly said.

Kelly discovered that much of the gasoline had been sabotaged with large quantities of soluble wax, which clogged gas strainers and carburetor jets so badly that they had to be cleaned hourly. The wax also contributed to a buildup in the gas tank itself. The men discovered that they could get rid of most of the wax by straining the gasoline through an army felt hat. Part of the problem may also have been the fact that many of the fuel drums had previously been used to store coconut oil.

When Kelly took Bulkeley to the offshore barges for an inspection, Bulkeley caught the Filipino watchmen eyeing him.

"Search these men," Bulkeley cried out, and four seamen jumped to obey the order. The Filipinos looked nervous as the sailors began to go through their effects. Kelly overturned one of the kegs of rice that the watchmen had brought aboard for cooking. In the bottom was a block of paraffin. Each of the other kegs contained a similar block. Bulkeley placed the men under arrest, charging them as saboteurs.

"I ought to shoot the bastards myself," Bulkeley said.

From then on, American sailors guarded the gasoline barges. But the damage had been done. Squadron 3 would fight constant battles against the wax, for there was no other gasoline available. All patrols were conducted with the knowledge that the engines could suddenly stop at any time.

All the spare parts were virtually blown away during the air raid on Cavite. And with the destruction of the navy base at Pearl Harbor, any hope of resupply was remote. The only parts that escaped destruction were the nine spare engines that Bulkeley had brought along on the voyage to the Philippines. He had stored them in various private garages around Manila. He would never get to use them, however. Three were lost early in January when the Japanese occupied Manila, another two were destroyed by bombers on Corregidor, and the other four had to be left behind when the PTs departed in March.

Winches and other equipment needed to change engines were not available, so most of the maintenance was performed by individual crews. After Cavite was destroyed, the only repair facility available to them was the old submarine tender *Canopus*, next door at Mariveles. Heavily camouflaged to avoid enemy aircraft during the day, the *Canopus*, or the "Old Lady," as she was called, worked around the clock every day until she was scuttled just before the fall of Bataan in early April.

Bulkeley would report to headquarters every morning aboard the 41-boat to get nightly assignments based on the shifting situation. Boats would be sent in pairs in case one got into trouble, but because there were so few of them and so little gasoline, this was not always possible.

The PTs would demonstrate their value in another way on the night of December 17, when three boats—numbers 32, 34, and 35—raced to the scene of the sinking of the USS *Corregidor* just off Bataan. The inter-island steamer, packed with almost 700 men, women, and children, was making a run for Australia when it hit a mine and quickly sank. The three PT boats, among the few craft to respond to this emergency because of the tricky minefields in the area, picked up a total of 296 passengers during the night, but 500 people, including many prominent Philippine political figures, lost their lives. The 32-boat, using a variety of rigged ladders and lines over the side, was credited with rescuing 196 passengers.

"Our shoulders got so weak pulling them up the sea ladder that we couldn't lift them," Bulkeley said. "So we'd throw lines out into the dark— it was like casting for trout—and haul them back with a dozen people hanging on. We'd just pull them on in—scraping off a few ears, and now and then a nose and plenty of skin, on the side of our boat—but they were drowning every minute and it was the only way. Our boat managed to rescue as many as 196. Had 'em lying and standing everyplace."

Most of the survivors were covered with oil. Beneath that were serious burn injuries. Bulkeley remembered that one burn victim screamed so much when his skin was touched during treatment that the nurses had to turn him over by grabbing the hair on his head.

Besides the high loss of life, the disaster claimed a large amount of artillery and ammunition destined for Brigadier General William Sharp on Mindanao.

A few days later, PT Squadron 3 was down to five boats when the 33-boat, investigating what was believed to be the lights of a submarine, went hard aground on a reef. After three failed attempts to pull her off, she was stripped and destroyed by fire so she wouldn't be of any use to the enemy. More bad luck followed a day later when the 32-boat suffered an accidental gasoline explosion in the engine room. There were no casualties, but the boat would be out of action for several weeks.

The health of the remaining boats was rapidly deteriorating due to lack of spare parts, bad gasoline, and crew fatigue. Still, the boats went on patrol just about every night, mostly along the west coast of Bataan.

The war news continued to worsen. At dawn on December 22, some 22,000 Japanese soldiers of Lieutenant General Masaharu Homma's Fourteenth Army, veterans of combat in China, came ashore on the broad, sandy beaches of Lingayen Gulf, in northwestern Luzon, and two other nearby places 125 miles north of Manila. Three untested Philippine divisions were rushed to the area to try to slow them down.

By the afternoon, all of Homma's forces had linked up and were marching down Route 3, the old cobblestoned military highway that leads to Manila. On paper, MacArthur had almost twice as many soldiers as Homma; the difficulty was that many of them were melting into the hills.

The attack came where everyone figured it would. The Americans and Filipinos had held joint maneuvers at Lingayen Gulf for years. Its broad, flat beaches were ideal for an amphibious assault. This time was different, however. The Japanese had complete control of the air and sea. Also, the Allies seriously underestimated the quality of Japanese equipment and the skill and bravery of Japanese soldiers.

Despite all the warnings, and the correct assessments by MacArthur that Lingayen Gulf was indeed the logical landing for a march on Manila, the ground forces were singularly unprepared. Beach defenses were in the hands of two raw Philippine army divisions, one of which had received only ten weeks' training; the other had no artillery.

The remnants of the air corps attempted to interfere with the landings. A few B-17s made the long haul up from Mindanao and caused some damage, but in the end it was the swell and the sea that caused the only disruptions to the Japanese timetable. At the end of the day the Japanese were ashore in strength. The raw recruits of the Philippine army fell back in disorder, while the veterans—the marines, the Scouts, and the 31st Infantry—waited passively on the sidelines. They could have turned the beaches red and made the enemy pay heavily had they been committed to battle.

Hearing of the invasion, Bulkeley called on Admiral Rockwell and asked permission to rush his boats to the scene and "raise hell" with the

Japanese landing craft unloading enemy troops and tanks.

"No," Rockwell said, "we know you boys want to get in there and fight, but there's no sense sending you on suicidal missions—just now."

The following day, the Japanese landed about 10,000 infantry and support troops at Lamon Bay, about sixty miles southeast of Manila, and began advancing on the capital. The Japanese obviously thought that MacArthur would make a stand in Manila, and they had devised a plan to destroy his forces in a pincer move on the city.

Not a single big gun and fewer than two infantry battalions protected this east coast. By 1200 hours on December 23, the Japanese were pushing toward Manila in three columns. The battle in southern Luzon was over before it started.

MacArthur's defensive plan, called War Plan Orange, called for his forces to execute a long retreat under fire into the Bataan peninsula, while delaying long enough to permit Bataan to be stocked with supplies and equipment. Brigadier General Albert M. Jones was to execute a fighting withdrawal north from the Lamon Bay area, through Manila, which would be declared an "open city," and then westward across the vital Calumpit Bridge into Bataan.

General Wainwright was to execute a fighting withdrawal of his northern forces to the south and follow General Jones' troops across the Calumpit Bridge into Bataan. One Japanese general described the scene by saying, "It was like watching a cat go into a sack." Had the Japanese pressed Wainwright hard, they might have turned the withdrawal into a rout, but General Homma was under orders to capture Manila, where he assumed that MacArthur's forces would be dug in and waiting to make a last stand in the capital.

Many of the Filipino troops had no transportation and were marching barefoot, their outsize GI shoes tied to their rifle barrels. They trudged along the hot, unshaded roads wearing blue denims and pith helmets.

The focus of the dual withdrawals was on the small Calumpit Bridge, just south of San Fernando. Two spans, one carrying the single track of the railroad and the other carrying a two-lane road, crossed the swirling Pampanga River and its surrounding marshes. Through this difficult defile all the troops, equipment, and supplies would have to pass. Every available piece of civilian transportation—cars, trucks, and even horse-drawn vehicles—was commandeered to speed the maneuver. All day and night they formed endless columns along the narrow Philippine roads as they moved men and munitions and military stores from Manila to Bataan. The scene was reminiscent of that critical point in World War I when every taxicab in Paris was mobilized to rush troops to the front to defend the Marne.

Why the Japanese air force did not choose to attack this most inviting of targets is a mystery. Not a bomb was dropped. Not a plane peeled off for attack. The pilots flew serenely south, oblivious of the panic below. The answer probably lies in the rigid code of military tactics employed by the Japanese. General Homma had orders to capture Manila and apparently had no flexibility to take advantage of opportunities along the way. Whatever the reason, MacArthur's entire force made its escape into Bataan virtually unmolested by the feared Zero.

The honor of blowing the bridge was given to one of Brigadier General Hugh J. Casey's demolition engineers, Colonel Harry Skerry. Later that day, Casey reported to MacArthur: "Sir, we've run clean out of bridges; now it's up to the infantry."

Colonel Skerry made a last-minute check of the four tons of dynamite on the highway bridge and the three tons on the railway bridge, which ran parallel fifty yards to the west. Wainwright extended the demolition time to 0615 hours to allow any stragglers to get across. He and General Jones, both groggy from lack of sleep, took a bottle of champagne from a commercial truck lying on its side in a ditch and toasted the New Year and the successful withdrawal of Jones' troops.

Everyone took cover, and Wainwright gave the order to blow the bridges at exactly 0615 hours. A terrific rolling roar was followed by a second one. The sky lit up the approaching dawn as debris from the two parallel bridges rained down. Wainwright and the demolition crew went down to the riverbank. Beneath the swirling waters of the wide, deep, unfordable Pampanga River, they saw tangled, curled masses of metal.

It was a close call, but Jones and Wainwright managed to get all of their forces into Bataan just ahead of the Japanese. However, they were forced to abandon stockpiles of badly needed food and supplies, a situation that would decide their fate in the weeks to come.

Supply troops and civilian workers, caught up by fear of the advancing Japanese, fled their posts. Railway workers deserted in large numbers. Drivers of the few trucks available sometimes made a headlong dash for Bataan—without freight. The important supply base at Fort Stotsenburg was, according to one historian, "evacuated long before the approach of enemy forces." An estimated 10 million tons of rice was abandoned at a government depot because of complicated Filipino laws and regulations that restricted its transfer across county lines.

The vast majority of the Filipino infantry marched into Bataan instead of melting into the countryside, as MacArthur's planners figured they would. In single file they trampled onward, looking more like a rabble than a disciplined army. Their baggy, once-blue trousers were now the color of chalk. They were just kids, really. Their American officers used sign language to communicate, for the young soldiers spoke no English.

More than 100,000 people, including civilian refugees, crossed into Bataan. Planners had figured on a fighting force of less than half this number. Supplying this much larger number of people would prove a nightmare.

Wainwright said that out of his original force of 28,000, only 16,000 made it to Bataan. He called them "a tired, pathetic lot."

Said Wainwright, "Some came in silent, blacked-out buses. But most of them came stumbling down the main highway from San Fernando, heavy with weariness and steeped in the knowledge that they were walking into little more than a trap. It was, in short, a sickening experience to withdraw into the peninsula. I issued the order with the greatest of sorrow."

One bright spot was the successful dash to freedom by the inter-island steamer *Mactan*. Loaded with more than 300 wounded, the ship, by sheer luck, pierced the blockade and made it to Australia; it was one of the few surface ships to slip through enemy lines.

Also evacuated from Manila were some eighty-seven army nurses, who were moved to hospital sites on Bataan and Corregidor. A dozen other nurses stayed behind with the seriously wounded at Sternberg Hospital in Manila and were taken prisoner a week later when the Japanese occupied the capital city.

Chapter Nine

An Open City

It may be a long, cold winter over here.
——Douglas MacArthur

All throughout the day on December 24, people scrambled to get out of Manila. The streets of the city were crowded with army trucks and commandeered squat, fat-bellied buses filled with soldiers and supplies. Everyone was going north to Bataan or across the bay to Corregidor.

Just before nightfall, President Quezon, his wife, Aurora, his daughters, Maria Aurora and Zeneida, and his son, Manuel, Jr., left the palace grounds by limousine for a pier next to the Manila Hotel. There they boarded the presidential yacht for the twenty-seven-mile trip to Corregidor.

An hour later, as night fell on Christmas Eve, MacArthur and High Commissioner Sayre, along with their families and staff, arrived in blacked-out limousines at another pier in downtown Manila and boarded the inter-island steamer *Don Estaban* for Corregidor. Also making the trip was a truckload of gold bullion, silver coins, and paper money, which had been removed from the national treasury for safekeeping.

Wrote POW survivor and author Edward Weiss, "As we were leaving the pier, overwhelmed by the emotion of the situation, I put Kate Smith's record of '*God Bless America*' on the ship's public address system and turned the volume to maximum. I made certain it was audible throughout the Port Area."

A little while later, as the big steamer picked its way through dozens of slow-moving barges, launches, and tugs loaded with men and ammunition, some of the passengers began to quietly sing "Silent Night." Jean MacArthur joined in, followed by Arthur and the general himself.

"Mummy," Arthur said. "I've had enough of Corregidor. Let's go back to the apartment now." Jean told him that they hadn't even started for Corregidor yet, but he was not impressed. "I'd rather go home," he murmured sleepily, according to one of MacArthur's aides, Lieutenant Colonel Sidney Huff.

Jean took Arthur to their cabin and got him ready for bed. Out of her own suitcase she pulled a fuzzy, stuffed white rabbit, which her son had loved since he was old enough for any toy and called simply "Old Friend." He slept with Old Friend every night, and in the next few years the toy rabbit became a widely traveled and somewhat battered but very important companion for the boy.

A couple of sailors looked over at the VIPs huddled against the railing of the ship and just shook their heads.

"The Japanese would give the emperor's right arm to sink this tub," one said to the other.

The following night, Admiral Hart, along with Rear Admiral William Glassford and a number of other navy staff officers, left from the same pier aboard the submarine *Shark* to rejoin Hart's scattered navy near Java, in the Dutch East Indies. Hart and his party had tried to get away the previous night in one of the few PBY patrol planes, but the aircraft struck a small boat in the harbor on takeoff. Because the plane could not be repaired quickly, the navy brass decided to exit by submarine.

Everyone else was heading to Bataan.

It was the last Christmas Eve for PT-33. The boat's skipper, Ensign Henry Brantingham, of Fayetteville, Arkansas, reported that all his engines had suddenly stopped shortly into the patrol at 2030 hours, probably because of water and dirt in the gasoline.

As a result, the boat dropped out of a formation with PT-31 and the USS *Pillsbury*, a destroyer escort (DE). Brantingham wrote in his after-action report, "At 2035, the engines were restarted, and an attempt was made to rejoin formation, using the formation's probable intentions as the best immediately useful information. An approximate course was selected and steered until a flashing light, construed to be signals, was seen on the port hand. PT-33 then headed in that direction, known to be towards Point Santiago."

The boat went aground at 2102 hours on a coral reef 1,600 yards from the mainland of Luzon, about five miles north of Point Santiago. Brantingham thought he could float her off at high tide, but that attempt failed. Three separate attempts over the next thirty-six hours were made by PT-31 and PT-41 to pull the destroyer off the reef. They, too, failed.

Lieutenant (j.g.) Ed DeLong, skipper of the 31-boat, wrote that he had "put over towing lines" and slowly revved his engines to about 800 rpms (about 15 knots)—until the towing lines parted without moving the 33-boat.

DeLong wrote in his report:

> Believing the PT-33 in no immediate danger and having no additional towing lines I returned to Mariveles. I transferred to the PT-33 a fire ax for use in cleaning around the propellers, struts and rudders and told the C.O. [Brantingham] that I would have at least two boats there at about 1700 (high tide) to make another attempt at clearing him.

At 1446 PTs 31 and 41 got underway and proceeded to the PT-33. We employed extensive lightening of the boat including the removal of all four torpedoes. At high tide another unsuccessful attempt was made at floating the P-33.

Upon conferring with the Squadron Commander it was decided to continue lightening the PT-33 during the night and to make one last attempt at the higher high tide during the morning of the 26th. This proving unsuccessful, the PT-33 was completely stripped and was destroyed by fire by the C.O. at 0758 on the 26th day of December, 1941.

Reluctantly, Bulkeley had given the order to set the boat afire to deny her use to the enemy.

In the eyes of the United States Navy, there are few things worse than a commander running his ship aground. The consequences often lead to loss of command and a black mark on one's record. Brantingham was ordered to hold himself in readiness to testify to the facts of the grounding before a court of inquiry. He was relieved of all duties pertaining to PT-33 and ordered to report to the commanding officer of PT-32 "for such duty as he may assign."

It would not be the last time that a ship ran afoul of a lethal coral reef in the Pacific. Old-timers described reefs as "instruments dreamed up by nature and the devil to punch holes in boat bottoms and tear flesh from unwary bodies." To others, the razor-sharp coral off the Philippines was often referred to as an "underwater barbed-wire fence."

Now there were only five PT boats in the Philippines.

Ashore, the exodus to Bataan became a stampede. Tons of food and equipment left on the docks in Manila seemed to be waiting for someone to come and get it. Attempts to ship supplies to Bataan and Corregidor from other areas had been abandoned when the various outposts were evacuated prematurely. On orders from MacArthur, more supplies were sent to Corregidor than to Bataan, even though Bataan would be occupied by eight times as many men.

The scene at the Manila docks was complete chaos.

Said Private First Class Michael Tussing, Jr., of the 27th Bombardment Group, "There was shipload after shipload of stuff that never got moved out of [Manila]. There were just acres and acres of crates and boxes. Once you got back there, it was no problem to load up. Somebody just forgot to organize the movement of these supplies to Bataan. They got the men in all right, but they forgot the food."

There was only one road into Bataan, Route 3. It was a two-lane highway with a four-foot shoulder on both sides that dropped straight down into a ditch. It was absolutely jammed with traffic going both ways.

Said Private First Class Michael McMullen, of the 27th Bombardment Group, "I took it upon myself to drive to Manila and load up whatever food I could get at Port Area and drive it back to Bataan. No one ever gave me an order or tried to stop me. When we got into Manila smoke was everywhere. We took things anywhere we could. If I found a dump somewhere and needed to sign my name, I signed. It didn't make any difference to me. In all honesty, my trucks were loaded with two-thirds food and one-third booze. The last time I was in Manila was December 31. The Japs were on one side of the city and I was on the other. The city was on fire and smoke made driving very bad. We loaded that truck strictly with chow. We also found some calico cloth and a few cuckoo clocks which we bartered for some booze at a barrio on our way back to Bataan."

Sergeant Nicholas Fryziuk, of the 192d Tank Battalion, was in charge of a detail guarding a road junction just outside Manila on New Year's Eve. He had a night to remember. Fryziuk told historian Donald Knox:

Nobody knew what the hell was going on and I'm scared shitless. I'm a tank maintenance sergeant, but right then I'm on the ground guarding my position. With me is a boy from Texas. I don't know who he was but he was a big guy and he had a submachine gun and two .45s. Typical cowboy. I had two bottles of Canadian Club whiskey, which I got from one of the barrios we went through. So he and I were going to celebrate New Years. Well, we celebrated. All of a sudden a big staff car comes roaring down the road with its head-lights on. So we stop it. A Filipino gets out. I start giving him a hard time. He tells me he's a colonel. I say, "I don't give a shit who you are, turn them goddamn lights off." Well, he keeps arguing and telling me he isn't turning them off. The Texas boy then steps into the middle of the road and shoots out both goddamn lights with his machinegun. We had orders. Nothing was to come down that goddamn road with its lights on and that was it!

One of the more interesting dashes into Manila after Christmas had been made by one of MacArthur's aides, Lieutenant Colonel Sidney Huff, who was sent to retrieve some prized possessions the general had been forced to leave behind in his penthouse.

Huff, a retired naval officer and MacArthur's top aide, was provided with several bodyguards for the mission, which went off without a hitch. MacArthur first met Huff in 1935 when the latter was a navy lieutenant stationed in Manila. Huff became MacArthur's adviser in naval matters with a special assignment to develop a Philippine PT-boat program. In 1941, MacArthur transferred Huff to the army, commissioned him as a lieutenant colonel, and made him his senior aide.

Huff later wrote of his orders from MacArthur: "While you're in my apartment look in the bedside table, where you'll find my Colt .45—the one I carried in the first World War. Bring that. And if you look in the cupboard, you'll see my old campaign hat. I'd like to have that. I think if you look in the dining room you may see a bottle of Scotch. Just as well bring that too. It may be a long, cold winter over here."

Bulkeley went back to Manila on New Year's Eve on a different mission. He and his crews were sent to destroy as many vessels as possible to keep them from falling into the hands of the enemy. Bulkeley accepted the mission grudgingly, mumbling under his breath that he'd rather destroy some enemy shipping.

"[Destroying our own vessels] made you feel bad," said Bulkeley. "[We] didn't dare go ashore. The little boats we'd just knock in the bottom with an ax. The big ones we'd climb aboard and set a demolition charge to. . . . The streets were deserted, and it was very quiet. Now and then, way off down a street, we'd see a column of Jap infantry or some cyclists go by."

After returning to base, PT-35 skipper Tony Akers asked Bulkeley why the Japanese didn't hear all the noise they had just made destroying the harbor craft.

"It was New Year's Eve so all the little bastards were drunk," Bulkeley said.

There was quite a bit of destruction going on ashore as well; anything that could be of use to the enemy was torched or smashed. Some of the local bartenders broke bottles of booze to prevent the Japanese from enjoying them. That was going too far in some eyes; one disgruntled sergeant told a reporter that the Filipino saloon keepers were engaged in a "scotched earth policy."

Another interesting foray into Manila that night was undertaken by Lieutenant Colonel Warren J. Clear, who was on temporary duty to MacArthur's staff. Clear had been sent to the Far East in July 1941 on a confidential military assignment by the Intelligence Division of the War Department and was trapped in Manila when war broke out. On New Year's Eve he was on a mission south of the city at Batangas. Clear wrote:

> *While I was there, the Japanese advance guard passed through; so when I finished my business, they were between me and Manila. There was nothing to do but drive up the Manila Road and see what would*

happen. Fortunately my Filipino driver, a corporal of the Scouts, was as cool and capable as they come. We started off at 2 a.m. New Year's Day. With the help of a Jesuit priest we had picked up on the road, we succeeded in fooling Japanese soldiers into letting our car pass.

We made our way through darkened Manila toward the glow of flame that was the waterfront. The thunder of distant artillery fire shook the air. Close by, terrific explosions followed successive enormous flashes of blue flame—Air Corps demolition men were blowing up aviation gasoline. To the east the shambles of Cavite still glowed like a white-hot inferno. To the north, just 500 yards away, all the remaining boats that might be used for a Japanese assault on Corregidor were being fired by our demolition men.

And directly across the street in front of me was the Manila Hotel. It, too, was ablaze—but not from explosives. A big New Year's Eve party was still going strong at 4:30 a.m. While Manila's solid citizens were at home preparing for the ordeal which would come in a few hours, the less stable element was engaging in one last, hysterical binge.

I went into the hotel. The gentlemen were in white ties and tails; their ladies wore formal evening gowns, gardenias, orchids. Mostly American, with some English, they were sipping tall cool drinks or swinging gracefully across the polished dance floor—while outside in a night of death and desolation, not five miles away, American boys were fighting in blood and filth to turn back the invading horde.

I passed between the tables looking for a friend who had a boat that might get me to Corregidor. Then I got out of there. I was glad to be outside. It was safer, I reflected—some irritated Japanese bomber might well drop a stick or two on the glitter and gaiety of the Manila Hotel.

I paced along the waterfront looking for anything that might float as far as Corregidor. I could see nothing. Then a welcome voice cried out, "Hey, Colonel, we're shoving off—last boat!"

I got in. We looked around to see if there was anyone else we could pick up. All around us on the waterfront the flames were leaping higher. Silhouetted against the fire we could see gangs of Quartermaster Corps men still plunging into the warehouses and carrying out ammunition, medicine, foodstuffs and clothing. . . . As we watched, one of the gangs went into the long warehouse in back of Pier 7 for another load. There was a blinding flash, a roar, and the warehouse disintegrated. No one came out.

We shoved off.

Colonel Clear was eventually evacuated from Corregidor on February 4 aboard the submarine *Trout*.

Lieutenant Kelly spent his New Year's Eve on Corregidor, where he was recuperating from a nasty infection of his right arm. As the only navy officer in the hospital ward at the time, he took a lot of guff from the army wounded.

"Where in hell's the Navy?" they continually asked Kelly, as if he had any knowledge of these matters. "Why aren't they bringing us tanks and planes and more men? It only takes two weeks to get here from Pearl Harbor." Kelly decided not to tell them what he knew about the bombing at Pearl Harbor.

Kelly got to see a lot of a young nurse called Peggy, even though she was dating a medical officer at the time. They even went to a dance that was put on by the nurses. Said Kelly:

It was a swell night, with a big moon hanging over Manila Bay—peaceful—and best of all, the girls had broken out with their civilian dresses. That doesn't sound like much, but one look at them after seeing nothing but uniforms for months was like a trip back home. Makeup too—they looked so goddamned nice you could eat them with a spoon, and Peggy had put just a touch of perfume in her hair—anyway if it wasn't that, it was something.

What did we do? Well, danced to a portable—I'll bet we played "Rose of San Antone" a dozen times—and Peggy and I figured out a way we could dance with my arm in a sling. And afterward we sat out on the grass and talked. I remember someone saying, "You think they'll ever bomb this place?" Of course we knew eventually they would, but that night the war seemed a thousand miles away. Only somebody spoiled it all by asking Peggy when this medical officer was getting back from Bataan, and she said she thought tomorrow.

Kelly spent New Year's Eve sitting by himself outside the entrance to Malinta Tunnel, feeling sorry for himself that his wound wasn't healing fast enough. Lost in thought, he barely noticed someone sitting down next to him. It was another nurse he knew, named Charlotte. Charlotte, who was about to go back on duty, began to cry as she told Kelly about her boyfriend, who had been badly wounded.

Just then, another figure sat down on the other side of him. It was Peggy, who was wearing a "cool-looking cotton-print civilian dress." Kelly continued:

Not very many nice things happen to you during a war, but this was about the nicest that ever happened to me then, or any other time. It made me feel so good that between the two of us, we managed to get Charlotte cheered up. She had to go back on duty presently, and she managed to sneak us out a couple of fairly cold bottles of Pabst beer, to celebrate on. But Peggy had been preparing. The island was on two meals a day, but she'd managed to hold back a couple of apples and a whole box of marshmallows. That was our New Year's Eve supper, and I'll bet that yours, wherever you had it, couldn't have tasted any better.

Chapter Ten

On Their Own

Sir, you are well aware that you are doomed.
——Masaharu Homma to Douglas MacArthur

More than sixty years later, the name Bataan still evokes chilling memories of death and desperation among those who served there or are students of American history. It was a place where young soldiers of both sides went to do hand-to-hand combat in early 1942 under the worst conditions imaginable. Rather than serving as a refuge, Bataan would become a trap in which disease, starvation, and fatigue would eventually grind down all of them, friend and foe alike. For the Americans, the only escape would be death or capture.

Twenty-five miles long and twenty miles wide, the Bataan peninsula is mostly jungle and mountains crisscrossed by streams and impassable ravines. Stretching down the center of the peninsula is a chain of mountains dominated by Mount Natib (4,225 feet) in the north and Mount Mariveles (4,656 feet) in the south. The coastline to the west on the China Sea is a mixture of sheer cliffs 60 to 70 feet high and little sandy beaches. A daunting coral reef runs along its length.

The town of Mariveles—Bataan's back door—lies at the southern tip, a scant two miles across the bay from Corregidor. It has one of the best harbors in the Philippines.

"Inland, except for crude roads cut by an army that knew where it would eventually hole up, the country is incredibly wild," wrote John Hersey. "There are great earthy hunches, precipitous rock walls, and deep gullies cut by cold streams. Thick groves of giant banyan trees with roots fanning outward have trunks big enough for men to hack out hutlets underneath. There are clumps of trees of hard grain, the famous Philippine mahogany . . . great snakelike vines wrestling with the trees— the kind that Tarzan uses; pure springs, [and] quiet pools.

"In the mansions of this jungle, before men ran in to kill one another, monkeys lived at peace with each other. Deer abounded. Little wild pigs scampered through the underbrush, flushing pheasant and quail."

More than 100,000 people were crowded into Bataan at the end of December—80,000 troops and about 26,000 civilian refugees. There was not enough food for half of them.

As the Allies dug in to defend themselves, an uneasy pall fell over Bataan. The officers tried to put the best face on their predicament, but the men knew a bad situation when they saw one.

On December 28, President Roosevelt issued a cheerful proclamation: "I give to the people of the Philippines my solemn pledge that their freedom will be redeemed and their independence established and protected. The entire resources, in men and material, of the United States stand behind that pledge."

That same communiqué closed with a promise to involve the U.S. Navy. "The Philippines may rest assured that while the United States Navy will not be tricked into disclosing vital information, the fleet is not idle. The United States Navy is following an intensive and well planned campaign against the Japanese forces which will result in positive assistance to the defense of the Philippine Islands."

MacArthur passed on these messages to his nervous troops and drew a measure of comfort in them himself. He told his men to hold on because reinforcements were really coming. He wanted to believe that with all his heart.

FDR quickly realized that he had been too optimistic and began the act of political backpedaling. When all was said and done, he knew he couldn't keep his promises. The Philippines had been written off. MacArthur knew it, too, but he naively clung to the hope that rescue was not only possible, but help was actually on its way. The men, however, weren't so sure that help wasn't on its way. The military had never deserted its troops before. In the absence of any concrete evidence, they lived on rumors. As long as there were rumors, there was hope.

Nat Floyd, of the *New York Times*, wrote at the time, "Bataan is in a constant ferment of rumors, mainly about the arrival of a convoy. It has gotten to the point where the price of coffee is one good rumor per cup. The definition of the word 'news' has become strictly limited. 'What is news,' means only 'What have you heard about the convoy?'"

Another correspondent, Melville Jacoby of *Time-Life*, reported that he had seen nailed to a tree above a table at a jungle headquarters a pretty calendar with a full-rigged sailing ship on it, idling along in a quiet breeze. Under the picture a soldier had scrawled: "We told you so; help is on the way."

With the departure of the remnants of Admiral Hart's tiny Asiatic Fleet, the PT boats became the only fighting surface craft in the Philippines. Hart's successor, Admiral Rockwell, was not about to throw them into action against Japanese cruisers and destroyers, no matter how hard Bulkeley pleaded with him.

In typical fashion, the outspoken Bulkeley viewed Hart's decision to pull his forces out of the Philippines with scorn.

"I was jolted by Admiral Hart's sudden departure," Bulkeley told writer William B. Breuer many years later. "Most of us felt that we had enough naval strength to make a fight of it in the Philippines, and sure as hell make the Japs pay a heavy cost, and could defend Corregidor long enough for help to arrive. But when Hart took off in the *Shark* he was simply washing his hands of a seemingly impossible situation. He had thrown in the towel."

With a remaining "fleet" of three old gunboats, three minesweepers, five tugboats, three Q boats, and five PT boats, Bulkeley's force was indeed the navy's first line of defense in the Philippines.

Their mission, like that of the infantry on Bataan, was to contest Japanese advances as best they could and buy time so that reinforcements could reach them and turn the tide. Even in the first week of January, when the enemy was consolidating its capture of Manila, the men seemed to know there would be no relief. But they continued to hope.

Bulkeley knew better. He flared up at one of his young ensigns, Barron Chandler, who reported that he thought he saw an American aircraft carrier on the horizon.

"Listen, Barron. I don't know what you saw or thought you saw, but I want you to understand this," Bulkeley said. "Our air force has been wiped out, our ships and submarines have left. No help is coming. Do you get the picture, Barron?"

Actually, there were a half dozen beat-up P-40s left in early January, but that total was quickly whittled down to two. One acquired the nickname of the "Phantom"; the other became known as the "Lone Ranger."

Things brightened a bit in Squadron 3 when Bulkeley was able to scrounge up some desperately needed personal items for the men to replace those lost during the bombing of Cavite. The new supplies included shirts, underdrawers, toothpaste, and razors. There weren't enough blades to go around, so most of the crews, to include many officers, developed a decidedly scruffy look.

Lieutenant Bulkeley's stiff black whiskers did famously well. They burgeoned daily and foliated until the boys said he looked more like a prophet than a navy man. In truth, all but one of the mosquito squadron's men appeared much like the sailors seen in old prints of Civil War days. The exception was young Ensign Cox, whose fuzz remained fuzz and who had to take a lot of ribbing regarding his bare face.

Squadron 3 took another hit on January 6, when PT-32 was temporarily put out of commission following a gasoline vapor explosion in its engine room. The accident happened at 0830 hours, about ten minutes after leaving Sisiman Cove for patrol duty. Although two men suffered secondary burns about the legs and arms, neither required hospitalization.

The accident was caused by sparks from the main engine generators, according to a report filed by the boat's skipper, Lieutenant (j.g.) Vincent Schumacher, of Kalamazoo, Michigan. "The accumulation of gasoline vapor in the bilges is attributable to water and other impurities in the fuel," he said in his official report. "Strainers, pumps or carburetors were removed for cleaning an average of ten times per day in order to keep the vessel running. Each removal caused the leakage of a small quantity of fuel."

The 32-boat would be out of action for nearly a month, leaving Squadron 3 with only four serviceable PT boats.

By the end of the first week of January, the Japanese had recovered from their surprise at having Manila given them and had regrouped their forces above Bataan. They were ready to strike. MacArthur, meanwhile, had regrouped his Bataan defense force into two camps: I Corps, under Wainwright, on the western flank and II Corps, under Major General George M. Parker, on the eastern flank.

Enemy artillery started falling on Bataan on January 7, and the long-awaited assault began on January 9. The next day, one of the Filipino Q boats took General MacArthur and several of his staff members from Corregidor to Bataan, the first and only visit the general would make to the embattled peninsula. His visit began at Cabcaben, on the eastern shore, early in the morning and took him across the front lines to Wainwright's headquarters, on the western perimeter, then down to Mariveles, where he had established a forward command post on Signal Hill. He was back on Corregidor at 1540 hours that afternoon. Said one of those on the scene, "The visitors from Corregidor seemed overdressed in immaculate out-of-place uniforms with neckties and smartly pressed pants."

Four automobiles were furnished MacArthur's party, which included a couple of zealous photographers. At each stop, the general delivered a brief pep talk about holding on because help was on the way.

"Jonathan," MacArthur said upon greeting Wainwright, "I'm glad to see you back from the north. The execution of your withdrawal and of your mission in covering the withdrawal of the South Luzon force were as fine as anything in history."

(Wainwright later wrote, "Douglas was a little expansive on some occasions, and I don't mean that unkindly. I just wondered if I deserved such praise.")

"And for that," MacArthur continued, "I'm going to see that you are made a permanent major general of the Regular Army."

(Wainwright later wrote, "That was nice, for I was only a temporary one at the time.")

MacArthur spoke to the other generals for a few minutes, then came back to Wainwright.

"Where are your 155-millimeter guns?" he asked.

Wainwright told him where the six of them were, and because two of them were fairly close he suggested that he walk over with MacArthur and take a look at them.

"Jonathan," said MacArthur, "I don't want to *see* them. I want to *hear* them!"

It would be their only meeting on Bataan.

Earlier that day, Japanese reconnaissance planes, called "Photo Joes" by the Americans, had dropped thousands of leaflets urging MacArthur to surrender. One of the staff officers showed the general the message, which read:

"Sir, you are well aware that you are doomed. The end is near. The question is how long you will be able to resist. You have already cut rations by half. I appreciate the fighting spirit of yourself and your troops who have been fighting with courage. Your prestige and honor have been upheld."

MacArthur read the leaflet quickly, then crumbled it in his fist and threw it to the ground. Told that many of the men had been using the message as toilet paper, the general displayed a cold smile.

There really was no excuse for MacArthur's failure to visit Bataan more often, but one of his aides, Court Whitney, tried to put a better face on the embarrassing situation in a memoir published in 1956.

"What galled MacArthur most of all was that he couldn't spend more time on Bataan," wrote Whitney, who actually joined MacArthur's staff in 1943 for the purpose of directing guerrilla forces in the Philippines.

"Not only was there no way to supervise the over-all strategy from any command post save Corregidor," Whitney wrote, "but the shifting battle positions in the peninsula's pathless jungle made a comprehensive inspection of front-line positions physically impossible."

MacArthur never visited the troops on Bataan again, though he continued to tell Washington that he was often on the front lines. To some it seemed an unforgivable breach of an officer's code and honor to lie in such a manner. Although the Filipinos adored MacArthur and revered his name, many American soldiers lost respect for the man. The general was to carry the epithet "Dugout Doug" with him to his grave; it was a stinging reminder from the campaign in Bataan that no amount of subsequent glory could purge.

Exactly a week later, on January 17, MacArthur would send a message to the men on Bataan. "Help is on the way from the United States," it read. "Thousands of troops and hundreds of planes are being dispatched. The exact time of arrival is unknown as they will have to fight their way through Japanese attempts against them. It is imperative that our troops hold until these reinforcements arrive."

Most wanted to believe what MacArthur was saying, but few among them did.

Said Private Leon Beck, of the 31st Infantry, "People lived on rumors. That was the only hope we had, so the rumor mill was quite active. We believed them even though, if we'd stop to analyse them, we knew they couldn't possibly be true. But we wanted to believe them and so we ended up actually believing them. Some rumors were even published. Once I saw a pamphlet announcing reinforcements were on the way and that our food was going to be increased. Not one rumor ever came to pass."

Meanwhile, General Homma's force of 22,000 experienced infantrymen, backed by artillery and hundreds of planes, began a punishing march down the Bataan peninsula, against varying degrees of opposition. The defenders, who were put on half rations after the first week of January, saw them cut again.

The untrained Filipino regulars bore the brunt of the initial assaults, because the highly trained American 31st Regiment and the two native Scout regiments were kept in reserve to reinforce pockets of weakness.

The Philippine Scouts, which was created in 1901 to help subdue the fierce and warlike Moro tribes and establish tranquility throughout the islands, were first-rate soldiers. Following World War I, they were inducted into the regular U.S. Army. By December 1941, the Scouts consisted of two crack regiments, the 45th and 57th, plus supporting artillery, engineer, quartermaster, and medical units. They were highly motivated, well trained, and ready to defend their homeland to the death.

The regular Philippine army troops were another thing entirely. Most of these troops were recent conscripts who were ill equipped and inadequately trained and lacked the proper motivation.

Said Sergeant Forrest Knox, of the 192d Tank Battalion, "The native infantry had a bad case of the runs so you could never tell for sure if the troops passing you in the night were friendly or not. They had a million excuses, to see the captain, to get more ammo, to find some medics, to get water. When they said, 'I go to seek my companions, Joe,' it was the last of them and we were on our own. They would hold up two fingers as they passed us and say, 'V for Victory, Joe.' We would do the same and answer back, 'V for Vacate, Joe.'"

Of the 80,000 Allied troops on Luzon, about 12,000 were American, including the 31st "Polar Bear" Regiment. Another 13,000 were the highly trained and highly motivated Philippine Scouts. The rest were recent native conscripts. These were the problem soldiers.

Said army nurse Leona Gastinger, "We used to get some Filipino soldiers who had been wounded in the back while running away from Japanese planes strafing the roads. They'd cry and be feeling real sorry for themselves. So to cheer them up I'd always remind them that they weren't wearing their helmets in the right place. That usually got a laugh out of them."

The American officers assigned to these units had a difficult time getting their orders obeyed. Brigadier General Clifford Bluemel, who commanded one of the native outfits, told a reporter that his Filipino enlisted men could do two things well: "First, when an officer appeared, to yell attention in a loud voice, jump up and salute and second was to demand three meals per day."

To compound matters, the families of many of these draftees, estimated at some 26,000, followed their men into Bataan, creating a logistical nightmare.

Often leaderless, these draftees performed dismally on the battlefield. The situation was so bad that the American 31st Regiment offered commissions to corporals and sergeants if they would go to one of the Philippine units. Many of these volunteers were killed when their companies deserted in the field.

Food shortages had reached critical stages by the first couple of weeks in January. Even the PT crews had to tighten their belts.

"Effective immediately, we will have breakfast, supper and a stomachache for lunch," Bulkeley told his boys.

At one point, Bulkeley noted that one of his dinner entrees was "boiled tomcat," which, he said, "required the consumer to hold his nose and close his eyes."

Further up the line, the 26th Cavalry, famed for being the last horse unit in the army, would be forced to eat their horses. General Wainwright gave the order to have his prized jumper Joseph Conrad be the first to give his life for the men.

The native carabao—or water buffalo—was also disappearing from the landscape. It was an acquired taste.

"Young carabao meat is not so bad, particularly if you have some kind of seasoning handy," Wainwright said. "But Bataan seemed to be a land reserved for carabao veterans. We would soak the tough old meat in salt water overnight and beat it for extended periods before we cooked it. But even then it was a test for the strongest teeth."

MacArthur and his generals had given up hope of any relief effort by early January, despite the rhetoric from Washington. They had the distinct impression that they had been written off, and they were correct. General Eisenhower would say as much in his book *Crusade in Europe*, published well after the war. In one passage, Eisenhower tells General Marshall, "It will be a long time before major reinforcements can go to the Philippines, longer than the garrison can hold out with any driblet assistance."

Marshall responded, "I agree with you."

The date of that exchange was December 14, 1941.

Court Whitney wrote in his memoir:

During the rest of December and January, while President Roosevelt and General Marshall kept promising that help was on the way, they knew that by formal policy already worked out with Churchill and the Joint Chiefs of Staff meetings in Washington, the priority would go to Europe first. It was that simple; they had handed MacArthur the stewardship of a military disaster. And what made it one of the cruelest deceptions of the war was that they not only did not tell MacArthur, but instead tried with every circumlocution possible to pretend the opposite of the truth.

By the end of January, even the most optimistic of men held little hope that they would be rescued. United Press correspondent Frank Hewlett summed up the feelings of the men in a verse that attained worldwide fame. It proclaimed:

> *We're the battling bastards of Bataan,*
> *No mama, no papa, no Uncle Sam,*
> *No aunts, no uncles, no cousins, no nieces,*
> *No pills, no planes, no artillery pieces.*
> *And nobody gives a damn.*

Another ditty, this one sung to the tune of "The Battle Hymn of the Republic," was just as popular.

> *Dugout Doug MacArthur lies ashakin' on the Rock,*
> *Safe from all the bombers and from any sudden shock.*
> *Dugout Doug is eating of the best food on Bataan*
> *And his troops go marching on.*

Chapter Eleven

On the Attack

We were aground on a reef.
As fast as you please—just floated over like a feather and stuck.
——Lieutenant (j.g.) Edward G. DeLong

Finally, on January 18, Admiral Rockwell decided to give the PT boats an offensive assignment to help relieve the pressure on General Wainwright's left flank near Subic Bay, along the west coast of Bataan. The Japanese had been attempting to land troops to Wainwright's rear while harassing his forces with naval gunfire.

"How'd you like to do a little fighting?" was the way Rockwell put it to an eager Bulkeley.

Bulkeley's eyes lit up when Admiral Rockwell told him that it was a Japanese cruiser that was shelling the army on Bataan.

"Sink her," Rockwell said.

Bulkeley decided it would be a job for two PT boats, half his available force now that the 32-boat was undergoing repairs for a gasoline explosion. He raced back to Sisiman Cove to tell his men. Although the four remaining boats were all in need of an overhaul, the 31- and 34-boats appeared to be in the best shape. They would go; the 35- and 41-boats would stay at home.

Lieutenant Edward DeLong, of Santa Cruz, California, would skipper PT-31, and Ensign Barron Chandler, of Gladwyne, Pennsylvania, would take out the 34-boat in place of Lieutenant Robert Kelly, who was still in the hospital on Corregidor with an infected arm. Bulkeley would go along on the 34-boat for command and control purposes.

Bulkeley always made a habit of going on missions with his junior officers to see for himself how they handled the men and how they reacted to combat situations. And if there was to be a fight, he wanted a piece of it. It was just his nature.

Bulkeley recalled, "We tested everything, tuned the motors, greased the torpedoes and got underway at nine o'clock chugging north along the west coast of Bataan. It was very rough. We throttled down to thirty knots, and even then we were shipping water, but we got off the entrance to Subic Bay about half an hour after midnight."

The two boats then separated as planned, intending to rendezvous thirty minutes later for a coordinated attack. It was pitch black, and soon the boats lost sight of each other.

Suddenly, as the 34-boat eased into the western reaches of Subic Bay, it was challenged by a light from land off her port beam. Bulkeley slowed from eighteen knots to ten knots and kept going. Artillery fire broke the silence, and Bulkeley turned to the southeast. As he made his way to the entrance to Binanga Bay, two lights sent their probing fingers seaward and were soon joined by fire from machine guns. Bulkeley idled PT-34 in lazy circles, waiting for PT-31 to join up as planned. When the latter didn't show after thirty minutes, he decided to go it alone.

Bulkeley later told writer W. L. White, "The lights and flashes from the shore batteries were a real help, for they enabled us to pick out the shore line, so in spite of the fact that it was blacker than hell, we knew where we were."

Bulkeley, who had taken the wheel from Chandler, guided the boat farther offshore into deeper water to get out of range of the guns. Bulkeley thought that the shore fire might have been directed at the 31-boat. Some of the fire was aimed straight up into the sky. Evidently the enemy mistook the noise of the PT engines for airplanes.

"Damn nice of them," Chandler said. "It's a hell of a lot easier to see where we're going with all this light—as long as they keep looking and shooting in the wrong direction."

A few minutes later, aided by the flashes from the gunfire and the glow of the searchlights, the 34-boat made out the entrance to Binanga. It was 0100 hours and past the rendezvous time, but still there was no sign of DeLong's boat. Said Bulkeley:

> To make the sneak, we cut the speed down to eight knots, skirted Chiquita Island, rounded Binanga Point, and entered the little bay on two engines at idling speed. Everything was quiet, no firing down here, and then we saw a two-masted auxiliary cruiser ahead in the dark not five hundred yards away. Creeping up on her, we had just readied two torpedoes when a searchlight came on and in dot-dash code she asked us who we were.
>
> We answered all right—with two torpedoes—but they had hardly been fired when I gave our boat hard rudder and started away. It isn't safe for an MTB [motor torpedo boat] to stay near a cruiser. One torpedo hit home with a hell of a thud—we heard it over our shoulders. Looking back, we saw the red fire rising, and presently two more explosions which might have been her magazines.

"One of them hit square!" Chandler shouted.

"Where's the other one?" Bulkeley wanted to know. He got his answer fast, as a breathless, dripping seaman lurched into the cockpit.

"Port torpedo didn't fire, sir. She's making a hot run in the tube," the seaman said.

While making a sharp turn and throttling up to clear the area, Bulkeley could see the second torpedo partially stuck in the tube, its propeller spinning away, a condition known as a hot run. With each turn of the propeller, the torpedo was nearing the point at which the warhead would be primed. After that, any eight-pound blow on the nose—even a good, hard slap from a wave—would set it off and blow them all to pieces. If they stopped to fix the situation, the shore batteries might get them. But with the torpedo hanging out as it was, it might be fatal to continue.

Said Bulkeley, "At this point our torpedo man, John Martino [of Waterbury, Connecticut], used his head fast. He ran to the head and swiped a handful of toilet paper. He jumped astride that wobbling, hissing torpedo like it was a horse, and, with the toilet paper, jammed the vanes of the propeller, stopping it."

All this was performed on the run. Bulkeley could not stop the boat, because shore batteries had opened fire and they would have been sitting ducks.

Though the propeller had been stopped, the torpedo was still hanging more than halfway out of the tube. A wave striking the warhead with enough force could still explode the torpedo. It had to be dislodged.

Outside the harbor, Bulkeley brought the boat to a full stop. As the crew wrestled with the jammed torpedo, the Subic shore came alive with searchlights and guns, seeking the intruder.

Bulkeley leaned over the cockpit and shouted, "We can't sit here forever! Can't you men shake her loose?"

"She's stuck fast," answered one voice.

"Then let it ride," Bulkeley said as he lowered the throttles, exited the area, and headed for the open sea, away from the enemy guns and searchlights.

Four nervous hours later as they approached the minefield off Corregidor, the rogue torpedo fell of its own accord into the sea. One could almost hear a sigh of relief from those aboard, particularly Torpedoman Martino, who would earn a Silver Star for his bravery and cool demeanor under fire.

When Bulkeley reported to Admiral Rockwell later that morning, he had good news and bad news. The good news was that a torpedo hit on an enemy cruiser, which led to several explosions. Rockwell told him that army observers posted on Mount Mariveles with 20-power binoculars saw the ship sink. It was believed to have been a two-masted, 5,000-ton merchant ship armed with 5.5-inch guns, but Japanese records obtained after the war failed to confirm such a sinking.

Later in the day, the crew got a good laugh when it was reported that Radio Tokyo had announced the unleashing of a new weapon in the Philippines by the Americans—a weapon that "roared, and flapped its wings, and fired torpedoes in all directions."

News of the attack made big headlines back home, and Bulkeley became a national hero to a public that had never heard of PT boats. Having suffered terrible losses at Pearl Harbor and elsewhere in the Pacific in recent months, the American navy was only too happy to put a positive spin on any of its ships.

News of the disappearance of PT-31 was not released, however.

Unknown to Bulkeley, PT-31 had scarcely started its slow patrol along the eastern shore of Subic Bay when it encountered trouble. The boat was running at seven knots on its center engine, because both wing engines were clogged with wax.

"The same old trouble," Lieutenant DeLong said, "wax in the carburetors." The 31-boat idled along on one engine while the sweating engineers hastened to clean the jets and strainers. The problem was just about licked when, without warning or apparent reason, something went wrong with the center engine and all of the water boiled out of the freshwater cooling system. The engineers had to shut it down while they refilled the system with water from the galley tank. While this was being done, the boat drifted—until there was an ominous grating of the propellers.

"We were aground on a reef," DeLong said. "As fast as you please—just floated over like a feather and stuck."

All efforts to free the boat failed. Said Gunner's Mate First Class James D. Culp, of Denver, Colorado:

> We swam out anchors and tried to pull off without success. The sharp coral had cut into the wooden hull and held us fast. The tide was going out, and we were in a progressively desperate state. We could hear the [34-boat] about midnight as it entered Subic Bay and again when it left at full speed.
>
> Finally, we tried to back off the reef with engine power. The props were ruined and the engines damaged. A decision was made to abandon the boat and set it afire. We built a raft of the engine-room canopy and bunk mattresses. Clothes and bedding were piled in the crew compartment and saturated with gas. The raft, with twelve of us aboard (and a black kitten), was to push off to the edge of the reef and wait for DeLong to set the boat afire. And what a fire it was! Gas, ammo and torpedoes!

At about 0300 hours, Ensign William H. Plant, of Long Beach, California, the boat's executive officer, and eleven crewmen shoved off on the raft. They quickly ran into trouble. They were unable to maneuver the awkward raft, which began drifting out of control.

"We tried to hold at the reef's edge, but soon found ourselves in deep water and being carried further out," Culp said. "We looked and waited for DeLong without result. The raft would have been very difficult to see. When the boat exploded we began to think that DeLong may have been trapped on board."

But as DeLong said in his after-action report, he had trouble getting the boat to burn. He wrote, "Finally after chopping holes in the gasoline tanks and blowing holes in the boat with hand grenades the boat was burning sufficiently and I took to the water at 0340."

For almost an hour and a half, while his boat burned and exploded, DeLong tried in vain to find the rest of his men on the raft. He finally gave up and swam to shore. The men on the raft reached the same conclusion. Ensign Plant, however, decided to stay with the raft with two nonswimmers, Rudolph Ballough, of Norwood, Massachusetts, and William R. Dean, of Ogden, Utah. The three men were captured shortly after their raft beached itself on the shore.

Culp, the senior man ashore, decided to head south toward the front lines, hole up at daylight, and attempt to filter through the lines the next night. He and his men hid in a clump of trees and underbrush on the beach and waited for daylight to reconnoiter the area.

Said Culp later, "At about 0800 someone was spotted on the beach. It was DeLong. We were sure happy to see him."

At dawn, DeLong had proceeded down the beach about a half mile when he picked up some fresh tracks in the sand. He followed them to a clump of bushes, where he found nine of his men. It didn't take long to discover that they were behind enemy lines and the only way to reach their own lines was by sea.

On the beach, the men could hear lots of small-arms and artillery fire inland. As it got lighter, they could see Japanese planes over their position.

Wrote DeLong, "During the morning the infantry fire discontinued and the artillery bursts drew farther north and west, leading me to believe that the Japanese were retreating. If this continued I was determined to make a run for our own lines around the beach at about 1500, believing that our chances would be better during daylight. In the meantime I had planned, as an alternate method, obtaining two or three bancas [native canoes] and making our way by night around into Bagac Bay to beach at dawn. From our vantage point I had already spotted one large banca about one half mile toward Moron. We had obtained canvas for use as sail and had stripped barbed wire entanglements for rigging."

DeLong sent some of his men out to investigate the *bancas* he had seen, with instructions not to engage any enemy. The sailors had a total of six pistols and one rifle at their disposal. The men returned at 1700 hours and reported that the two *bancas* appeared to be in good condition.

At about the same time, DeLong decided to forage for some food and water and took Culp with him. They found some coffee grounds in an abandoned shack and, after building a small fire, they each enjoyed a cup. They found no food.

At twilight the men began moving toward the water, dragging the *bancas* with them. They thought they heard some Japanese voices in the distance, but they knew that the growing darkness would help cover their getaway. Said Culp:

> We left at intervals of about 40 to 50 feet. It was a mistake—we left too early. I was rear guard with the only rifle. As the first of the crew topped some sand dunes they were silhouetted against the setting sun. An immediate outcry to our rear told us the Japs had found us. We carried on with the plan and managed to get the boats launched. I laid [sic] behind the last sand dune on the beach with the rifle, as the others prepared the boats. I could hear, but not see, the Jap forces closing in.
>
> Four men, including myself, were in the small banca and six, including DeLong, were in the large banca. Both capsized as we tried to get on board. We lost some paddles and bailing cans. DeLong's boat lost its rudder and its outrigger was damaged. I took them in tow and headed south, DeLong advising by stars and land sight.
>
> The bancas were barely wide enough to squat down in, and then you dared not move, except to paddle. The four of us paddled until about midnight. I stopped and sent the three men with me, one at a time, back to the large boat to be replaced.

Around midnight they ran into a strong headwind and made little progress. Finally, when the men were nearing exhaustion, DeLong gave the order to head for the beach, hoping that they were beyond the enemy lines. After reaching the shore and picking their way painfully through the tangled barbed wire, they huddled together on the beach until dawn, when a patrol of Philippine Scouts spotted them and guided them to a nearby army outpost. They had come ashore just inside the front lines at a spot where it was impossible to move along the beach at high tide. It was also at the base of the only trail leading over the cliff.

The final bit of luck, of course, was that the outpost was manned by friendly forces, who provided not only food and water but transportation back to their base at Sisiman Cove, where they arrived at 1730 hours on January 20.

Bulkeley was happy that DeLong had managed to save most of his men, but he was more than a little chagrined that he had lost a precious PT boat after it had drifted onto a reef. Now without a boat, DeLong would be reassigned on February 25 to command the seagoing tug *Trabajador*. Most of his crew from the 31-boat, including Culp, would join him in this new assignment.

DeLong was to meet a tragic and unlucky end after escaping from Corregidor just before the fortress surrendered on May 6. On May 2, DeLong was among some thirty passengers, including twenty nurses selected to be evacuated from Corregidor aboard two seaplanes. His plane suffered some damage to one of its pontoons after striking a submerged object on Lake Lanao, on Mindanao, where they had stopped to refuel, and could not continue on its next leg to Australia. The passenger list for the undamaged PBY was reworked to get as many nurses on the aircraft as possible, then it flew off to Australia.

The other passengers, including DeLong and a handful of nurses, were captured a few days later on Mindanao and taken off to prison camps. DeLong was executed later in the war following an unsuccessful escape attempt. Ironically, the damaged PBY that took DeLong to Mindanao was patched up a few days later and was able to be flown to Australia.

Equally tragic was the fate of Ensign Plant and the two crew members, Dean and Ballough, whom Plant had helped swim to shore. According to Culp, who ran into Plant in a prison camp several months later, the three men reached shore and promptly fell asleep at the jungle's edge. When they awoke they found three Japanese soldiers standing over them with their rifles. Plant allegedly lunged at one of the soldiers and was shot in the leg.

"[Dean and Ballough] were tied up to trees," Plant told Culp, "and [Plant] was interrogated, primarily about the minefield around Corregidor. They told him they did not take prisoners in the field. They were roughed up and remained tied to the trees for some time, several days I believe. Plant's leg became badly infected, and he was in and out of consciousness. He awoke to find the ropes cut where Dean and Ballough had been. He was told they had been executed."

Plant was taken to Manila and had his leg attended to before being sent to Bilibid Prison, near Manila. He died in 1944 aboard a prison ship en route to Japan when the ship was torpedoed by American submarines.

Culp said of the young ensign, "Although inexperienced and commissioned after three months of training, and not (yet) a leader, he was a fine, young gentleman and well liked by the crew."

Despite the loss of the 31-boat, Bulkeley managed to convince Admiral Rockwell to step up combat patrols along the west coast of Bataan in the vicinity of Subic Bay. Because of fuel shortages, some of the patrols would have to be one-boat missions.

On the night of January 22–23, Bulkeley took the 34-boat into action with Ensign Chandler at the wheel and Lieutenant Kelly along for his first mission since being hospitalized with a life-threatening infection. An hour into the patrol, they ran into a barrage of small-arms fire from shore. One of the bullets ricocheted off something and penetrated both of Chandler's ankles.

Said Chandler many years later:

> *There was a hell of a [racket] going on and bullets were flying everywhere. John Bulkeley was a short distance from me when a burst of Japanese machinegun fire seemed to just zip past our heads. I yelled to Bulkeley, "Boy that was close." Then I fell to the deck, but really didn't feel anything at the time. However, one of the Jap bullets that I thought had come "real close" had gone through both of my ankles.*
>
> *Buck and Kelly dragged me below. I was bleeding like a butchered hog. Reynolds, the cook, was also acting as the boat's pharmacist and he tried to do the best he could. He poured almost an entire bottle of iodine on my wounds and I almost went through the overhead. Bulkeley put tourniquets on both of my legs. Soon I was hurting like hell, but was aware that our boat was still circling the Jap launch, and that lead was flying around. Throughout the fighting, John Bulkeley would often dash below, call out, "How're you doing Barron?" and then bolt back up to the firing deck. I wasn't doing so well, but I didn't tell him that.*

Because they couldn't return through the minefield until daylight, Bulkeley decided to continue his patrol and give Chandler what first aid he could. Still several hours before dawn, Bulkeley spotted a small enemy launch in the distance off Luzon Point heading away from the beach.

With all guns blazing, PT-34 bore in for the kill. Enemy fire was light and was soon silenced. When the boats closed to within a few yards of each other, Bulkeley, to make certain that no tricks were played, lobbed two hand grenades into the launch. It was on fire and sinking when PT-34 pulled alongside.

Looking much like a twentieth-century pirate, Bulkeley jumped on board the enemy craft with his pearl-handled .45-caliber pistol in hand. He saw at once why the resistance had been so light. There were only three men aboard: one dead, one dying, and one badly wounded. One was a captain and the other two were privates. Apparently, they had already landed their troops during the night. The officer fell to his knees and pleaded: "Me surrender! Me surrender! Don't kill!"

Said Kelly, "Ten minutes before we'd all been pumping steel, hating every Jap in the world. Now we were sorry for these two. They were so abject, sitting on the deck—little half-pint guys—the youngest boy in our crew looked like a full-grown man beside them. Our crew all came up to take a look. People had been scared of these guys? It seemed impossible! Any man could handle two of them in a fight. There they were, avoiding our eyes, and yet we had to hand it to them—they'd put up a damned good fight.... The little private who sat there puffing the cigarette had five holes in him."

Bulkeley managed to gather up a few weapons, two sets of charts, and a dispatch case containing a muster list of the infiltration force and the operation plan. He grabbed Kelly's hand and scrambled onto the 34-boat as the enemy boat went down under him.

Bulkeley concluded his after-action report by stating: "Two wounded Japanese (including one officer) were taken prisoner after surrendering on their knees and were hoisted aboard the PT-34 as prisoners of war. A third Japanese already dead was left in the launch. The launch sank beneath the Squadron Commander while he was rescuing the wounded who were apparently too weak to swim." (The Japanese private died on the way to the hospital.)

A total of fourteen bullet holes through the port and starboard staterooms and topside conning station were counted on PT-34.

Ensign Chandler was taken to the hospital on Corregidor, where he eventually became a prisoner of war when the Rock fell on May 6.

Following the war he was liberated, after having spent more than three years in Japanese prison camps.

After only one night's rest, Bulkeley was at it again, this time going on a combat patrol with Lieutenant DeLong and Ensign George Cox on the 41-boat.

Creeping silently into Subic Bay on one engine, Bulkeley spotted an enemy ship believed to be a 4,000- to 6,000-ton transport lying anchored close to shore. At 2,500 yards, Bulkeley gave the order for all engines ahead full speed, and PT-41 roared to life in a great surge. At 2,000 yards, Bulkeley noticed some "floating entanglements" in the water, designed to snare the propellers of his little speedboat.

The 41-boat slowed somewhat to evade the nets, then Bulkeley gave the order to fire a torpedo at 1,000 yards. Lieutenant DeLong pressed the key, which brought forth a quiet swishing sound as the 2,300-pound fish left the tube. At the same time, the enemy began firing at the noise of the roaring PT engines, but Bulkeley continued to close, firing a second fish at 400 yards amidst a hail of .50-caliber machine-gun fire from both sides. The sky was red with tracers. It seemed as though everyone aboard PT-41 had grabbed a rifle to get in some licks on an enemy vessel "just for the hell of it," according to Bulkeley.

The first torpedo ran hot, straight, and normal; it struck the transport amidships and exploded. Everyone aboard saw and felt the explosion, then saw debris falling about the PT. The second torpedo never reached its target. Its tail had struck the deck of PT-41 on leaving the tube and went off course.

"As the PT turned hard left, strafing the transport, a shore battery of four to six 3-inch guns opened fire. Shells splashed on both sides, astern and ahead," Bulkeley said. "The 41 zigzagged out to sea at top speed, clearing by only 20 yards an obstruction net at the entrance of the cove that could have held the little boat like a fly in a web."

The one fish doubtless was enough, wrote historian Stewart Holbrook, but John Bulkeley is a man who likes to be certain of a job. He ran his PT to 500-yard range, then let go another torpedo. The crash and explosion were magnificent, and the PT's crew got a good view from their foaming stern.

Now a searchlight found the PT and played on her, and from shore came 3-inch shells, howling overhead. It was beginning to be time to get out of there, but Bulkeley didn't want any Japs from the sinking tender to drown. He ran in again, this time to within a hundred yards, then turned his machine guns on the Japs. The sinking tender's decks were alive with men, but only for a few minutes. Twice the PT swept past, her .50 calibers rattling and sweeping the tender's sides and decks and the water around her.

It was, as the lieutenant later admitted, a most satisfactory evening. "As I understand war," he said, "you've got to kill the enemy, a lot of him."

Initially, Bulkeley thought that his boat had sunk an aircraft tender, but it was later changed to a 5,000-ton transport. Nonetheless, everyone was feeling good about this raid. The 41-boat had stolen the cheese from an enemy trap and escaped, leaving behind a telling blow to the enemy.

Bulkeley was so pleased by the operation that he had a broom attached to the masthead on the return trip as a symbol of a good hunt.

Squadron 3 got the 32-boat back in late January after extensive repairs following the gasoline fire aboard some five weeks earlier. With the destruction of Cavite and the evacuation of surface naval craft, the only machine shop available to the PT boats in the Manila area was the *Canopus*, the submarine tender left behind for just this purpose. Docked at Mariveles, the *Canopus* was understaffed, overworked, and vulnerable to enemy air attacks during the day when repairs were conducted under a large camouflage net.

Though the 32-boat was held together by braces and wires, Bulkeley was anxious to include the boat in his normal patrolling routine to give the other three boats (34, 35, and 41) some rest and time to perform necessary maintenance.

The 32's patchwork repairs had reduced her maximum speed to twenty-two knots—good enough, Bulkeley thought, to send her on patrol the night of February 1, along with the USS *Maryanne*, a small commandeered yacht augmented by several machine guns. Lieutenant (j.g.) Vincent Schumacher and Lieutenant DeLong would lead the patrol along the west coast of Bataan.

A navy signalman on Bataan had spotted a dozen large barges filled with Japanese troops sailing down the west coast for a probable landing. He notified navy headquarters on Corregidor recommending that Bulkeley's PT boats, already on patrol, be sent to the vicinity. As the flotilla drew nearer under a bright, full moon, shore batteries opened up with everything they had. Also getting into the act were four patched-up P-40s, virtually MacArthur's entire Far East Air Force. They dropped 100-pound fragmentation bombs and swooped down to strafe the landing barges.

At around 2130 hours, Schumacher spotted a large ship he thought was an enemy cruiser heading toward Subic Bay. He closed as rapidly as he could. At 5,000 yards the cruiser caught the 32-boat in its searchlight and lobbed a two-gun salvo. The shells, estimated by Schumacher as 6 inch, exploded in the water 500 yards ahead. Schumacher fired his starboard torpedo just as a second salvo from the enemy ship landed 200 yards ahead and a third salvo landed 200 yards astern. Schumacher fired his port torpedo, then beat a hasty retreat—at about twenty-five knots now that the boat had gotten rid of the weight of the torpedoes.

"There was an explosion below the searchlight, definitely not gunfire, and debris came up into the searchlight beam," Schumacher reported. "There was a pause in firing, although the searchlight continued on and the ship apparently slowed as the range started opening. This was undoubtedly the second torpedo hitting as PT-32 drew away indicating the ship had slowed to about 15 knots. Fire was resumed and was excellent, continuing until the PT-32 succeeded in losing the searchlight about 2230 by a hard right turn."

Americans and Filipinos on the cliffs along the shore watched the combined sea, air, and land assault on the Japanese barges in the brilliant moonlight. They were sure the landing had been completely smashed. Several of the barges were sinking, and others were fleeing the scene as best they could.

The following morning, the army informed Bulkeley that PT-32 had foiled a cruiser's attempt to land a party near Moron. Although it is impossible to state with certainty the results of this action, it appears definite that no Japanese ship was sunk. Japanese records do show that on February 1 a Japanese minelayer suffered minor damage. Although this was attributed to shore fire, it is possible that the real cause was PT-32's attack.

Chapter Twelve
Matter of Time

We spit on our hands and waited for the enemy to come again.
——Jonathan Wainwright

There were long stretches during January and much of February when the battlefield on Bataan was relatively quiet. The weather cooperated as well; the days were bright and sunny. The Japanese probed constantly and tried to land troops behind Allied lines on the west coast, but, for the most part, they seemed content to harass the American and Filipino forces with their artillery and airpower. The Japanese seemed in no hurry, believing that it was only a matter of time until the Allied forces, plagued by rising disease and falling food stocks, would run out of ammunition and have to surrender.

According to *New York Times* correspondent Nat Floyd, who spent two and a half months with the men on Bataan, lack of food was the biggest problem. In a dispatch that, because of censorship rules, wasn't printed in the *Times* until April 22, Floyd wrote:

Bananas and other fruits were gone by the middle of January. Early in February rice stocks ran low and part of the Filipino troops *were put on bread. The bakery output ran up to 30,000 pounds a day. Eggs went quickly. While I was sick at Limay I had two eggs. They cost 25 cents each. Just before I left Bataan eggs were bringing $1 each in the black market. Cigarettes gradually increased to $3.50 a package.*

In the later days of the campaign, however, the going got tougher. More and more trimmings were dropped from meals. Men went on two meals a day late in January. Usually breakfast was around 8 o'clock and dinner between 4 and 5.

Breakfast was a pancake with a little corned beef hash of poor grade and locally roasted coffee. Dinner often consisted of salmon, beans and bread or rice. There was carabao steak or stew once or twice a week and beef when blockade runners got in.

Surprisingly, the men got along well together and there was little griping. Continued Floyd:

The communal life of Bataan, with its pervasive spirit of practical give and take, cleansed the whole body of men. The only fist fight I heard of was started by a man who had done time under observation in a mental hospital two years before. All were in the same boat with the same problems, tied together by the common threat to their lives and freedom. The men had nothing to fight each other about.

When they weren't manning a security post, the men had to invent ways to stay active during their idle hours. Gambling and listening to the radio were the two main pastimes. Wrote Floyd:

There was not a single store in Bataan, no movies and no recreation except in the amusement we found in Japanese propaganda broadcasts and in poker. Poker was the only use we could find for our money.

At night men clustered around battery radio sets in their own or neighboring camps to hear news broadcasts from Bataan's own station (actually aired from Corregidor) and afterward to listen to popular songs broadcast from Manila by the Japanese. The Japanese propaganda was without exception good for the American troops. They either laughed heartily or became very angry.

Tokyo Rose was on every night, doing her best to make a bad situation worse.

"You're out on the end of a 6,000-mile limb," she said in her condescending dulcet tones. "The Japanese Imperial Forces are sawing that limb in two. Get smart and give up. Why starve in the stinking jungle while the folks back home make big profits?"

Writer Steve Mellnick wrote, "Though we grinned at most of her barbs, and conceded that some had merit, we bristled at reports of labor strikes and picket lines in the states. Viewed against our background of bursting shells and slow starvation, such actions seemed incredibly selfish and shortsighted."

Initially, the struggle on Bataan went badly for the untested American and Filipino forces. The ground troops, which had become a kind of "Hooligan's Army," had fallen back on their last defensible line on January 24.

The shortage of dependable combat formations and the need to keep a reserve in readiness to watch both the front and the beaches meant that units in the line were never relieved. There were no rest areas into which the men could be withdrawn. This, perhaps, was one of the worst features of the campaign. Except for the climate, the trench warfare conditions resembled the Western Front in World War I. In that campaign, however, units in the line were relieved after a spell at the front and retired to reasonable rest areas. It made all the difference then; at least it gave the men something to look forward to and a target date to survive. There was nothing to look forward to in the Philippines. Most had already given up any hope of relief or rescue.

MacArthur was beginning to show signs of desperation in his messages to the War Department in Washington. On January 22, MacArthur cabled Washington the following:

Heavy fighting has been raging all day (on Luzon). The enemy has been repulsed everywhere. He seems to have finally adopted a policy of attrition as his unopposed command of the sea enables him to replace at will. My losses during the campaign have been very heavy and are mounting. They [are] now approximately thirty-five percent. My diminishing strength will soon force me to a shortened line on which I shall make my final stand. I have personally selected and prepared this position and it is strong. With its occupation all maneuvering possibilities will cease. I have not the slightest intention in the world of surrendering or capitulating the Filipino forces of my command. I intend to fight to destruction on Bataan and then do the same on Corregidor.

I wish to take this opportunity while the Army still exists and I am in command to pay my tribute to the magnificent service it has rendered. No troops have ever done so much with so little. I bequeath to you the charge that their fame and glory be duly recorded by their countrymen. In case of my death I recommend that my chief of staff, General Sutherland, be designated as my successor. Of all my general officers, he has the most comprehensive grasp of the situation.

On the receiving end of these messages was MacArthur's old chief of staff, Eisenhower, who was now a brigadier general and working for

General Marshall in the War Plans Department. Eisenhower wrote most of the responses and also kept a private diary of day-to-day events that recorded his true feelings toward his old boss. In late January and early February, for example, he wrote:

> *In many ways MacArthur is as big a baby as ever. But we've got to keep him fighting. . . . Today, in a most flamboyant radio (message), MacArthur recommends successor in case of "my death." He picked Sutherland, showing that he still likes his boot lickers. . . . MacArthur has started a flood of communications that seem to indicate a refusal on his part to look facts in the face, an old trait of his. He has talked about big naval concentrations; he complains about lack of unity of command, about lack of information. He's jittery! . . . Looks like MacArthur is losing his nerve. I'm hoping that his yelps are just his way of spurring us on, but he is always an uncertain factor.*

An ebullient MacArthur would report that the withdrawal into Bataan was executed "without the loss of a man or an ounce of material" and "would have done credit to the best troops in the world."

The truth of the matter was that the American and Filipino troops learned quickly and gave the Japanese all they could handle. General Homma had never expected the Americans to defend Bataan in such strength or with such tenacity. His intelligence officers had assured him that MacArthur would pull the Americans onto Corregidor and leave the Filipinos to their fate. Instead, the Allies, Filipino and American, though they had to give a little ground, had fought the Japanese to a standstill.

"We spit on our hands and waited for the enemy to come again," General Wainwright wrote in his memoirs.

Along the front, Homma's brigades had been severely mauled, and to their considerable battle casualties must also be added the sick. It is doubtful whether the enemy could have mustered more than three full-strength battalions, perhaps no more than 2,000 men, in the whole of Bataan by the third week of February.

The men had seen their half rations cut again, and all hope of eventual rescue gave way to a gloom and doom scenario. Without much to eat, the men were nourished on rumors of rescue missions that, with each passing day, grew less and less likely. Many of them gazed aimlessly out to sea, hoping to see the U.S. Navy steaming into sight. The men painted Vs on their helmets. The V wasn't for "victory"; it was for "victim."

One soldier asked a war correspondent to deliver the following message to Roosevelt: "Dear President Roosevelt, our P-40 is full of holes. Please send another."

Even the army brass had long ago considered the situation hopeless. Once when General Wainwright's car was strafed, he and an aide bailed out in a roadside foxhole that turned out to be an abandoned latrine.

A few minutes later while trying to clean himself up, Wainwright remarked to his orderly: "Who could ever imagine MacArthur in a mess like this?"

Indeed.

Wainwright was a heroic figure and a true inspiration to his men. Never one to complain, he simply did the best with what he had. When an aide, navy lieutenant Malcolm Champlin, asked him why he recklessly exposed himself to enemy fire while he toured his front lines, his answer was illuminating.

"Champ," Wainwright said with a slight smile and a slow drawl, "think it over a minute. What have we to offer these troops? Can we give them more to eat? No. We haven't any more food. Can we give them any more ammunition? No, it's running low. Can we give them supplies or equipment or tanks or planes or medicine? No. Everything is running low. But we can give them morale and that is one of my primary duties.

That's why I go to the front every day. Now do you understand why it's important for me to sit on sandbags in the line of fire while the rest of you run for shelter?"

Many of the men turned on MacArthur, and he couldn't help but hear the things they were saying about him, sometimes in verse.

> *Dugout Doug, come out from hiding.*
> *Dugout Doug, come out from hiding.*
> *Send to Franklin the glad tidings*
> *That his troops go starving on!*

A few miles away on Corregidor, the situation was less dangerous but filled with the same degree of pessimism as on Bataan. The island, built to accommodate about 4,000 people, was overcrowded with 10,000. Many of them lived like rats in bunkers; others rarely left the safety of Malinta Tunnel.

At first, MacArthur refused to live or take refuge in the tunnel during air raids and artillery attacks. He and his family lived in a cottage in an open area called Topside. While his wife and young son raced to shelter in the tunnel during air raids, the general would remain behind, standing in the open, daring the Japanese gunners to kill him if they could. He was determined not to let the enemy drive him underground. As the enemy attacks increased in intensity, however, he finally agreed to heed the advice of his wife and aides to take cover. Still, he could often be seen standing at the tunnel entrance shaking his fists and glowering at the enemy bombers.

Large telephone poles strung with cables were put up along the approach to the tunnel to prevent suicide bombers from crashing into the entrance. Also, flash walls were erected at an angle to prevent the enemy from "skipping" a bomb inside. The only problem with these defensive barricades was that they blocked the flow of air into the tunnel, making an already uncomfortable situation almost intolerable.

Each small lateral tunnel was crammed with more than two dozen people, who shared a single portable toilet and one washbasin. Visitors came and went at all hours of the day, often bumping into or stepping on wounded men lying in the aisles. The clatter of typewriters and the wailing of the wounded made sleep difficult. All had to cope with the smells of unwashed bodies and overworked latrines.

Other than the hospital complex, the busiest area of the tunnel was the communication center, which provided MacArthur his one lifeline with the outside world. Operational twenty four hours a day, it kept hope alive when everything seemed so grim.

The foul air, crowded conditions, and claustrophobic atmosphere took some getting used to.

"The smell of the place hit me like a blow in the face," wrote Carlos Romulo, the radio "voice of freedom" in the Philippines. "There was the stench of sweat and dirty clothes, the coppery smell of blood and disinfectant coming from the lateral where the hospital was situated, and over all the heavy stink of creosote, hanging like a blanket in the air that moved sluggishly when it moved at all."

Romulo, a marked man with a price on his head, would later become the Philippine ambassador to the United States and president of the General Assembly of the United Nations.

Pessimism was just as rampant on Corregidor as it was on Bataan, maybe more so. By the middle of January, few people could have any doubts about the outcome.

"I believe it is accurate to say that all of the top military personnel on Corregidor and Bataan had reached the conclusion that there was neither escape nor rescue in store for us," Lieutenant Colonel Sid Huff wrote. "I know I had resigned myself to that fate. And I have no doubt in my mind that MacArthur had given up hoping for help."

MacArthur fought hard to keep a positive frame of mind and set a good example for his staff and the soldiers under his command. He took each day as it came, always looking for a ray of hope. But deep down inside, he knew there wasn't any.

MacArthur was particularly distressed with the news of the fall of Singapore on February 15. He knew that meant the Japanese would have additional planes, ships, and battle-hardened troops to throw at the Philippines within the next few weeks.

Three ceremonies of note took place on Corregidor in the early days of the siege. Manuel Quezon, wracked with tuberculosis, rose from his wheelchair to be sworn in for his second term as president of the Philippines on December 30, and a somber MacArthur quietly celebrated his sixty-second birthday on January 26.

A much happier occasion took place on February 23 at a party for Arthur MacArthur, who turned four years old. A tiny birthday cake was made for him with four candles. One of his gifts was a little amber cigarette holder. Arthur was always putting a twig or a pencil in his mouth and pretending that he was smoking. He thought it was a fine present, Lieutenant Colonel Huff said, and later would strut around the tunnel "smoking" his cigarette holder.

Arthur would have his lunch most days with the nurses, where he would get to swing in one of their swivel chairs. He was a happy little child, providing an unwitting relief from the tensions of the surrounding war. He was a gentle reminder of another life and another world.

He would return salutes in a military fashion but didn't like being called a "little general." He preferred "sergeant" to "general," because sergeants got to drive the jeeps and trucks. He became a sort of mascot to those who lived and worked in the tunnel.

There were few quiet moments on Corregidor, for in the background one could always see the bright flashes and hear the harsh growl of guns on Bataan.

The fall of Singapore on February 15, with the surrender of 130,000 local, British, Indian, and Australian troops—the worst defeat ever for the British army—had a ripple effect on events in the Philippines. The Japanese success sealed the fate of the Allied troops on Bataan and Corregidor, freeing up more resources for the Philippine campaign, making it all the more difficult for supply convoys to run the Japanese blockade.

In late February, sensing a change in fortunes, the two highest-ranking civilians in the Philippines were evacuated from Corregidor aboard the submarine *Swordfish*. President Quezon left on February 20 with a party of ten for the Philippine island of Panay. A week later, the *Swordfish* took U.S. high commissioner Frances B. Sayre and a party of thirteen, including his wife and young son, to Australia.

Before Quezon boarded the tender *Perry*, the small boat that would take him to the submarine waiting in the deeper waters off Manila Bay, MacArthur took Quezon in his arms. "Manuel," he said, "you will see it through. You are the father of your country and God will preserve you." Quezon slipped from his bony finger a signet ring that he used to stamp his official documents, and he placed it on MacArthur's finger. "When they find your body," Quezon said brokenly, "I want them to know that you fought for my country."

Quezon also promised to give MacArthur $500,000 in gold, the amount he would have made, plus a bonus, had he completed his term as military adviser. This fact remained a secret for thirty-seven years, until historian Carol Petillo discovered a printed copy of the transaction in General Sutherland's papers.

MacArthur also saw Sayre off a week later on what would be a seventeen-day trip to Australia. "You will have a hard trip but when you come up at the end, you will be in a different world," MacArthur told him.

Earlier that month, the submarine *Trout* took away some twenty tons of gold and silver that had earlier been moved from the Philippine treasury in Manila to Corregidor. The sub commander signed for 583 gold bars and eighteen tons of silver coins, which were packed in heavy sacks. After reaching Pearl Harbor, it was discovered that one of the bars of gold, worth $14,500, was missing. After an inch-by-inch search of the sub, the gold bar was found in the galley. One of the cooks was using it for a paperweight.

MacArthur was able to receive supplies on Corregidor as late as mid February, when small vessels could reach the island at night. But by the end of the month—with the navy still unwilling to risk a single sailor on convoys—only submarines, light planes, and, occasionally, a lucky small craft were able to bring MacArthur supplies. During the five-month investment of Luzon, not a single American soldier, warplane, or warship reached the Rock.

The only reliable report about reinforcements, according to one wag, was that one of the army nurses was pregnant. Like most of the rumors, it proved to be untrue. But there were two weddings performed on the Rock, both involving nurses.

It was at this point that MacArthur gave to his superiors in Washington a somber yet dispassionate report that made it clear that his situation on Bataan and Corregidor was very shaky, at best. He wrote:

> *My estimate of the military situation here is as follows. The troops have sustained practically 50% casualties from their original strength. Divisions are reduced to the size of regiments, regiments to battalions, battalions to companies. Some units have entirely disappeared. The men have been in constant action and are badly battle worn. They are desperately in need of rest and refitting. Their spirit is good, but they are capable now of nothing but fighting in place on a fixed position. All our supplies are scant, and the command has been on half rations for the past month. It is possible for the time being that the present enemy force might temporarily be held, but any addition to his present strength will*

ensure the destruction of our whole force. We have pulled through a number of menacing situations, but there is no denying of the fact that we are near done. Corregidor itself is extremely vulnerable. This type of fortress, built prior to the days of air power, when isolated is impossible of prolonged defense. . . . Since I have no air or sea protection, you must be prepared at any time to figure on the complete destruction of this command.

A few days later, MacArthur again reminded Washington that he planned "to fight to the complete destruction of our forces on Bataan and then to do the same on Corregidor," adding that he planned to "remain and share the fate of the garrison. My family, with whom I have consulted, wish to remain with me to such end and I will not interfere with their decision."

The PT boats, short of gas, torpedoes, and ammunition, were now being utilized in a variety of noncombat roles.

Said Lieutenant Kelly, "Early in February they started sending submarines up from Australia and our boats would always meet them outside the minefields and bring them in, Bulkeley getting aboard to ride as pilot. The subs had news. They said America was building a big Australian base—that supplies were rolling down there."

Chief Machinist's Mate Carl Richardson, of Newcastle, Texas, kept Squadron 3's spirits up during the downtime with his elaborate wagers on the outcome of the war. Not the outcome, really, but when the Americans would win. His odds shifted almost daily and seemed to be predicated on all sorts of unrelated subjects, such as the daily health and disposition of the 41-boat's mascot, a monkey the men had christened Admiral Tojo.

As the days wore on and the Japanese got stronger, the men realized that the chances of getting out grew dimmer.

In the wartime publishing sensation *They Were Expendable*, author W. L. White wrote, "Doomed, but bracing themselves to look fate in the face as it drew nearer, knowing that they were expendable like ammunition, and that it was part of the war plan that they should sell themselves as dearly as possible before they were killed or captured by the Japs. But a handful of us secretly knew that we, and only we among these many brave thousands, would see home again, and soon."

Water buffalo, horses, and monkeys all became food for the starving infantry on Bataan. Even the navy had to do a bit of scrounging to survive.

Said Bulkeley, "On our boat we got so tired of salmon we ate a tomcat. It had been bothering us at night, and one of the men plugged it with a .45. We boiled it to get all the good out of it, and it wasn't bad. All dark meat—reminded you a little of duck. Of course we didn't have to eat it— if you didn't like tomcat, there was always plenty of canned salmon."

Squadron 3's last combat action in the Manila area came on the night of February 17–18 when Lieutenant Bulkeley again entered Subic Bay, this time aboard PT-35, which was commanded by Ensign Anthony Akers. Ensign Cox, aboard the 41-boat, accompanied the 35-boat as far as the entrance to the bay, where it lay to. Bulkeley was hoping he could get an enemy destroyer to chase him past the 41-boat so the latter could torpedo it.

Bulkeley charged into the bay and fired a torpedo at a small diesel-driven fishing trawler of about 200 to 400 tons, but the missile appeared to have passed under the ship without exploding. Moving on, PT-35 fired off another torpedo at what appeared to be a tanker, then retired immediately, strafing the beach along with PT-41 on the way out.

Cox ran the 41-boat close to shore and held his fire until he could see the figures of enemy soldiers running for cover. His twin .50s strafed the enemy campsite unmercifully for 200 yards. When he got to the end of the camp, Cox spun his boat around on her heels and started back the way he came. His four guns poured hundreds of rounds at fleeing soldiers, covering his deck with spent casings. Enemy gunners returned fire, but most of the rounds soared well overhead.

At the end of the encampment again, Cox shouted for a quick turn. "Let's do it again!" he cried, and sure enough they went right over the old route and shot away every bullet they had except a string for possible emergencies on the way home.

Bulkeley reported that a fire was seen in the area after retirement. What it was from could not be ascertained, because no explosion from the torpedoes was heard, possibly due to strafing during retirement.

That last raid used up all their "spare" torpedoes and much of their .50-caliber ammunition in stock, but the boats continued to make strafing runs along the west coast of Bataan over the next few weeks. One of those runs caught the attention of Admiral Rockwell's chief of staff, Captain Harold G. Ray, who wrote the squadron commander a quick note that said:

> *Dear Bulkeley: I really think your gang is getting too tough. The latest report is that "three dive bombers were seen over Mariveles Mountain chased by a MTB." Don't you think that is carrying this war a bit too far! Sincerely, Ray*

Bulkeley was determined not to have any of his men fall into enemy hands. After many discussions with his men, Bulkeley came to a decision that their best chance lay in making a dash for the coast of China, where they would burn their boats and join forces with General Chiang Kai-shek.

Said Lieutenant Robert Kelly, "At first glance you'd say that was crazy—the Japanese holding most of the Chinese coast—but not the way the skipper had it thought out. He knew China from the years he'd spent out there on a gunboat while I was there on a destroyer."

Bulkeley, left, and his father, Frederick, admire a model PT boat at
Bayonne shipyard. *Frank J. Andruss Sr.*

John Wayne, Donna Reed, and Robert Montgomery in *They Were
Expendable*. Montgomery, who had served as a PT commander in the
war, played the Bulkeley-inspired Lieutenant John Brickley. *World War
II PT Boats Museum and Archives*

The first American PT boat based on the seventy-foot British design. Too short to carry upgraded torpedoes, it was sold to the British in 1941. *Frank J. Andruss Sr.*

Upside-down construction of a PT boat. *Frank J. Andruss Sr.*

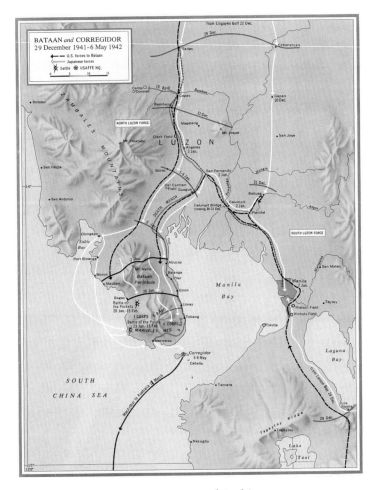

World War II PT Boats Museum and Archives

Mosquito fleet emblem. *World War II PT Boats Museum and Archives*

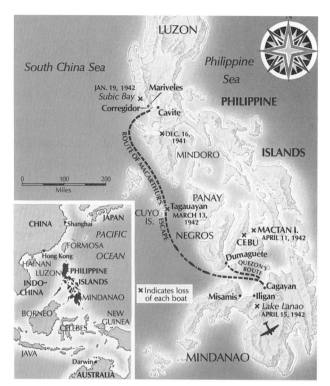

From left to right: George E. Cox, Jr., Robert B. Kelly, John D. Bulkeley, Anthony Akers. *World War II PT Boats Museum and Archives*

Lieutenant Bulkeley's PT41 cradled aboard the tanker *Guadaloupe* en route to the Philippines in 1941. *World War II PT Boats Museum and Archives*

Lieutenant Bulkeley, second from left, and General MacArthur, right, pay their respects to an unidentified American soldier in Melbourne, Australia, in April 1942. *World War II PT Boats Museum and Archives*

Navy recruiting poster (circa 1942) featuring Lieutenant Bulkeley. *World War II PT Boats Museum and Archives*

Lieutenant Kelly, front row center, poses with his crew, including Ensign Brantingham, front row second from left, in the Caribbean in 1941. *World War II PT Boats Museum and Archives*

Ensign Henry J. Brantingham stands by the entrance to the mess hall on Bataan in early 1942. *World War II PT Boats Museum and Archives*

Lieutenant Bulkeley, second from left, is shown with three of his senior enlisted men, John L. Houliham, left, Otis F. Noel, right, and George W. Winget in late 1941. *World War II PT Boats Museum and Archives*

President Roosevelt presents Bulkeley with the Medal of Honor at the White House as Admiral King looks on. *World War II PT Boats Museum and Archives*

Lieutenant Bulkeley, right, stands next to his wife Alice and Lieutenants Akers, left, and Kelly at a New York war bond rally. *World War II PT Boats Museum and Archives*

Captain Bulkeley, left and his wife, Alice, meeting with President John F. Kennedy at the White House in the early 1960s. *WWII PT Boats Museum and Archives*

Top row left to right: Major General Richard K. Sutherland, Brigadier General Richard J. Marshall, Brigadier General Spencer B. Akin, Brigadier General William F. Marquat; second row: Brigadier General Hugh J. Casey, Brigadier General Harold H. George, Colonel Charles P. Stivers; third row: Colonel Charles A. Willoughby, Lieutenant Colonel Francis H. Wilson, Lieutenant Colonel LeGrande A. Diller; fourth row: Lieutenant Colonel Sidney L. Huff, Lieutenant Colonel Joe R. Sherr; fifth row: Major Charles H. Morehouse, Captain Joseph McMicking; sixth row: Master Sergeant Paul P. Rogers. Navy personnel, bottom right, first row: Rear Admiral Francis W. Rockwell, Captain Harold G. Ray; second row: Lieutenant John Bulkeley, Lieutenant Robert B. Kelly; third row: Lieutenant George E. Cox, Lieutenant Anthony B. Akers. *World War II PT Boats Museum and Archives*

The squadron began hoarding gas and food for the trip, which caught the attention of a couple of correspondents—Clark Lee, of the Associated Press, and Nat Floyd, of the *New York Times*—who were covering the fighting on Bataan. Both men had gone on patrols with the PT crews and wanted in on the plan.

"We've got only about enough gasoline for one good operation and we have only a few torpedoes left," Bulkeley told Lee. "I have suggested that we fill up our boats with the gas that's left and go out and raid Jap shipping along the China coast. After firing all our torpedoes we'll land along the coast, destroy the boats, and hike overland to Chungking."

Said Lee, "Buck [Bulkeley] had served with the Asiatic Fleet and done valuable intelligence work which had won him the nickname of 'Charlie Chan' in the Navy. He was well acquainted with the China coast."

Lee told Bulkeley that he had a Chinese officer friend, a Lieutenant Colonel Chi-Wang, stationed in Bataan who had contacts with Chungking, and he arranged a meeting.

Said Lee:

> *The colonel agreed to send a wire to Chungking asking permission for us to land and requesting facilities to get us to Chungking. In a few days an answer came back. Chungking approved the plan and all arrangements were being made. . . . Nat Floyd of the* New York Times *heard about the project and decided to go along, one way or another.*
>
> *Bulkeley and his officers originally figured on taking seventy-eight men in three boats. . . . We estimated that with the element of surprise and with the firepower furnished by the boats, we would have a good chance to overcome the Jap garrison on the Swatow waterfront.*

Bulkeley discussed the matter with Admiral Rockwell, and they agreed that, to ensure some measure of secrecy, the torpedo boats would take the correspondents and Colonel Wang with them.

Destiny would have something else in mind for Squadron 3, but the plan for a 600-mile dash to China was all the men could talk about for several weeks.

"In a way I shall always regret that we didn't get a chance to capture Swatow," Lee wrote. "Bulkeley's wife was born there and it would have been a nice, sentimental gesture."

Chapter Thirteen

Exit Strategy

General, it'll be a piece of cake.
———John D. Bulkeley

The first hint Bulkeley had that something was in the works to get MacArthur off Corregidor came on February 18 in a conversation with one of the general's aides, Lieutenant Colonel Sid Huff. Huff casually asked Bulkeley whether his boats were capable of making a "sea run of a few hundred miles."

Huff was nonspecific and evasive, but there was no doubt he was feeling Bulkeley out on an escape attempt by MacArthur.

Bulkeley hesitated for only a moment. "No question about it," he said. "You have something specific in mind?"

"Maybe," Huff said. "I'll be able to tell you a little more about it later on—maybe toward the end of the month. If you were to do it, would you need any special material?"

Bulkeley thought of new gaskets, unadulterated gasoline, additional torpedoes, ammunition, and food, then said, "Nothing that would be available here."

Bulkeley thought the destination was China.

"We had just about enough gas to get us [to China], with hardly a barrel to spare," Bulkeley said. "If we were ever to make the run, we must make it soon. And it was getting plain that we couldn't do much more for Bataan, which was on its last legs."

President Roosevelt and his chief of staff, General George Marshall, had long ago given up any hope of relieving the Philippines. All their efforts in early 1942 had been to stockpile men and equipment in Australia for offensive action many months down the road. The two men wrestled with the problem of what to do with MacArthur. As early as February 5, Marshall had raised the possibility of MacArthur leaving Corregidor to organize a guerrilla resistance on Mindanao, then proceed to Australia. He also made it clear that if MacArthur did leave, it would be by direct order of the president.

MacArthur didn't make it easy on his superiors. He let them know that he had no thoughts of surrendering. On the contrary, he told Roosevelt, he fully intended to take his command headquarters to Bataan and fight to the end and then do the same on Corregidor. His wife and son would stay with him and share the fate of his decision.]

Despite MacArthur's stubbornness and massive ego, Roosevelt and Marshall grudgingly realized that they needed MacArthur if they were to win the war in the Pacific.

"Marshall had second thoughts about the prospect of losing his Far East commander," wrote William Manchester. "MacArthur was the only Allied general who had proved that he knew how to fight the Japanese and in whom the public therefore had confidence. He was the best informed U.S. officer in the Far East, America's one hero in the war thus far, an irreplaceable man who could provide leadership and example in the Pacific campaigns that lay ahead."

Roosevelt also knew that MacArthur wouldn't leave Corregidor unless he was ordered to do so.

Yet, Manchester added, it is almost certain that MacArthur would have been left to die on the Rock had Australia not intervened to still the sense of panic that was developing throughout the entire southwest Pacific area. Panic reigned following a heavy Japanese air attack on Darwin on February 19. The government of Australian prime minister John Curtin, still reeling from the shock of losing 20,000 men in the debacle at Singapore, was threatening to demand the recall of two of its veteran divisions from the Middle East to defend the homeland.

Roosevelt knew that the presence of MacArthur would be a big boost to the morale of the people of Australia and New Zealand. This was the primary consideration that caused the president to order MacArthur's departure from Corregidor, but it was not the only one. Roosevelt knew that Bataan and Corregidor would soon be captured by the Japanese and realized that MacArthur's death or capture would be a propaganda victory for Japan and a psychological blow to the American people, who regarded the general as a popular military hero.

The presidential order arrived at the communications center on Corregidor at 1123 hours on February 23.

> *The president directs that you make arrangements to leave [Corregidor] and proceed to Mindanao. You are directed to make this change as quickly as possible. . . . From Mindanao you will proceed to Australia where you will assume command of all United States troops. . . . Instructions will be given from here at your request for the movement of submarine or plane or both to enable you to carry out the foregoing instructions. You are authorized to take your chief of staff General Sutherland.*

There were no directions given to use the PT boats.

At a staff meeting that day, MacArthur said he faced an impossible dilemma. If he disobeyed Roosevelt, he faced a court-martial. If he obeyed, he would be accused of deserting his men. Therefore he intended to resign his commission, cross to Bataan, and enlist as a single volunteer. He even waved a piece of paper that he said was his written resignation. No one knew for sure whether or not this was a bit of theatrics.

His staff protested, arguing that there was a good reason for the order. He was being sent to lead a great relief effort assembling in Australia. MacArthur agreed to sleep on it.

The next day MacArthur radioed Roosevelt and told him he would go but asked that he be permitted to choose the right "psychological time" to depart. "I earnestly hope that you accept my advice as to the timing of this movement. I know the situation here in the Philippines, and unless the right moment is chosen for this delicate operation, a sudden collapse might occur. . . . With regard to the actual movement, I deem it advisable to go to Mindanao by combined use of surface craft and submarine and thence to destination by air, further movement by submarine being too time consuming. A flight of three B-24s or B-17s will be able to fight through if intercepted. . . . Advise the Navy that no, repeat no fuel is available here for a submarine."

Back in Washington, Eisenhower wrote in his private diary:

> *I've always been fearful of this plan. I think [MacArthur] is doing a better job in Bataan than he will anywhere else. . . . I'm dubious about the thing. I cannot help believing that we are disturbed by editorials and reacting to "public opinion" rather than to military logic. "Pa" Watson is certain we must get MacArthur out, as being worth "five Army corps." He is doing a good job where he is, but I'm doubtful that he'd do so well in more complicated situations. Bataan is made to order for him. It's in the public eye; it has made him a public hero; it has all the essentials of drama; and he is the acknowledged king on the spot. If brought out, public opinion will force him into a position where his love of the limelight may ruin him.*

MacArthur thought he would be able to leave on March 15. He asked Washington to coordinate the availability of a submarine and some aircraft. General Marshall sent a radiogram to Major General George Brett in Australia informing him that "General MacArthur will call upon you in the near future, probably shortly before March 15, to dispatch in a single flight three long range bombers to Mindanao. You are to be prepared to respond promptly to his request, and he has been authorized to communicate with you directly for arranging details. . . . This matter is highly secret."

Marshall then had Admiral Ernest King notify Vice Admiral William A. Glassford in Australia to "allocate submarines so that one is always at the disposal of General MacArthur."

One assumes that MacArthur's mention of "surface craft" refers to Bulkeley's PT boats. Before he made it official, however, he had one important test to conduct to reach his final decision.

On February 28, word came to Bulkeley that MacArthur himself wanted to inspect the squadron the next day. The inspection would include a run in Manila Bay, with the general as a passenger.

The officers and men of the squadron worked feverishly to get the boats slicked up for the commander's eyes. The next morning, the four battle-scarred mosquito boats rumbled proudly across the two miles of water to the Rock and picked up their passengers, who included the general's wife, Jean.

"With the four remaining P-40s flying security cover over Manila Bay, MacArthur and Jean went for a test run in a PT-boat on March 1," Manchester wrote. "The placid bay was a poor example of what they would face on open ocean. Tame as it was, Jean was a bit queasy."

Nonetheless, MacArthur's "finest soldier," as he often called his wife, said she was perfectly willing and able to endure a long trip in one of these rough-riding speedboats.

For a half hour, the general and his wife stood on the bridge of the 41-boat watching Bulkeley's boats go through their paces. When they returned to the dock, the general, to disguise the real purpose of the trial run, announced that, in recognition of his combat services, Bulkeley was being awarded the Distinguished Service Cross. He then invited Bulkeley to lunch at his quarters on Corregidor. Said Bulkeley:

As soon as General MacArthur and I reached Topside, I became aware that this was more than just a social occasion. MacArthur led me into a bomb-pocked open field away from prying ears, and while we strolled around side by side, he revealed that President Roosevelt had given him a direct order to leave Corregidor and go to Australia to take command of an Army for eventual return to the Philippines. He indicated that he hoped to lead the Army back in time to rescue his force on Bataan.

Although alert, the general looked gaunt. He'd lost thirty pounds in two months on skimpy meals of fish, rice and mule. He ate what his soldiers ate.

All of this he was telling me was top-secret stuff—I wasn't to say a damned word about it to anyone until it was nearly time to shove off.

General MacArthur said he wanted my PT-boats to break through the Nip sea and air blockade around Corregidor and carry him and his party some 580 miles south to the Philippine island of Mindanao. Then he would hook up with airplanes flown up from Australia for the final leg of the trip.

"But, General MacArthur, sir," I said, "wouldn't it be safer for you to get to Mindanao by submarine or by air?" But he smiled and said no, that the Nips would expect him to leave like that and would make every effort to intercept him. "They won't be expecting me to make the breakout by PT-boat," he added. "Besides I've got great faith in you and your boys!" The general paused briefly, then asked, "Well Johnny, do you think you can pull it off?"

Having been young, cocky, and brash, I replied, "General, it'll be a piece of cake."

Bulkeley admitted some forty-five years later that "no way" should probably have been his answer. He continued:

The nearly 600 miles of largely uncharted waters, with unseen jagged coral reefs waiting to rip apart our thin-skinned wooden boats, much of our route covered at night, alone should have warned of impending danger. And the Japs knew that MacArthur would make an effort to get off the Rock to avoid capture. Seizing him would have been a devastating propaganda victory for the Nips. Tokyo Rose had been gleefully bleating for days that General MacArthur would be captured and publicly hanged as a war criminal on the Imperial Plaza in Tokyo, in front of Emperor Hirohito's royal palace.

MacArthur told Bulkeley he wanted to leave on March 15.

Even MacArthur's aide, Lieutenant Colonel Sid Huff, was caught off guard by his boss's decision to leave by PT boat.

"Washington obviously expected us to go by submarine as others had already gone," Huff said. "That's what I expected too. In fact, it hadn't entered my mind that we would go any other way. Furthermore, all of those on the list with whom I talked—and I talked with almost all of them then or later—not only assumed we would go by submarine but definitely wanted to do it that way."

MacArthur told Huff that he had already talked with Bulkeley, who said it wouldn't be easy but it could be done.

Said Huff, "As [MacArthur] talked it was obvious that the general preferred the PT-boats to a submarine. I'm not sure why, but it was almost as if he suffered a touch of claustrophobia. He had, I remembered, shown the same attitude by refusing to sleep in the underground tunnel and I felt he instinctively disliked the idea of being cooped up. He was, as always, perfectly willing to take plenty of risks, but he wanted room to move about and to see what the enemy was doing; and most of all he needed to feel that he could fight back if necessary even if he had only a pistol with which to fight."

It was also possible that MacArthur discounted leaving on a PBY because of all the dangers involved in landing the aircraft in the water off Corregidor, though this was later done (in early May) to evacuate some nurses. It was also a fact that MacArthur had never flown before.

There is no doubt that MacArthur was enamored with the PT boats and had great confidence in Bulkeley, whom he called that "bold buckaroo with the cold green eyes."

Said Lieutenant Robert Kelly,

> *When General MacArthur had served as Chief of Staff of the Army during the 1930s, he had recommended to the Navy Department that small craft such as the PT-boats would be a valuable adjunct to the Fleet as defensive weapons. The Navy had derided and turned down this recommendation. MacArthur never forgot nor forgave this rebuff.*
>
> *After the start of the war, when he was assigned the responsibility for the defense of the Philippines, he took a personal interest in the operations of the PT-boats and had Lieutenant John D. Bulkeley, their squadron commander, report to him daily in person. In this way, over a three-month period he became not only familiar with their capabilities and accomplishments but he had an excellent opportunity to get to know and evaluate their commander, Lieutenant Bulkeley. It was on the basis of this personal evaluation that he seriously considered the use of the PT-boats for his evacuation from Corregidor.*

Lieutenant Bulkeley was an outstandingly dynamic and compe-tent young officer. His sincerity and resoluteness to duty were unquestioned. General MacArthur recognized and respected these characteristics. When he queried Bulkeley concerning the feasibility of the PT-boats accomplishing such a mission, he received an unqualified affirmative. There was no question in Bulkeley's mind that he could successfully complete this mission despite the long odds. This fortified General MacArthur's tentative decision.

Having served with Lieutenant Bulkeley as his second in com-mand on this and a prior assignment, I was privy to much of what transpired during his conferences with General MacArthur during the decision making process. MacArthur's decision to use the PT-boats for the evacuation of his party dramatically emphasized to the American public the over-whelming odds against which the United States forces were fighting in the Philippines. It evened an old score with the United States Navy. And since he had a tendency toward claustrophobia and did not relish making the trip on a submerged submarine with a commander whom he did not personally know, it provided an acceptable alternative which he elected to exercise.

The PT boats would give MacArthur a glamorous platform to fight his way out if necessary. They also offered him an opportunity to get to Australia faster than on a submarine. The quicker he got to Australia, the quicker he could begin preparations to return to the Philippines.

But the biggest reason why MacArthur chose the PT boats may have been a personal one. He wanted to show Washington, and especially the navy, that the much-vaunted Japanese blockade was penetrable, and at the same time it would allow him figuratively to thumb his nose at the enemy as his parting gesture. MacArthur knew the Japanese, and he knew what a defiant gesture such as this would do to the morale of the enemy command.

MacArthur apparently didn't ask anyone on his staff for an opinion and later told Huff that he had made up his mind from the beginning not to go by submarine.

This differs somewhat from an account given by noted historian and MacArthur biographer William Manchester, who claims that MacArthur switched to the idea of traveling by PT boat on March 9, only after he learned that the submarine *Permit* would be late in getting to Corregidor. MacArthur cabled Roosevelt on the ninth telling him he planned to leave on March 15 and reach Australia on March 18 and that he planned to leave aboard the submarine *Permit* but realized it would arrive too late.

The same view is held by navy historian Robert J. Bulkley, who said the "original plan was to make the first leg of the journey by submarine, using PTs to assist in escort and disembarkation. The submarine USS *Permit* was to put into Corregidor, pick up the party and leave on the 14th." When it was determined that the submarine would be late in getting to Corregidor, MacArthur switched plans and decided to leave on the PT boats and use the *Permit* for backup on the second leg.

Some historians believe that this plan simply made no sense.

Wrote historian Curtis Nelson, "One is hard pressed to imagine how four PT-boats could escort a submarine through 500 miles of enemy-infested waters, then be on hand to disembark its passengers afterward. It could not be done, nor would there have been any sense in trying. PTs depended on high speed for their survival; diesel submarines depended on slow, deep submergence for theirs. PTs were ill-equipped to signal, detect, or otherwise keep in contact with a submerged submarine."

As for safety, using the submarine was clearly the better choice. With the PT boats forced to carry an extra thousand gallons of gasoline in drums on their decks, one stray machine-gun bullet or hot piece of shrapnel would vaporize the little boats in an instant. Still, even with the lives of his wife and son at stake, MacArthur decided to risk it all and go by PT boat.

Nelson, among others, comes down hard on MacArthur's decision.

"MacArthur need not, and should not, have used the PTs of Squadron Three for the first leg of his escape," Nelson wrote. "The reason he did was devoid of sober military considerations. He thereby unnecessarily risked his life and the lives of all the others on the trip, including his family, and needlessly—even recklessly—sacrificed the squadron, consigning it to inevitable destruction in southern Philippine waters."

Although those close to him were sworn to absolute secrecy, word of MacArthur's plans began to leak out. The news spread to his staff on Bataan, and then Bulkeley's men knew that something was in the works.

Still, many could only guess at the destination.

Bulkeley told his boat crews to get busy overhauling their boats to prepare for a rough ocean journey. All of the engines had more than twice the recommended mileage on them and were in dire need of an overhaul. There were no spares. All the boats had been reduced to half speed. Some were worse than others.

"Overhauling those motors without any replacement parts was a terrible job," Lieutenant Kelly said. "For instance, any tank-town garage which overhauls a flivver back in the states always replaces the gaskets with new ones. Only we didn't have any. Or any sealing compound. So those old gaskets had to be carefully removed, handled as gently as though they were precious lace, and laid back in place when the motors were reassembled."

Planks were laid over two portions of the deck to accommodate twenty 50-gallon drums of extra gas for use on the trip. The added weight of more than three tons was spread out for balance. With the boats fully loaded with torpedoes, their top speed was reduced to around thirty knots, significantly less than that of an enemy cruiser or destroyer.

Bulkeley met with MacArthur and Admiral Rockwell every day to go over details of the breakout. Together they worked out an elaborate plan to have the four PT boats leave from four different locations so as not to arouse the curiosity of enemy spies, then meet up at the entrance of Manila Bay before heading south.

The first leg would take them to the Cuyo Island group, about 50 miles west of the island of Panay and 250 miles south of Corregidor, where they would rest during the day. On the second night, they would proceed to Cagayan, on Mindanao, to waiting B-17 bombers that would fly them to Australia.

They were to avoid enemy ships; but if they did come under attack, PT-41, with MacArthur and his family aboard, was to make a run for it while the other boats engaged the enemy. Alternate rendezvous points and hideaways were designated, and the submarine *Permit* would be available at the halfway point to take on passengers if the situation warranted.

There were few maps and no radar. Much of the trip would be through rough seas and under the surveillance of enemy planes and ships. Luck would be needed—lots of it.

Departure day was moved up to March 11 to ease apprehensions in Australia and to take advantage of a "very thin" moon.

Because of a lack of space aboard the PT boats, Bulkeley had to leave behind a total of thirty-two men, which included two extra crews and some ground personnel. Most of them were reassigned to infantry units on Bataan. Also remaining behind were Lieutenant Edward DeLong, who had been recently transferred to command the tugboat *Trabajador*, and Ensign Barron Chandler, who was still hospitalized on Corregidor with ankle wounds.

DeLong, who had lost the 31-boat the previous month off Subic Bay, was living the "good life" aboard the *Trabajador*, according to Kelly.

"We all sat around envying him because here he was, living like an admiral—a cabin, a wardroom, a real galley (not just a hot plate, which was all we had on the MTBs), and even a mess boy who could bake pies," Kelly said. "It was big-ship life, and Bulkeley and I used to find some excuse to go every night and eat his dessert and drink coffee. DeLong liked it so much he later decided to stay on Bataan rather than leave with the rest of us."

MacArthur, who had initial approval to take his chief of staff, General Sutherland, with him, had to make some tough life-and-death decisions about who else he would bring along. The anxiety level among senior officers on Bataan and Corregidor was off the chart.

"Roosevelt had authorized the departure of the general and no one else," according to historian William Manchester. "The War Department had amended this to include Jean and Arthur but MacArthur wasn't going to let George Marshall or anyone else decide who would accompany him on such an occasion."

If he was to properly prepare for an eventual return to the Philippines, he would need the nucleus of his staff, but because of the already over-crowded conditions of the PT boats, he was limited to the number of people he could select.

Besides his faithful chief of staff, Sutherland, he would select thirteen army officers, two naval officers, and Master Sergeant Paul P. Rogers, his secretary-stenographer.

Said MacArthur, "They were chosen because of their anticipated contribution to the liberation of the Philippines and largely formed the subsequent staff of the Southwest Pacific area. Two naval officers, Rear Admiral Francis W. Rockwell and Captain Harold G. Ray, were selected on the basis of their general usefulness to the United States."

Rockwell and Ray were originally scheduled to depart by submarine, but orders were changed at the last minute when the departure date was moved up. MacArthur may have felt that a couple of senior naval officers might come in handy on a seaborne evacuation by speedboats.

Word of the escape attempt reached Bataan, of course, and there were more than a few who harbored hopes that they would be among the chosen few to accompany MacArthur on the daring plan.

Bulkeley, it seems, was a popular young man during this period, an experience he thoroughly enjoyed. He said:

> *During the few days prior to General MacArthur's departure from the Rock, I received several and various luncheon and dinner invitations from a number of the general's generals located in Bataan. In each case, the meal was at best meager, but far superior to the edibles available at my camp.*
>
> *The point of discussion at each of the meals was to relay to me that "the end was near." As I had the boats and a small reserve of fuel, I was solicited to consider picking each of my hosts up in one of the boats when "judgment day" arrived. . . . The other generals, and MacArthur of course, knew nothing of the conniving being initiated by their fellow officers. With the situation deteriorating as it was and my being junior to the troubled generals, I concluded that I would tolerate their unclear thinking, but in no way condone their near-panicked escape plan.*

When the departure day arrived, many of the overlooked generals were at the dock to wave good-bye to MacArthur.

Bulkeley said many years later:

> *It didn't take a genius to read the faces of the scared generals—they thought the "jig" was up and the "Old Man" [MacArthur] had been informed by me of their plotting. Without a doubt, they were convinced that the general was about to chew them up and out for attempting to submarine his command by trying to save their "yellow" skins. The bastards!*
>
> *A machete could not have cut the emotion, fear, and sense of abandonment felt by all who were there. It was pure relief to the small clan of "escapists" that I had kept their personal secrets to*

myself. Even to this day, I would not divulge the identity of the general's generals who, for some fleeting moments, had placed their own personal safety and survival above the requirements of war.

Many of the enlisted men and junior officers looked upon MacArthur's departure with bitterness, feeling that they had been left aboard the sinking ship while the captain sailed away in the only lifeboat.

Meanwhile, Bulkeley's PT boats scrounged for food and gasoline, all the while continuing with scheduled maintenance. They were replaced for patrol duty by diesel-powered launches and native Q boats. While Bulkeley met regularly with MacArthur and his staff, his crews and boats just sat and waited.

"To keep the men occupied and also to keep our secret, we went right on with plans for developing our shore base at Sisiman Cove," Lieutenant Kelly said. "We installed a good cook's galley, fixed up the mess hall, screened in everything, as though we hoped to live there for months."

A dinner party was arranged with a couple of nurses and a doctor that made good use of the new galley. The meal consisted of fruit cocktail, pot roast with brown gravy and a whole can of mushrooms, rice, canned peas and beans, apple pie, and coffee.

It would be the last good feed for a long while.

Chapter Fourteen

Escape

You may cast off, Buck, when you are ready.
——Douglas MacArthur to John D. Bulkeley

The Japanese had also gotten wind that a rescue attempt was in the works. On March 9 there was a marked increase in the activities of enemy surface craft on Subic Bay, north of Corregidor. A surface patrol was reported off Corregidor, and a destroyer division was sighted steaming north at high speed in the southern Philippines. The conclusion drawn was that the Japanese High Command had issued orders to prevent MacArthur from leaving Corregidor.

The Japanese were aware of the possibility that the general would try to leave, because the radio-press had been "repeatedly broadcasting to the world an insistent and growing demand that General MacArthur be placed in command of all Allied Forces in Australia." In light of these factors, according to Admiral Rockwell, MacArthur decided not to wait for the submarine *Permit*, scheduled to arrive some time after March 13, but to take the four PT boats "as soon as preparations could be completed."

On the morning of March 10, Bulkeley, armed with maps and charts of the Philippines, met with MacArthur and Admiral Rockwell on the Rock to discuss an evacuation plan that he had worked out the day before. Bulkeley outlined a run south that would best steer clear of enemy strongpoints and hidden reefs. When the men nodded their approval, MacArthur said they would leave the next night. Bulkeley was taken aback but said he and his men would be ready to go. Bulkeley sensed that MacArthur knew for several days that he would be leaving on the eleventh but had kept it to himself for security reasons.

When Bulkeley returned to Sisiman Cove, he told Kelly but no one else. That could wait until the next day.

The part of the plan that did not change was to have the four PT boats leave from different locations, to arouse as little suspicion as possible. Bulkeley's 41-boat, with MacArthur and his family aboard, would leave from the North Dock on Corregidor at 1930 hours. Also riding in the 41 was MacArthur's chief of staff, General Sutherland, as well as Captain Ray, Lieutenant Colonel Huff, and Major Charles H. Morhouse, the general's physician.

The other three boats would depart from Bataan. Lieutenant Kelly's 34-boat and Ensign Akers' 35-boat were to leave from Sisiman Cove; PT-32, skippered by Lieutenant (j.g.) Schumacher, would depart from the Quarantine Dock at Mariveles. Their passengers would be taken to the departure sites from Corregidor by launch earlier that afternoon.

Admiral Rockwell would sail with Kelly, along with Brigadier General Richard J. Marshall (deputy chief of staff), Colonel Charles P. Stivers (operations officer), and Captain Joseph McMicking (assistant intelligence officer). Traveling aboard PT-35 would be Colonel Charles A. Willoughby (chief intelligence officer), Lieutenant Colonel LeGrande A. Diller (press relations officer), Lieutenant Colonel Francis H. Wilson (aide-de-camp), and Master Sergeant Paul P. Rogers. Sailing with Schumacher aboard the 32-boat would be four brigadier generals—Spencer B. Akin (chief Signal

Corps officer), Hugh J. Casey (chief engineer officer), William F. Marquat (chief antiaircraft officer), and Harold H. George (air officer)—and Lieutenant Colonel Joe R. Sherr (assistant Signal Corps officer). (See Appendix Two.)

The most controversial member of the group was Arthur MacArthur's nurse, a Chinese woman named Ah Cheu. Some felt that an American army nurse would have been a better choice, but MacArthur argued that had Ah Cheu been left behind, she would have been a marked woman for Japanese reprisals.

All four boats were to rendezvous at 2000 hours off the turning buoy just outside the Corregidor minefield at the entrance to Manila Bay. At the same time, two Philippine Q boats were to stage a diversion off Subic Bay, to the north, to give the enemy the impression that the PT boats were involved in some kind of action there.

If the boats were spotted en route, evasion tactics were to be used. If the boats were attacked, the senior boat carrying MacArthur was to turn away and attempt to escape while the others engaged the enemy. The captain of the submarine *Permit* was instructed to investigate the midway area of Tagauayan Island at daylight on March 13. Should one of the PT boats be hit by enemy fire, the captain of the submarine would be signaled at Tagauayan to prepare to take passengers aboard. The *Permit* might also pick up MacArthur and his family at Mindanao if plane transportation failed at the Del Monte airfield.

Should any boat break down, she was to transfer her passengers to another boat and proceed independently, or, if necessary, transfer all personnel and scuttle. All boats were to lay over in the lee of Tagauayan during the daylight hours, then get under way at 1700 hours on March 12 for Cagayan, on Mindanao, to arrive at 0700 hours on March 13.

MacArthur had Sutherland call Wainwright on Bataan, telling him that the general wanted to see him. He didn't tell him why.

Wainwright, who was called "Skinny" by his men, arrived on Corregidor with his aides, Major Johnny Pugh and Captain Tom Dooley, just after noon on March 10. Wrote Wainwright:

> *MacArthur was not at the pier when we tied up, naturally. He was not at his office in Malinta Tunnel either. But his chief of staff, Major General Sutherland, was in the office. He took me aside, and in a quiet voice he let me have it quickly: "General MacArthur is going to leave here and go to Australia," he said. "He's up at the house now and wants to see you. But I'll give you a fill-in first.*
>
> *"The President has been trying to get him to leave Coregidor [sic] for days, but until yesterday the general kept refusing. He plans to leave tomorrow evening around six-thirty by motor torpedo boat for Mindanao. A plane will pick him and his party up there and fly us the rest of the way. Tell no one—no one—of this until the morning after next, the morning of the twelfth."*

Sutherland told Wainwright that MacArthur planned to divide his Philippine forces into four subcommands, which would be under his control from Australia. Wainwright would assume command of all troops on Luzon. (Washington would later countermand that order and give Wainwright command over the entire Philippines, which, as it turned out, gave him the authority to surrender the entire archipelago upon the fall of Corregidor.)

After explaining that Colonel Lewis C. Beebe would be promoted to brigadier general and made MacArthur's deputy, carrying out his orders from Australia, Sutherland said, "You look hungry, Skinny."

I shrugged, but I was, Wainwright said.

"Come on," Sutherland invited, "have some lunch and then we'll go up to the house."

Wainwright shook his head. "Nope, I think not," he said. "I don't want to pick up any habits I could not keep on Bataan. We eat only twice a day over there."

After a few minutes, the two generals walked out the east end of the tunnel, then through the scrub jungle for a quarter of a mile to MacArthur's slate gray cottage.

Said Wainwright:

> *MacArthur came out on the porch, after saying something to Mrs. MacArthur and the boy inside. He was tired, but he grinned and shook hands with me. He calls me Jonathan, the only person in the world who does.*
>
> *"Jonathan," MacArthur said as we sat down, "I want you to understand my position very plainly. I'm leaving for Australia pursuant to repeated orders of the President. Things have gotten to such a point that I must comply with these orders or get out of the Army. I want you to make it known throughout all elements of your command that I'm leaving over my repeated protests."*
>
> *"Of course I will, Douglas," I told him warmly.*
>
> *Then MacArthur repeated substantially what Sutherland had told me about the altered command and turned to the tactical situation on Bataan—by that time simply desperate.*
>
> *"We're alone, Jonathan," MacArthur went on, turning to the tactical situation on Bataan. "You know that as well as I. If I get through to Australia you know I'll come back as soon as I can with as much as I can. In the meantime you've got to hold." He gave me a cigar.*
>
> *I told him that holding Bataan was our aim in life.*
>
> *"Yes, yes, I know," said MacArthur. "But I want to be sure that you're defending in as great depth as you can. You're an old cavalryman, Jonathan, and your training has been along thin, light, quickhitting lines. The defense of Bataan must be deep. For any prolonged defense you must have depth."*

"I know that," I said. "I'm deploying my troops in as great depth as the terrain and the number of troops permit."

"Good!" replied MacArthur. "And be sure to give them everything you've got with your artillery. That's the best arm you have."

We stood in silence for a few seconds as cannon fire could be heard across the water on Bataan. I was lost in reverie, perhaps thinking of MacArthur's dwindling ammunition and food supply, his air force of two battered P-40s, of the spreading malaria and dysentery and lack of medicine.

"You'll get through," I finally said.

"And back," MacArthur added, with all the determination the man has.

MacArthur then explained briefly why he was taking certain officers and men with him and why he was leaving others behind. I told him again that I understood.

Sensing that it was time to leave, I stood up. MacArthur rose and we walked down the porch steps. MacArthur gave me a box of cigars and two large jars of shaving cream.

"Good-bye, Jonathan," he said, shaking my hand. "When I get back, if you're still on Bataan I'll make you a lieutenant general."

"I'll be on Bataan if I'm alive," I swore.

Wainwright turned around and walked slowly back to Malinta Tunnel, where he would join his aides to catch the boat that was waiting to take them back to Bataan. As he walked, his head was filled with the day's events. And many times in the days and months and years that followed their last meeting on Corregidor, he thought of his parting promise—a promise he could not keep.

When Bulkeley went over to Corregidor the next morning for his regular briefing, he could feel the excitement in the air. By then, everyone knew that MacArthur and his party were leaving that very night.

Said Lieutenant Kelly:

Bulkeley went over early in the morning and returned to us at noon. He called in not only me but the other officers, Akers, Cox and Schumacher, and for the first time showed them copies of our secret orders and the charts he had worked out for our route. He made the point that we should all keep together, but if one broke down, the rest would go on, leaving it to make its way the best it could.

If we met the enemy, we were to avoid them if possible. But if they gave chase and were gaining on us so that an attack was necessary, the 41-boat, in which [Bulkeley] would carry the General, his wife and his son, would turn and run, and my boat, since I was second in command, would lead the attack to give the others time to escape.

The last thing he told us was that we were leaving that very night.

Lieutenant Colonel Huff and Jean MacArthur spent much of the afternoon of the eleventh collecting tins of food for the four PT boats and packing for the trip.

Each passenger was allowed one suitcase weighing not more than thirty-five pounds.

"Ah Cheu's belongings were folded in a handkerchief," according to Manchester. "Jean was taking one dress, her coat and a pantsuit. Arthur was wearing a blue zipper jacket, khaki trousers, and his prized overseas cap. He was holding his stuffed Old Friend and the six-inch-long toy motorcycle; his tricycle had to be left behind. His father was wearing civilian socks with loud checks and brown civilian shoes—wing tips with decorative little holes in them—and he carried not an ounce of baggage, not even a razor; he planned to borrow Bulkeley's."

Jean's suitcase had a label attached to it that read "New Grand Hotel—Yokohama." Five years earlier, the MacArthurs had stayed briefly at the hotel on their honeymoon. Three and a half years later, after the war had been won, MacArthur would spend his first night in Japan in what was left of the New Grand Hotel.

Huff also procured a mattress to be placed on the floor below for the MacArthurs. Rumors were spread later that the mattress was stuffed with gold bars and money. The most incredulous story told of the withdrawal "suggested" that seriously ill American nurses had been left on Corregidor so that the PT boats could transfer furniture (one version even included the piano) from the MacArthur's Manila penthouse.

In midafternoon, the passengers leaving aboard the 32-, 34-, and 35-boats were transported across the North Channel to Bataan. Among the luggage was a duffel bag full of canned food for each boat; it had been collected by Huff and Jean MacArthur on Corregidor.

MacArthur made the rounds, saying good-bye but also telling everyone that he was coming back. He seemed to be in pain. The look on the faces of those left behind would haunt him for the rest of his life.

Late in the afternoon, Lieutenant Colonel Huff had two staff automobiles driven into the tunnel to load any luggage to be taken on the trip. Jean, Arthur, and Ah Cheu would ride in the first car to the dock. Huff was ordered to take the four-star license plates off MacArthur's car so they could be used in Australia.

Just before dark, Bulkeley's 41-boat appeared at the bomb-damaged North Dock and sat there idling softly.

"It was a tense and unhappy and uncomfortable few minutes," Huff wrote. "Nobody said much. . . . Quickly and quietly, the MacArthurs stepped into the first automobile and left the big tunnel in a kind of stunned silence. At the docks the torpedo boat, with its extra gasoline supply, was loaded to the limit above and below deck."

At the dock the party walked slowly along a wide concrete pier to the waiting PT-41. Along the way they shook the hands of a few spectators. Each of them carried a bag or a suitcase. Lieutenant Bulkeley greeted the MacArthurs and carried their two suitcases aboard PT-41. In the growing darkness Lieutenant Colonel Huff stumbled a bit helping Jean MacArthur and Ah Cheu aboard. Arthur, clutching Old Friend, hopped aboard with little help.

While Mrs. MacArthur, Ah Cheu, and Arthur boarded, General MacArthur talked with Major General George F. Moore, who commanded the harbor defenses. Previously, MacArthur had cautioned Moore "that in case of the ultimate fall of Corregidor [he] was to make sure that the armament was destroyed to such an extent that it could not be used against an American effort to recapture the Philippines." Now, telling Moore "to hold Corregidor until he returned," MacArthur said, "George, keep the flag flying. I'm coming back."

Lieutenant Commander Melvyn H. McCoy, the radio material officer for the 16th Naval District, gave MacArthur a hand as he stepped aboard PT-41. He was followed by Morhouse, Sutherland, Ray, and Huff. Seeing Colonel Frederick A. Ward, who commanded the Army Transport Service, among the spectators, Huff waved and yelled, "We're coming back up here, Freddy."

To Morhouse it was like a dream. The day before he had been surgeon of the Provisional Air Corps Regiment on Bataan. Though he had never met MacArthur before, the general had chosen him, on the recommendation of others, to be the attending physician on the rigorous trip to Australia. When everyone was aboard, MacArthur turned and said to Bulkeley, "You may cast off, Buck, when you are ready."

It was 1945 hours, fifteen minutes before the scheduled rendezvous with the other three PT boats.

MacArthur, looking forlorn, his jaw clenched in defiant rage, stood topside and looked back on the outline of Corregidor receding in the darkness. It was a dramatic moment for a dramatic general. Then he raised his cap in a silent salute.

Chapter Fifteen

By Guess and by God

Oh, some PTs do forty-five
And some do thirty-nine;
When we get ours to run at all
We think we're doing fine.

After passing through the minefield, Bulkeley's 41-boat took the lead and Kelly's 34-boat dropped back to the rear.

The course from Corregidor channel was designed to keep the boats at least five miles offshore of the western end of Cabra Island, but stronger-than-expected currents and perhaps a compass error brought them within two miles. As they approached the island, they sighted many white lights coming from bonfires, which were often used as navigational aids for aircraft flying between Mindanao and Bataan. The lookouts obviously mistook the noise from the PT boats as the roar of aircraft.

"First we went five miles straight out to sea in the deepening twilight," Bulkeley said. "We'd hoped to get out unnoticed, but suddenly we saw a light glimmer and glow on one of the Japanese-held islands. It was a signal fire warning to the mainland that they'd seen us pass. If they had seen it on Luzon, that meant trouble for us—maybe bombers at dawn, maybe destroyers later on in the day. By eleven o'clock we made out the outline of Apo Island against the stars (there was no moon) and checked our navigation, which we were doing entirely by compass and chart. MacArthur and General Sutherland were pleased with the way it was going."

The boats swept around Cabra Island and turned sharply to the southeast through the Mindoro Strait and into the Sulu Sea. To the navy personnel the sea was moderate. It was a different story for the army personnel, however. Young Arthur and Ah Cheu quickly became seasick on the bumpy ride, and MacArthur was drenched from the spray that bounced off the curved hull. Without any sea legs, MacArthur retired to the mattress on the floor of the lower cockpit with Jean by his side.

Every twenty minutes or so, Bulkeley, who was navigating for all four boats, turned the wheel over to Ensign Cox, noted the compass bearing, and went below to the day room. There, at a temporary chart table he had rigged up, he would take the compass bearing and the rpm reading and make an educated guess at windage to chart the course.

Not long after midnight, the boats lost track of one another. Each of them had to stop to clean clogged gas strainers at various times, which made staying together impossible. Without much of a moon, visibility was practically zero.

Kelly's 34-boat, the only one of the four that hadn't been thoroughly overhauled, began to lag far behind. Soon the other three were out of sight. Bulkeley, realizing Kelly's separation, slowed to allow him to catch up. Kelly, meanwhile, had jury-rigged the carburetors on his engines by tying down the throttles at full power. Suddenly, Kelly's engines roared to life, and the 34-boat not only caught up to Bulkeley but shot past him, throwing up a huge rooster tail of water in its wake.

Said Kelly, "In the darkness I could see the Admiral [Rockwell] had squared around and was giving me a doubtful look. I could tell he thought he was riding with a madman."

Though a very senior navy man, Rockwell had practically no experience with PT boats. He didn't know quite what to make of Kelly's seamanship. He decided to find out. Pointing to a nearby island to starboard, he asked Kelly how far he thought it was to shore.

"About four miles, sir," Kelly responded, trying to exude confidence.

"Looks farther than that to me," Rockwell answered. "Take a bow-and-beam bearing."

Lacking the proper instrument for the measurement, Kelly used his thumb and index finger to make a forty-five-degree angle and sighted along them to a point ahead.

"Don't you have a pelorus?" Rockwell asked, referring to a common navigational instrument with two sight vanes.

"No, sir," Kelly responded.

"Hmm, I suppose the flagship has better means."

"No, sir," Kelly said. "They don't."

"How in hell do you navigate?"

"By guess and by God, sir," Kelly said.

"My God!" said the admiral, and this time he didn't say it as softly. "I hope," he added wistfully, "that we get there."

The weather was worse than forecasted. All the passengers were sick within the first hour, some having a tougher time than others. A strong easterly wind whipped up fifteen- to twenty-foot swells, and the boat trembled as though it was going to break apart.

MacArthur, unable to stay on his feet, remained below with his family in the tiny cabin, where he suffered in silence.

The general later wrote: "Towering waves buffeted our tiny, war-weary, blacked-out vessels. The flying spray drove against our skin like stinging pellets of birdshot. We would fall off into a trough, then climb up the near slope of a steep water peak, only to slide down the other side. The boat would toss crazily back and forth seeming to hang free in space as though about to breach, and then would break away and go forward with a rush. I recall describing the experience afterwards as what it must be like to take a trip in a concrete mixer."

Another passenger aboard the 41-boat called the conditions "murderous," much like hanging on to "a bucking bronco or riding in a wallowing tub." The whipping wind made the temperature feel twenty degrees colder than it actually was. Bulkeley, Kelly, and the other skippers, Lieutenant (j.g.) Schumacher and Ensign Andy Akers, had trouble keeping their binoculars dry. The lookouts, some standing on the flying bridge, had to hang on for dear life to keep from being washed overboard.

"MacArthur, little Arthur and Ah Cheu were in agony," Manchester wrote. "Ironically it was Jean, about whom the General had been most concerned, who was the least distressed passenger on the 41-boat. Arthur and his nanny lay below on the two officers' bunks, Arthur running a fever. On the floor beside them MacArthur sprawled on a mattress, his face waxen and his eyes dark-circled. He kept retching, though his stomach had been emptied in the first spasms of nausea. The anguish of his defeat, and the mortification at being sent away from his men, were now joined by unspeakable physical suffering. For a sixty-two-year-old man it could have been fatal. His limbs were so rigid that he was unable to move them. Jean, kneeling alongside, rubbed his hands hour after hour."

By midnight it was clear that the boats were struggling to stay together and the rough seas were taking a heavy toll on the passengers. Bulkeley decided to run closer to shore to find some calmer water, taking the chance of drawing some fire from enemy batteries. This also meant he had to keep an even keener eye open for uncharted reefs.

By 0300 hours, the boats had become completely separated. Each was on its own.

Kelly's 34-boat was the first to reach the rendezvous point of Tagauayan Island. It arrived at about 0800 hours, an hour late. At least Kelly thought it was Tagauayan Island; Bulkeley had the only detailed map of the area. Kelly managed to convince a highly skeptical Admiral Rockwell that they were in the right spot. Kelly circled the island, then entered the cove. There was no sign of the other three boats.

"My God," Admiral Rockwell said to Kelly in a nervous manner. "What's happened to the general? Where can he be?"

Kelly tried to put the best face he could on the situation, explaining that Bulkeley probably decided not to take any chances with women and a child aboard and made for the first island he saw. It sounded reasonable to Kelly, but he could tell by Rockwell's facial expression that he wasn't so sure.

Kelly dropped anchor and waited for the others to show.

Said Kelly, "As soon as we had entered the calm waters of the cove, the Army, which had been down in the cabin all night and miserably seasick, began stirring and soon showed definite signs of life—emerging into the sunlight, straightening their uniforms, and even mentioning the subject of breakfast, which wasn't unusual, considering the food that had gone over the side during the night."

Breakfast would have to wait. The first priority was to gas up the boat so they would be able to make a quick exit should the enemy appear. All of the refueling was done by hand, pouring the gas through strainers to try to eliminate as much wax as possible. Because of the flammable nature of the 100-octane gas, all electricity on the ship had to be turned off to avoid risking a fatal explosion. The process took most of the morning, and breakfast was delayed until around noon.

Meanwhile, Kelly sent two men ashore with semaphore flags to climb the island's 500-foot hill and stand continuous watch for the other three boats, as well as enemy aircraft. The rest of the men spent the morning assisting the refueling and making minor repairs. They wouldn't see another PT boat until 1700 hours.

What Kelly didn't know was that Bulkeley and MacArthur were almost blown out of the water by the 32-boat in a case of mistaken identity.

The skipper of PT-32, Lieutenant (j.g.) Vincent Schumacher, was chugging along on one engine just before dawn when he sighted a "strange, unidentified craft" closing on him from his rear. Believing that he was miles behind the other three PT boats because of his struggles during the night, Schumacher thought the mystery vessel must be an enemy patrol boat or destroyer.

Schumacher asked Brigadier Generals Casey and Akin, who were on the deck with him at the time, if he should open fire. He was cautioned to wait until the boat was in range. Schumacher ordered his crew to man the .50-caliber machine guns and stand by to launch torpedoes. General Akin prepared to drop overboard a barracks bag filled with code devices.

Schumacher then proposed they make a run for it, and the generals agreed. Orders were given to jettison the twenty drums of extra gasoline— nearly four tons of fuel—that were lashed together on the deck, to give them more speed and maneuverability.

In the increasing light of dawn, Schumacher took another look through his binoculars at the pursuing ship. He saw that it was another PT boat. As it came closer, Schumacher could see Bulkeley and General MacArthur standing on deck, the latter wearing his familiar cap and field jacket. Neither was smiling.

As Schumacher would later explain, he was fooled by two lookouts posted high on each side of the 41's flying bridge, which gave a "super-structure" appearance to the PT boat's otherwise low, smooth silhouette.

Said Schumacher, "Although the size and distance of PT-41 as it came up astern were next to impossible to determine in those conditions of light and sea, I do recall that it was my impression that it was larger than a PT-boat, and that it appeared to be further away than it actually turned out to be.... I mistook two men for substantial parts of the ship's superstructure."

Bulkeley was livid with Schumacher for this "error in judgment," which could have resulted in the death of MacArthur and his family.

Bulkeley ordered Schumacher to try to recover the gas drums he had dumped overboard. It proved to be slow work trying to drag the heavy barrels aboard a bobbing ship. They also made inviting targets if enemy aircraft should show up. After Schumacher had recovered only a few drums, Bulkeley took his boat out and ordered the gunners to shoot holes in the drums that were still floating.

Just as Kelly had earlier conjectured to Admiral Rockwell, Bulkeley headed for the nearest and best island he could find as it began to get light.

"It wasn't much of an island—only a quarter of a mile wide—but it had plenty of shallow water to keep off Jap destroyers," Bulkeley said. "We hid in the cove and stayed aboard—although we posted one lookout on the island's opposite shore. It was an untouched tropical desert islet right out of a movie travelogue. Palm trees waved lazily over a snowy white beach. The cove had a coral bottom and the water was clear as an emerald. The place was inhabited by one lone dog—a very thin one—although there were four deserted huts.

Mrs. MacArthur, Arthur, and Ah Cheu came up to sit in wicker chairs on deck in the bright sunshine. The general, looking much the worse for wear, paced the deck in silent deliberation. While breakfast was served and the boats were gassed up, Arthur played with the cook's pet monkey.

"It was too bad little Arthur couldn't have played on the beach but I told the General no one should go ashore," Bulkeley said. "Because if dive bombers came over and spotted us, we would have to get the hell out of that cove quick, leaving even the lookout behind."

As the day wore on, MacArthur became restless. If they missed the rendezvous at Tagauayan by waiting too long, he believed, they would jeopardize the entire mission. He conferred with Sutherland, Bulkeley, and Ray. Captain Ray, the only navy man in the discussion, pointed out that if spotted they might not be able to outrun an enemy ship, but if they remained in the cove they might be sighted by enemy planes. It was only an hour and a half to Tagauayan, but it would be a rough trip.

Said Bulkeley, "I figured the morning would be the dangerous time for bombers if they knew we had slipped out, so by two o'clock I felt it was safe to get underway. We threaded down through the little shoaly channels between the islands, which would defy a destroyer or cruiser to follow. When we arrived, Kelly in the 34-boat was already there and waiting."

No one had seen PT-35.

The three boats anchored in a cove overlooked by a low cliff. MacArthur called a powwow aboard the 41-boat to decide what to do next. Should they wait for the *Permit*, scheduled to arrive at daylight the following day, or continue that night by PT boat to Mindanao, as planned? The scene, as described by William Manchester, would have made quite a photo opportunity.

"There was General MacArthur sitting on a wicker chair, soaking wet; beside him Mrs. MacArthur, also soaking wet but smiling bravely; and then the Chinese amah holding little Arthur MacArthur, both soaking wet and very seasick. You could see [Arthur] was most unhappy but wouldn't admit it, and his jaw was set—just the exact angle of his father's."

The question of the hour was whether to switch to a submarine the next day for the final leg of the trip, or continue on in the PT boats, as planned.

Admiral Rockwell argued that they should stick to the original plan, because there was always the possibility that the *Permit* would not appear the next day. Sutherland agreed. Bulkeley warned that the weather ahead would be even rougher than that on the first leg.

"The afternoon trip had been rough, and I had to answer the General frankly that I thought the night trip would be rougher, because we would head away from the island into the open sea," Bulkeley said. "Seasickness may be a joke to sailors but it isn't to landsmen."

But Rockwell, obviously anxious to proceed, assured MacArthur that the weather would be good and the sea calm.

MacArthur had decided to stay with the PT boats, and, to make sure they weren't late for their air transportation to Australia, they would take the chance and leave at 1800 hours, while it was still light.

Then, to add some levity to the situation, MacArthur turned to Sutherland and said: "Dick, I can't do anything to Rockwell. But if it's rough tonight, I'll boil you in oil."

Bulkeley's weather forecast would be proved correct, but MacArthur's promise to Sutherland turned out to be nothing but hyperbole.

Schumacher was directed to remain behind to make contact with the *Permit* the following day to relay a message that the 41- and 34-boats had gone on to Mindanao. The army passengers aboard the 32-boat were divided between the other two boats for the last leg. Schumacher was to proceed the next day to Panay, about 125 miles distant, for repairs and fuel before continuing on to Cagayan, on Mindanao.

Although technically "commander" of this now two-boat squadron, Bulkeley was heavily outranked during these discussions of how to proceed with the mission. Typically, it didn't stop him from rendering his opinion in the strongest of terms. Still, it was MacArthur who made the final decision to proceed in daylight, over the strong objection of Bulkeley. Bulkeley did win one argument, however. One of the army generals suggested reducing the number of crew members on the 34- and 41-boats to accommodate the dispersal of officers from the 32-boat. Bulkeley argued against it and won.

As they readied to get under way, there was still no word from Ensign Akers and the 35-boat.

Chapter Sixteen

Into the Jaws of Death

I wouldn't do duty on one of these for anything in the world.
——Rear Admiral Francis W. Rockwell

Under cover of approaching twilight, PT-34 and PT-41 slowly crept away from Tagauayan Island on a southeasterly course across the Sulu Sea. The wind and waves rose up with a vengeance to greet them.

The 34-boat went first in the hopes that it would bear the brunt of the heavy seas while the 41-boat could ride in the relative calm of its wake, thereby providing a smoother ride for MacArthur's party. It sounded good in theory, but both boats took a pounding over the next twelve hours.

Less than an hour after leaving Tagauayan, a Japanese cruiser was spotted on an easterly course in the twilight to the south. It was on a path that would cross right in front of the PTs. Bulkeley issued orders for the PT boats to turn at maximum speed due west into the setting sun. But because of the crowded conditions aboard both boats, they could do only about twenty knots, much slower than the speed of an enemy cruiser.

MacArthur, lying on a mattress below, overheard the crew's conversation regarding the sighting, but he said nothing. He was too seasick to move, gritting his teeth as Jean rubbed his hands. After about twenty minutes of anxious waiting, the danger passed. Apparently, the Japanese lookouts failed to see the two small boats in the glare of the setting sun.

Bulkeley said later:

> I think it was the whitecaps that saved us. The Japs didn't notice our wake even though we were foaming away at full throttle.
>
> During the excitement, the General was lying down in the cabin with his eyes closed, but Mrs. MacArthur, who was with him, heard everything that went on and she didn't turn a hair. She took it like a lady—went right on rubbing the General's hands to keep up his circulation, though she was seasick herself.
>
> I never went below, and all my men stayed at battle stations, so the people in the cabin took care of themselves—there was no one to wait on them.

The winds howled like a wolf at a full moon. The waves slammed into the tiny ships and swept across the slippery decks, now empty of the extra barrels of gasoline. The sailors and passengers hung on to whatever they could grab. Lightning flashed across the sky, which only signaled worse weather ahead.

The boats steered for the coast of Negros Island, where they could hug the shore and get a smoother ride. The southern tip of Negros would also mark the entrance to the Mindanao Sea.

Admiral Rockwell remembered, "At dark we headed to the eastward to cross the traffic lane, and then slipped along the coastline of Negros Island as close inshore as we thought was safe. Our navigation was pretty sketchy but we finally made a landfall on Silino Island at 0200 and laid our course for Cagayan. The weather was very bad from 0100 to daylight, with heavy seas and frequent rain squalls, but as we passed through the most likely patrol area during this time we were probably lucky at that."

The two boats were lucky in another sense: the Japanese shore batteries mistook the roar of their engines for the drone of warplanes and directed their searchlights on the sky and not out to sea.

Neither Bulkeley nor Kelly had ever sailed in this part of the Philippines. This night, they were literally sailing blind.

"We were going in the dark entirely by dead reckoning," Bulkeley said later. "At midnight we figured we'd be off the strait—so we turned into the pitch blackness, holding our breath, but still we didn't hit anything. I had no charts, I'd never been there before. I could see absolutely nothing, but since we didn't crash into a beach, we kept on going, and at last I knew we were through and safely into the Mindanao Sea—our dead-reckoning navigation had been right."

The sea was particularly angry, and it seriously threatened to sweep people overboard. Navigation was hit or miss and strictly by feel. The magnetic compass on Kelly's boat swung wildly and varied by twenty-five to thirty degrees. Said Kelly:

> *Big foaming waves fifteen or twenty feet high thundering over the cockpit, drenching everybody. Our binoculars were full of water and our eyes so continuously drenched with stinging salt that we couldn't see, in addition to which it was pitch-black. We were making good speed through strange waters with islands all around us. We could see the outlines of the big ones—Negros and Mindanao—very dimly against the horizon through the storm. But there were dozens of small ones and probably hundreds of reefs.*
>
> *You had to keep one hand in front of your eyes to avoid the slapping force of the water and yet you needed both to hold on.*
>
> *The Admiral was pretty wrought up. "I've sailed every type of ship in the Navy except one of these MTBs," he shouted at me above the wind, "and this is the worst bridge I've ever been on. I wouldn't do duty on one of these for anything in the world—you can have them."*

Of course, conditions were just as tough on any enemy craft that was in the area looking for boats trying to run the blockade.

Kelly's boat, which was in the lead, had an especially tough time keeping Bulkeley's boat in sight. Visibility was less than a hundred yards, and the waves seemed to grow larger every minute.

Remembering that he had told MacArthur that the seas would be calmer on the last leg to Mindanao, Rockwell shouted in Kelly's ear: "The General's going to give me hell for this in the morning. Damned if I thought Bulkeley knew what he was talking about—but he surely did."

Rockwell kept Kelly company on the bridge the whole way during one of the most miserable nights of his life. Several of the passengers hung on to the torpedo tubes while retching into the sea. Others remained below, too drained of energy to move.

The weather was doubly hard on the crew, who hadn't slept in more than forty-eight hours. Ensign Cox passed out at the wheel. Then, with Chief Morris Hancock at the helm, the 41-boat started to veer slowly off course. Hancock was dozing while standing up in a howling gale. Bulkeley noticed in time and took over the wheel.

On the 34-boat, Admiral Rockwell's teeth were chattering, but he would not leave the bridge and get some rest. Kelly insisted on bringing the admiral a sweater.

"When I went down to hunt for it I stepped on something soft and produced a groan," Kelly said. "It turned out I had gone over my shoe tops into the soft abdomen of a general. But while I was getting my flashlight turned on to see what it was, I managed to step on another general who was too weak to even groan. I don't think he cared if he lived or died. The only person enjoying the trip was an air corps captain. You can no more make one of them seasick than you can a sailor. He was snoring in his bunk, happy as a baby."

The situation was similar on Bulkeley's boat. All the passengers were wiped out. A staff officer described MacArthur's seasickness as "almost a paralysis, a stiffness and rigidity of the limbs that made it practically impossible for him to move. It must have been a nervous reaction. We were afraid, for a time, that he was going to die."

MacArthur was suffering as much mentally as he was physically. He couldn't stop thinking about all the men left behind on Bataan and Corregidor and what they must be thinking of him. He knew they were making up new verses to go with his nickname of "Dugout Doug." It tormented him. He couldn't sleep.

His aide and trusted confidant, Sid Huff, was like the rest aboard. He had hardly slept in the past forty-eight hours. Just after midnight, Huff squeezed into a spot on the steps of the lower cockpit, right above the MacArthurs, and finally dropped off to sleep. He thought he was dreaming when he heard a voice crying out, "Sid? Sid?" Huff quickly realized it was MacArthur.

"Yes, sir?" Huff answered, trying to pull himself together. It was dark but he could see MacArthur sitting below him on the mattress. Jean seemed to be asleep.

"I can't sleep," MacArthur said.

"Sorry, sir."

"I want to talk."

"Yes, sir. What about?"

"Oh, anything. I just want to talk."

"Yes, sir."

That began a couple of the strangest hours of his life, Huff wrote nine years later in a series of *Saturday Evening Post* articles.

Up on deck, Bulkeley was sending the torpedo boat along at a good clip in the darkness, the lookouts were alert for every craft, we were all soaked with the salt spray and a dash of coffee—and the General was sitting on the mattress talking about what we had gone through in the last four years or so.

What had happened, I soon realized, was that he had had time to think back over our defeat in the Philippines and he was now trying to analyze it and get it all straight in his mind. And to do that, he wanted to think out loud. He talked about the program he had drawn up for preparing the Philippines to defend themselves by 1946. He recalled how difficult it had been to persuade the legislature to provide enough money, and how that money had been whittled down in the next few years. He remembered his differences with Washington and how orders had been prepared for his recall and how he had, more or less, been forced into retirement in 1937.

Occasionally I remembered something that had slipped his mind, but most of the time MacArthur just talked, his voice slow and deliberate and barely distinguishable above the high whine of the engines. I was soon wide-awake, especially when his voice choked up as he expressed his chagrin at being ordered to leave Corregidor.

It was all a little uncanny. But it was bitterly dramatic, too, and gravely sad. I thought then that on this bouncing voyage to Mindanao, on this rough passage that brought us not only mental but physical wretchedness, he had been thrust downward from the crest as far as a man could go.

I was wrong, of course. I was wrong because we could not realize the greater trouble that lay ahead. But I was wrong, too, if I thought that MacArthur was merely looking back at what might have been. He was in the trough of the wave at the moment, but he had no intentions of staying there. His jaw was set. His face was grim. When he said he would return to the Philippines, he meant it, and he was already planning how he could do it.

It was two o'clock in the morning when he stopped thinking out loud and was silent for a few moments. Then he added, "Sid, if we ever get to Australia, the first thing I'm going to do is make you and [LeGrande] Diller full colonels. Good night."

"Thank you, General," I said. "Good night." I then put my head
back against a bulkhead and tried going back to sleep.

The dawn brightened everyone's mood. The wind had died down and
so had the waves. But, because of the storm, the 41-boat was two hours
behind schedule and forced to travel through a heavily patrolled area of
the Mindanao Sea in daylight.

Said Kelly, "Dawn came at six and we saw land ahead, a point which I
thought was the peninsula just west of Cagayan, our destination. I showed
it to the admiral and he shook his head with satisfaction.

"Good navigation, Kelly," he said. "I wouldn't have believed it possible."

As soon as Kelly was sure they were approaching the correct landfall,
he slowed his boat and let Bulkeley take the lead, because he had the channel charts. Bulkeley asked Huff to tell MacArthur, and the general came
topside with Jean to witness the boat pull up to the dock.

"We were not at all sure that we would not find a Japanese warship in
the harbor," a nervous Huff wrote. "Everyone was alert and craning his
neck as we rounded the last bend. The harbor without a Japanese flag
looked mighty good."

William Manchester wrote that MacArthur, unshaven and rubbing his
bloodshot eyes, "had miraculously recovered from his ordeal" and stood at
the prow as the 41-boat came into the dock, "looking very much like
Washington crossing the Delaware."

An emotional MacArthur approached Bulkeley and told him that he
would award every officer and man of his unit the Silver Star for gallantry
for their efforts in getting his party to Mindanao.

"You've taken me out of the jaws of death, and I won't forget it," he
said. He would more than keep his promises.

After shaking hands with the greeting party, MacArthur politely asked
General Sharp where the nearest latrine was. The party then sped off in

automobiles for some rest at the Del Monte plantation.

A few hours later, Bulkeley delivered the news that Ensign Akers and the missing 35-boat, with MacArthur's intelligence officer, Colonel Willoughby, among others aboard, arrived in port after a long voyage. It had missed the assembly point at Tagauayan Island by several miles that first night and had laid up in the lee of an uninhabited island during the day. Finally reaching Tagauayan at nightfall, Akers learned from PT-32 skipper Schumacher that the other two boats had already departed for Cagayan.

MacArthur was greatly relieved that his entire staff had safely arrived on Mindanao, once again praising Bulkeley and his crews for their valiant seamanship.

"If the boats never accomplish anything more and were burned now, they'd have earned their keep a thousand times over," MacArthur told Bulkeley, promising that once he reached Melbourne he would try to get him and his key men out.

MacArthur's party would have to survive three more days of delay and intra-service bickering before his planes arrived and they could complete their trip to Australia. Four B-17 bombers were scheduled to be waiting at Del Monte airfield for the MacArthur party on March 13, the day they arrived at Mindanao. An embarrassed General Sharp told MacArthur that his planes had not yet arrived.

The following day a lone, patched-up Flying Fortress landed at Del Monte. Four had left Australia. Two had turned back with engine trouble and a third had crash-landed in a heavy rainstorm in Cagayan Bay. The fourth, piloted by a fresh-faced Lieutenant Harl Pease, limped in with damaged turbo superchargers and faulty brakes. MacArthur took one look at the plane and the young pilot and declared that he wouldn't risk his family in "that broken-down crate with a boy at the controls." The twenty-four-year-old Pease, who would earn the Medal of Honor five months later for heroism at Rabaul, left that evening without MacArthur's party but with sixteen other grateful passengers. He arrived safely in Australia.

MacArthur was told that these were the best planes the U.S. Army commander in Australia, Lieutenant General George Brett, had been able to scrape up. He had tried to borrow four of the dozen brand-new Flying Fortresses assigned to Vice Admiral Herbert Leary, the senior American naval officer in the Australia–New Zealand theater, but had been turned down.

"I'd like to help you, Brett," Leary had said, "but it is quite impossible. We need those planes here and can't spare them for a ferry job, no matter how important it is."

MacArthur fired off an angry message to Chief of Staff George Marshall in Washington, demanding that "the best three planes in the United States or Hawaii" be made available to him "with completely adequate and experienced crews. To attempt such a desperate and important trip with inadequate equipment would amount to consigning the whole party to death and I could not accept such a responsibility," he said.

When Brett got this message, he once more called on Admiral Leary, this time determined to be more forceful. To his amazement, Leary didn't raise a single objection. A radiogram from Washington had seen to that, evidently. Brand-new bombers were instantly made available, but it took another day to prepare them for the long flight.

They were scheduled to arrive at 2000 hours on the sixteenth. Two arrived at 2200 hours. The third never left Australia because of an oil leak. It was decided that all the passengers could make the trip in the two bombers if their luggage was left behind.

Said Colonel Francis H. Wilson, "Each passenger, with the possible exception of General and Mrs. MacArthur, was directed to leave his one piece of hand luggage on the field [so] that it might be sent to Australia later. No one objected. We would gladly have removed our clothes if that had been ordered. Our baggage did arrive later on another plane."

According to historian Eric Morris, MacArthur's "arrogant" attitude enraged some of the airmen stationed at Del Monte, who noticed that the two bombers were being stocked with cases of apple juice and pineapples, footlockers and mattresses. Private First Class Dick Osborn overheard the copilot of the bomber that crashed two days earlier, a Lieutenant Fitzgerald, tell MacArthur that he badly wanted to get back to Australia to get another plane and get back into the war.

"I'm glad to hear it, son," the general replied, "but I'm sorry, we don't have any room."

Osborn decided he was going to do something about that. He walked up to the frustrated flier and promised to get him out. He grabbed an oxygen bottle, a mask, and a parachute from the service trolley and thrust them at the young officer, then led him around to the rear of the plane. Osborn took out a cloth and started to polish the rear turret. The gunner pulled back the side window.

"Hey, fella," Osborn said to the gunner, "when I give you the nod I want you to open the escape hatch, and this lieutenant here is going with you all the way."

A few minutes later a small crowd gathered to watch MacArthur, "godlike," wave as he and his party of VIPs board the plane. Osborn signaled, the little escape hatch opened, and the pilot scrambled aboard.

If people thought MacArthur was a little cranky at Del Monte after his exhausting escape from Corregidor, it was nothing compared to the attitude he developed on an equally arduous journey through Australia.

Crammed like sardines, the two bombers lumbered down the blacked-out runway and barely made it into the sky, their engines backfiring like old jalopies. Instead of seasickness, there was airsickness all around during the ten-hour flight. One of the planes was fired upon as it crossed over the Dutch East Indies.

On approach to Darwin they learned that the designated airfield was under attack by Japanese planes. The two aircraft carrying MacArthur's party were rerouted to Batchelor Field, forty-five miles south of Darwin.

MacArthur's plane landed first at about 0900 hours and the other landed forty minutes later.

Upon disembarking, Jean MacArthur told her husband that she would never fly again. Arthur, who had been very airsick on the flight, was put on intravenous fluids by Dr. Morhouse, who told MacArthur that the boy couldn't tolerate a long, overland trip. MacArthur had no choice. He and his party continued on by air to Alice Springs in mid Australia, taking off just before a Japanese bombing raid.

After MacArthur and his family stayed overnight at a dilapidated hotel, train transportation was arranged for them the rest of the way. Most of MacArthur's staff flew ahead to Melbourne. At a stop at the small town of Burra, fifty miles north of Adelaide, MacArthur was briefed by his deputy chief of staff, Brigadier General Richard Marshall, who had just come from a fact-finding jaunt to Melbourne. He told MacArthur that there were not sufficient forces in Australia to offer any hope of saving the beleaguered Philippines now or in the near future. Washington's claim of a buildup of troops, tanks, and planes had been a myth.

For the first time, MacArthur realized fully that his beloved Philippines were doomed, and it filled him with outrage. He felt he had been led astray and lied to by his superiors in Washington. He would never forget it.

The Australians sensed his mood, of course, and were put off by it.

"There has been too much publicity about General MacArthur," remarked former secretary of war Patrick J. Hurley, who was serving as a brigadier general in Australia. "That may be all right in the States, where the people don't know anything more about war than what they read in the papers, but it's different here. After all, there are thousands of soldiers in Australia, who lived through Tobruk and the Western Desert, Singapore and Java. They won't look on the men who came out of the Philippines as supermen. . . . McArthur's staff won't help. To hear them tell it, they're the greatest heroes and finest soldiers the world ever saw. That won't sit well with a lot of people."

At a stopover at Adelaide just before the final destination of Melbourne, MacArthur put on a brave face and told those in the audience, "The President of the United States ordered me to break through the Japanese lines and proceed from Corregidor to Australia for the purpose, as I understand it, of organizing the American offensive against Japan, a primary object of which is the relief of the Philippines. I came through and I shall return."

When word of the short speech filtered back to Bataan and Corregidor, some of the men mocked the ego of MacArthur for using the first person singular when the first person plural would have been more accurate. It soon became a joke among the men, who used it derisively: "I'm going to the latrine but I shall return."

Bulkeley had orders to keep his three boats under cover while MacArthur was in Mindanao. There was no need to draw any more attention to the area than necessary.

Bulkeley continued to report to MacArthur and his staff daily. Bulkeley had been given a new mission: to conduct offensive operations against the empire of Japan in waters north of Mindanao.

"I, a lowly lieutenant, had in effect been named commander of the United States Fleet in the Philippines," Bulkeley said. "A thought struck me: that's a hell of a lot of water for my 'fleet' of three beat-up PT-boats to cover."

The disappearance of the 32-boat weighed heavily on his mind during the next few days. Over the next few weeks he took several trips in a light plane over the rendezvous point around Tagauayan Island and off the coast of Negros, but he saw nothing.

He wouldn't find out what happened to the 32-boat until a month later, when he arrived in Australia and overheard some scuttlebutt filtering in from Fremantle. Until then, Bulkeley had listed the crew members as missing in action and presumed lost.

As it turned out, Lieutenant (j.g.) Schumacher decided back on March 13 that the 32-boat was in no condition to continue and had the submarine *Permit* sink it with its deck guns to keep it from falling into the hands of the enemy. The *Permit* then took on the fifteen-man crew and continued on its mission to Corregidor. Eight members of Schumacher's crew were offloaded on Corregidor. Schumacher, his executive officer, Ensign Cone Johnson, and five others among the PT-32 crew remained aboard while the submarine took on forty new passengers, most of them code breakers.

The *Permit*, one of the navy's first modern fleet boats, large and roomy as submarines went, left Corregidor on March 17 with 111 people on board, including its crew. It was more than twice the number of people the boat had been designed to accommodate. The submarine was forced to endure twelve depth charges and remain submerged for more than twenty-two hours under difficult breathing conditions. On April 7, after a voyage of twenty-three days, the *Permit* arrived in Fremantle, Australia.

In the investigation that followed, Bulkeley said that the condition of the engines and hull of the 32-boat were good when he last saw it at 1800 hours on March 12. Even without other minor repairs, the boat should have been able to make twenty knots, he claimed. Furthermore, Schumacher had sufficient gas to carry out his orders to proceed to Cagayan, Mindanao.

A livid Bulkeley had previously cited Schumacher for a lack of judgment for an engine fire aboard the 32-boat in late December. To that he now added a failure to recognize the silhouette of PT-41 on March 12, which endangered General MacArthur and his party, and a failure to report the disposition of the ship or its men to the commanding officer. Furthermore, he was clearly disappointed that no attempt was made to salvage any of the 32's ordnance, which was badly needed elsewhere.

Schumacher would claim that two of his engines were out of commission and the third unreliable when he made his decision to scuttle the ship. He said he had been given verbal orders from Bulkeley to remain overnight at Tagauayan Island in order to deliver a message to the *Permit* that MacArthur had continued on to Mindanao, then to use his judgment and "make out as best you can."

Bulkeley said Schumacher was directed to stay for forty-eight hours at the Tagauayan Island rendezvous for orders in case the bombers did not reach Mindanao, then proceed to Iloilo, Panay, a distance of 100 miles, for gas, then continue on to Cagayan, on Mindanao. No orders to "make out as best you can" were given, according to Bulkeley. The record showed that the *Permit* destroyed the 32-boat at 0600 hours on the thirteenth, just after its arrival, then immediately got under way. No attempt was made to repair any of the problems with the 32-boat, though tools were available for a "patch job."

The end result of the investigation was that Schumacher was reprimanded for the loss of his boat, cited for poor naval judgment, and transferred to the submarine service.

Chapter Seventeen
A Kidnapping

At the time I didn't give two cents for our chances for survival.
——John D. Bulkeley

Shortly after arriving in Mindanao, Bulkeley was summoned by MacArthur to Del Monte plantation for another rescue assignment. MacArthur had decided that Philippine president Manuel Quezon, as sick as he was, had to be evacuated to Australia to keep him from falling into enemy hands and becoming a "puppet" of the Japanese.

Quezon, wracked with tuberculosis, had left Corregidor by submarine back on February 20 with his wife, son, two daughters, and several members of his staff for the island of Panay. He had since moved to the neighboring island of Negros as the Japanese began closing in on him.

MacArthur had also become concerned over some of the things that a bitter Quezon had been saying lately. Feeling that he had been abandoned by President Roosevelt, Quezon began advocating neutrality for the Philippines in the hope of getting both the Americans and Japanese to leave the country.

MacArthur felt that decisive action had to be taken to squelch this kind of defeatist talk, so he summoned his "pirate" for one more mission. Bulkeley said of his arrival at Del Monte on the morning of March 18:

> General MacArthur took me out on the porch of the old club-house. I was shocked over the general's appearance. His shirt and trousers, usually immaculate, were soiled and wrinkled, and he had a heavy beard stubble. His eyes were bloodshot from lack of sleep and illness from the long trek.
>
> I'd never seen the usually calm general so agitated. His jaws were clenched and his face was flushed red. He said he had another crucial job for me to do, wanted me to hop over to Negros, find Quezon and bring him and his whole tribe back to Del Monte. "I don't care how you get them here, just do it!" he said, almost snarling. The general even was swearing on occasion, and I'd never heard him swear.
>
> MacArthur added that "we're sending Quezon to Australia to form a Philippine government in exile, whether he likes it or not." I hadn't been aware of all the high-level machinations, so I was quite puzzled by it all. But if General MacArthur wanted Quezon back there, then I intended to bring the son of a bitch back—one way or the other.

MacArthur introduced Bulkeley to a former aide to Quezon, who would act as interpreter and guide on the rescue operation. There was something about the man that rubbed Bulkeley the wrong way, and he vowed to keep a close watch on him during the mission. Bulkeley told himself that if he didn't survive the mission, neither would the "suspicious" Filipino. He needn't have worried.

As Bulkeley turned to go, MacArthur put his arm on him and said, "Don't forget, Johnny, bring him back—by whatever means is necessary."

Rescue mission? It sounded more like a kidnapping to Bulkeley.

Two boats, PT-41 and PT-35, were available for the mission, which was scheduled for the night of March 18–19, the day after MacArthur left for Australia.

Lieutenant Kelly's 34-boat would have been the logical choice to accompany Bulkeley, but it had run aground on a coral reef the day after it arrived at Cagayan. An anchor line had snapped, allowing the boat to drift onto a reef in the harbor, causing major damage to the boat's propellers, shafts, and struts.

After a tow from the 41-boat failed to dislodge her, Kelly had to wait until high tide the next day for another try. That, too, failed, and Bulkeley hinted that the boat might have to be destroyed if it couldn't get free. Kelly called his crew together and challenged them to save their boat.

"Someone suggested maybe we could hire work gangs of natives to help us, whereupon the whole crowd started pulling money out of their pockets and piling it on the table," Kelly said. "They'd had no pay since the start of the war, but since they'd been down here in Mindanao, they'd had shore leave and a chance to play poker with the Army. The government could cut the cost of the war by just paying the Army and then giving the sailors a chance to play poker with them."

After a day of digging the 34-boat out of the coral, another line was hitched to an army tug to wait for high tide. The boat didn't budge on the first pull, but on the second it suddenly lurched free. The tug remained to tow the boat to a nearby repair yard. Ten days later, it was able to limp across the Mindanao Sea at twelve knots to a bigger repair facility at Cebu City, where it remained out of action until April 8.

In the meantime, Bulkeley and Ensign Akers took out the 41- and 35-boats on the rescue mission of Philippine president Quezon. They left Cagayan at 1900 hours on March 18.

The first leg of the trip was a hundred-mile dash across the heavily patrolled Mindanao Sea to the small port of Zamboanguita, on the southern tip of Negros. Bulkeley took his boat to a small dock at Zamboanguita while Akers, in the 35-boat, patrolled two miles offshore to prevent a possible surprise enemy attack from the sea.

Bulkeley waited an hour at the dock before Quezon's aide, Major Andres Soriano, arrived to request that the PT boats proceed to Dumaguete, fifteen miles up the coast. Only the 41-boat would be able to proceed, however, because the 35-boat had struck a submerged object while on patrol, causing a gaping hole in her bow. The boat quickly filled with water and was in danger of sinking. The crew was transported to the 41-boat before PT-35 was beached; she could be recovered at a future date.

It was learned upon arriving at Dumaguete that Quezon was at a town called Bais, about twenty-five miles up the coast. Bulkeley, armed with a tommy gun, left Ensign George Cox in charge of PT-41 and continued on by automobile with Major Soriano and a couple of guards to Bais, where they finally found the president of the Philippines.

Quezon was reluctant to leave. He showed Bulkeley a telegram from General Wainwright advising him that the trip was too dangerous because of enemy warships in the area. He had decided he wasn't going.

Bulkeley, who had been told not to take no for an answer, advised Quezon in the strongest language he could muster that General MacArthur had ordered that he be evacuated to Mindanao, then to Australia. That was the way it was going to be.

Bulkeley noticed that the president's hands were trembling. Part of Quezon's uneasiness may have resulted from his first good look at John Bulkeley, who resembled a reincarnated pirate. The skipper wore no uniform, only an old oilskin. His boots were mud caked, and his unruly black beard and longish hair tied around his head with a bandanna gave him a menacing appearance. Embellishing that sinister look, Bulkeley strode around with a tommy gun, two pearl-handled pistols strapped to his waist, and a nasty-looking knife tucked ominously in his belt.

Said Bulkeley:

It was now about oh-two-thirty [0230 hours] so I had no time to waste on idle chitchat. If we were to get Quezon, his family, and assorted straphangers across the hundred miles to open sea before daylight, to avoid Nip warships and planes, we had no time to lose.

As soon as I told Quezon that we had come to take him to MacArthur, he dug in his heels. Said he wasn't going. I stared hard at the bastard, and minced no words, reminding him of repeated Japanese treachery in the Far East, but not letting on that I knew he intended to go over to the enemy.

By now, fifteen minutes had gone by. I said to him sternly, "Well, Mr. President, are you ready to come with us?"

Quezon listened very carefully to this wild-looking man who claimed to be a United States naval officer. The president's hands were shaking uncontrollably as he moved his head up and down, finally mouthing the words, "I am ready to go."

An hour later, the party arrived at the pier at Dumaguete. It included President and Mrs. Quezon, their two daughters and a son, Vice President Sergio Osmena, Major General Basilio Valdes, Major Soriano, and nine members of the cabinet, all with a vast quantity of luggage. Already aboard were the crews from two PT boats.

"There was more luggage than the boat could safely carry, especially considering the number of people aboard," Bulkeley said. "I had heard and seen enough. 'That's it, folks. Everyone get aboard and forget the damn suitcases!'"

According to Bulkeley's biographer, William B. Breuer, everybody scrambled aboard except Quezon, who approached Bulkeley and said: "I've changed my mind. I'm not going to go." Bulkeley assured him in a loud, forceful voice that he was, indeed, getting aboard whether he liked it or not.

Breuer also wrote that among the luggage that made the trip were "seven bulging mail sacks filled with United States currency, estimated at twelve to fifteen million dollars." (Historians believe that this money represented the total assets of the "free Philippine government in exile.")

As the boats entered the Mindanao Sea for a sixty-mile dash to the little town of Oroquieta, the wind and sea picked up to almost gale force. Thirty minutes into the voyage, a crushing wave snapped the shear pins of the two after torpedoes, jolting the missiles halfway out of their tubes and starting hot runs.

The electric firing circuits failed, probably shorted out by the sheets of water that came pounding over the bow. While the boat rose and fell in heavy swells, two men crawled out on the tubes and tried to kick them loose. After causing no end of anxiety, the torpedoes were finally ejected by a small charge.

"Before we blew the torpedoes out, their backend, where their motors are, turned pink and then bright red from the heat," Bulkeley said. "On a normal run, of course, the surrounding water keeps them cool. But out of the water, they're not nice things to crawl around on."

Both sailors, Torpedoman First Class John L. Houlihan and Chief Torpedoman James D. Light, along with Bulkeley and Ensign Cox, were later awarded the Philippine Distinguished Conduct Star by a grateful Quezon. All four men were cited for "extraordinary coolness" and credited with saving all those on board "from an impending death." Bulkeley was also commended for "his timely action in holding Houlihan and preventing him from falling overboard."

Bulkeley later described the near-death experience as a battle with Lady Luck.

"Everyone was hanging on to anything he could grab as the little boat was tossed about by the relentlessly rolling sea. Many were unceremoniously throwing up. Others were in a state of terror, too frightened to say or do anything. With Ensign Cox handling the wheel, [My] job was to head off a panic.

"At the time I didn't give two cents for our chances for survival," Bulkeley said. "But now President Quezon came up to me and said that he wanted to go back to Negros. I was fed up with him and told him he'd sure as hell have to walk on water to get there."

The storm, which probably kept the Japanese navy close to shore this night, petered out quickly, and PT-41 arrived at its destination at 0600 hours on March 19. The passengers staggered to shore to awaiting automobiles for the ride to Del Monte and its B-17 airfield. Quezon exited the boat wearing a red bandanna over his face in an attempt to hide his identity. But several natives waiting at the dock waved their hats in recognition as he walked down the pier, hanging on to the arm of one of his aides.

Quezon and his party eventually flew to Australia, on March 26, but not without further incident. It was Quezon's first ride in a plane, and because of his poor health he was reluctant to get aboard. He had heard stories about the difficulty of breathing at high altitudes and was terrified that he might die from a lack of oxygen. To some at the airport it appeared that he was being forcibly pushed into the Flying Fortress.

One of the engines on Quezon's plane would not start, and the presidential party was transferred to another plane. As the new plane began taxiing to the runway, the engines sputtered, then stopped. Some passengers started to disembark. Quezon, it was learned, had ordered the pilot to cut the motors so he could get off. Quezon couldn't find his chaplain and refused to fly without him aboard.

After a delay of about fifteen minutes, the chaplain, a Father Ortiz, was discovered in another part of Quezon's plane. After seeing for himself, the president allowed the flight to proceed.

Quezon survived and was greeted warmly by his old friend MacArthur in Melbourne. Both men now had another thing in common. Each had been snatched from the "jaws of death" by the same man, John Bulkeley.

Bulkeley thought he had seen the last of Quezon, but their paths would cross once more. Several weeks later after he himself had arrived in

Australia, Bulkeley was invited by MacArthur to a small luncheon honoring Quezon.

Bulkeley's appearance had changed quite a bit since he and the Philippine president first met. He was clean shaven, for starters. His hair was trimmed to regulation length, and he wore a brand-new official navy uniform. Said Bulkeley:

> During the lunch, Quezon proceeded to relate the story of his rescue, in detail, to the luncheon party. When he first referred to the "American sea wolf" who had convinced him to leave his island country, I didn't know who in hell he was talking about.
>
> He then turned to me and expressed his "sincere admiration" and spoke of the "true courage of your father, Lieutenant Bulkeley." Everybody roared with laughter at Quezon's confusion. I politely told him that I was the "sea wolf" to whom he was referring and that I regretted any embarrassment he may have from his mistake.
>
> He put his hand to my clean-shaven chin and studied my face for nearly a minute. When the recognition became complete, he, too, bellowed with laughter and slapped me on the back. "Your father should be proud of Lieutenant Bulkeley," he said. "You not only saved me, my family, and my vice-president, but you saved this great general, General MacArthur, from certain death. Thank you from the bottom of our hearts."

After arriving in the United States the following month, Quezon entertained the Washington press corps with an even more colorful and dramatic version of his first meeting with Bulkeley, according to the *New York Tribune.*

"It was stormy night," Quezon began in fractured English. "Suddenly my aide, Colonel Soriano, appears out of darkness and introduces me to man who looks like a fierce Spanish pirate, a sea wolf, with a formidable black beard and a cloth tied round his head like a turban.... A month later a young naval officer was presented to me in Australia. It was Lieutenant Bulkeley. Only this time he had no beard. He was no pirate. In fact he looked like a young boy. 'Goddamn,' I told him, 'if I had seen your face I would not have gone with you.' "

The whole room erupted in laughter.

Chapter Eighteen

Taking on the Big Boys

I'll tell you one thing about war: one of the handiest weapons
to have is a commander who knows his business.
——Iliff Richardson about John D. Bulkeley

A couple of days after dropping off Quezon and his party, Bulkeley returned across the Mindanao Sea to find the 35-boat right where they had beached her the night of March 18. After a patch was applied to the hole in her bow, the 41-boat towed her north to a modern machine shop and repair facility at Cebu City, run by a seventy-one-year-old American named "Dad" Cleland.

A few days later, Lieutenant Kelly's 34-boat, which had undergone emergency repairs at Cagayan, joined the 35-boat at the Cebu City facility for more extensive refitting, leaving only the 41-boat available for patrols. Bulkeley, after making several aerial flights to try to find PT-32, was forced to write off the boat and its crew as missing.

The war slowed down a little for Squadron 3 over the next couple of weeks. While waiting for their boats to be repaired, many of the crew members helped load Allied transports stopping off at Cebu City with food and ammunition for runs to Bataan and Corregidor. They even managed to con a few torpedoes from submarines passing through.

Cleland treated the PT-boat crews as though they were family. He got along especially well with Bulkeley and Kelly. Cleland, who enjoyed a snort of whiskey every now and then, had been in the Philippines since 1914. A feisty character, he was never at a loss for words, particularly when it came to the Japanese.

"A swell gent he was—originally from Minnesota and a typical hulking frontiersman," Kelly recalled. "[He] didn't look a day over fifty. He was a great gourmet, too."

Kelly remembered one particular meal that included crabmeat cocktails, lobster Newburg, roast duck, canned asparagus and corn, pickles, and sweet potatoes—all washed down by bottled beer.

When Bulkeley asked the old man how he was going to pay him for all the repairs, Cleland remarked: "You fight 'em and I'll fix 'em. It's the least I can do."

The war news was not good. Bataan and Corregidor were taking an awful pounding, and the Japanese were pressing southward. It was only a matter of time before the enemy overran Cebu City.

Bulkeley asked "Dad" Cleland what he was going to do when the Japanese came.

"[I] have my dignity to think about," the old man said, clenching his huge fists. "I'm not going to the hills. I'll stay right here and face them. They can get me if they can, but they'll have a fight on their hands first."

Cleland, whose given name was Morrison, survived the war and died in Cebu City on January 9, 1948, at the age of seventy-seven.

The 34-boat went back into the water on April 8 and was in action that night. Bulkeley had learned from army intelligence that two enemy destroyers were proceeding south through a strait between Cebu and its western neighbor, Negros, and should clear the southern tip of the former around midnight. The enemy ships were probably hunting for inter-island steamers packed with supplies and bound for Bataan and Corregidor. If the two PT boats could get there first, they might be able to ambush them.

"To man the boats I called for volunteers," Bulkeley said. "I had no trouble about that. I guess they understood by now that any man who doesn't volunteer won't be in the squadron long if I can get rid of him."

Bulkeley's 41-boat, with Ensign Cox at the wheel, would take the lead ahead of Kelly's 34-boat, with Ensign Iliff Richardson at the helm. Around midnight, Bulkeley spotted a Japanese ship about five thousand yards ahead gliding slowly eastward just two miles off the tip of Cebu. It wasn't a destroyer, however. It was a light cruiser of the *Kuma* class, armed with 5.5- and 3-inch guns. It was a little bigger ship than they had expected, but what a beautiful target.

The 41-boat idled quietly to within five hundred yards of the cruiser's port bow and fired two torpedoes. They ran erratically, straddling the target bow and stern. As the 41-boat increased speed and circled to the right, Bulkeley fired her last two torpedoes. Both Bulkeley and Cox saw the torpedoes run true, one to the bow and the other beneath the bridge, but observed no explosion.

Kelly, meanwhile, had maneuvered the 34-boat into firing position on the starboard side of the enemy ship and fired two torpedoes, which also missed. Then the 34-boat became caught in the cruiser's powerful searchlights. Bulkeley saw this and, out of torpedoes, he circled the cruiser's starboard side to strafe her decks in an effort to draw fire away from Kelly's boat.

With enemy shells whistling overhead, Kelly pressed the attack, raking the cruiser's searchlight and deck with his .50-caliber machine guns. He closed to within three hundred yards, taking heavy fire. One of his gunners, Chief Commissary Steward William J. Reynolds, was shot through the throat and shoulder, and the boat's mast was shot away.

To remain and slug it out with the cruiser would have been fatal. Kelly fired his last two torpedoes and ordered a hard right rudder to leave the area. Under a hail of fire, Kelly noticed that two ships were firing at him. The second ship was a destroyer, which began following him with her searchlight.

Just then two detonations were heard and two columns of water spouted high in the air. The cruiser's searchlight dimmed and went out, and all her guns ceased firing. At first, Kelly thought the cruiser had been hit by fire from the destroyer, but Chief Torpedoman John Martino saw the hits and reported that they were torpedoes.

Ensign Richardson, who had the wheel aboard the 34-boat, had a ringside seat for his boat's last charge toward the enemy cruiser, and it scared the daylights out of him. Said Richardson:

> We kept going at full tilt, and Kelly wouldn't fire. There were match flares flickering all up and down the cruiser from the guns shooting at us. We were so close to them that I began to feel crazy. I guess Kelly felt crazy, too, because he wouldn't fire. I think maybe for a crazy moment there he wanted to ram that ship because there we were, already so close that I had to pull my head back and look up to see the cruiser's searchlight, and still he wouldn't fire.
>
> Finally I couldn't stand it any more. "Mr. Kelly," I yelled, "we are going aboard."
>
> But he didn't answer, just stood stock-still for another long crazy lifetime and then said, "Right a touch."
>
> Then he let go the Number 1 and Number 2 torpedoes, beautiful new ones with great big beautiful warheads that we had swabbed lovingly with Marfak [an oil-based lubricant made by Texaco] and seen to [sic] that the pressure was okay on them, and they went gushing through the water, making the most wonderful bubbling little blurp of music anybody ever did hear.
>
> When I looked back, all I saw were big black chunks of torn cruiser debris flying through the searchlight beam and making a rain

of splashes in the water. I thought, it's the cruiser and destroyer firing at each other. . . . But as we passed about two hundred yards astern of the cruiser I saw the cruiser was dead in the water and I saw its searchlight begin to dim and then turn orange and then deepen into red and finally ruby red and finally glower out altogether, stone cold and black.

Bulkeley, out of torpedoes and ammunition, saw the action from a distance and said, "There was no doubt" that Kelly's torpedoes "polished off" the enemy cruiser. Bulkeley continued:

I saw her searchlight fade out, and heavy yellow smoke arise. Her stern was under in three minutes—the destroyer put the searchlight on her decks, where the Japs were all running around, not knowing where to go—and she had sunk in twenty.

But I was running around with three destroyers after me, which were firing all they had, and I could see another one hot on Kelly's tail. That was the last I could see of him and I thought he was a goner.

A few seconds later, the 41-boat had problems of her own when a second destroyer picked her up with a searchlight. Five quick salvos from the destroyer bracketed the 41, wetting down the decks. Now the 41 started to run, with the enemy after her like an express train.

Bulkeley retired to the east at top speed and found an enemy destroyer blocking an escape route to the north and two more to the east. He quickly turned south and ran to Port Misamis, on Mindanao, where the waters of the inlet were too shallow for the enemy ships to follow. Kelly's 34-boat was cut off from following suit by another destroyer, which had caught her in its searchlight. Kelly barely had time to get out of the way as the two ships roared past each other at a relative speed of more than sixty knots, barely avoiding a collision.

"I started zigging to squirm out of that light—wouldn't let my gunners fire a shot; it would help him keep our position," Kelly said. "I was getting away, all right, but he kept firing for ten minutes, although his accuracy was going to hell. By oh-one-thirty [0130 hours] I could barely see his light, which was waving around, searching the water back of us."

Kelly slowed and made his way north back toward Cebu City. Ten miles from the entrance to the channel, the 34-boat ran aground on a coral reef. It was about 0400 hours.

Unable to immediately rock the boat off the reef, Kelly sent Ensign Richardson ashore in a rowboat to get an army doctor and an ambulance for the injured Reynolds and a tug for the 34-boat. With the help of a rising tide, the boat finally broke free, but Kelly decided to wait for daybreak to risk further travel. The dawn brought a thick fog, further delaying the last leg to Cebu City.

Shortly after getting under way at around 0800 hours, a flight of four cruiser-based Japanese seaplanes swooped over the 34-boat and bombed and strafed the helpless craft for thirty minutes. The first 100-pound bomb landed ten feet off the port bow. It blew a large hole in the crew's washroom, tore the port machine gun off its stand, shattered windshields, and covered the entire boat with mud. The men never heard the planes coming, because their own engines were making too much noise.

One of the enemy planes went off trailing smoke and crashed just before the 34-boat's last .50-caliber gun was silenced, but no one saw the plane go into the water. Kelly remembered:

> We were chugging up the channel at fifteen knots. Reynolds, our wounded gunner, was feeling better and sitting on deck. We had only three guns, the others having been shot away in the night fight. Suddenly, out of the sun, four Jap planes jumped us, loosing bombs and strafing. For thirty minutes they hit us.

Machine gunner David W. Harris was killed on the first strafing pass just before Albert Ross got credit for shooting down one of the seaplanes with his .30-caliber machine gun. Ross was then shot in the leg on the next pass, one that silenced his gun.

The Nips were coming lower and lower to within a hundred feet of us. Our boat was riddled with holes. We couldn't return fire, had only two engines and could only try to dodge in the narrow channel. Then our engineer yelled that the engine room was full of water. We were sinking, so I had to beach the boat on a tiny island if we were to save our wounded men.

Kelly went down into the engine room and found his chief machinist's mate, Velt F. Hunter, with his arm practically blown off. A bullet had entered his elbow and gone out his forearm, leaving a three-inch hole, but he was still manning the engines. Kelly gave the order to abandon ship. Said Kelly:

> *It turned out that there were only three of us unhit, so it was a job getting the wounded out while the Japanese dived to rake us. We made the mistake of taking off our shoes, and the coral cut our feet to ribbons as we staggered carrying the men.*
>
> *I found [William J.] Reynolds, who had been wounded in the throat during the night, now lying with his hand over his belly.*
>
> *"Mr. Kelly," he said, "leave me here. I'm done for, sir. I'll be all right here. You get out [with] the others."*
>
> *Well, the hell with that. So in spite of his protests, Martino and I carried him ashore. Then we went back for a last trip. Only Harris was left, lying where he had tumbled into the tank compartment. But the radioman and I carried his body ashore, because we hoped to give him a decent burial.*

Ensign Richardson had been waiting at Pier One with an ambulance for the arrival of the 34-boat. He could see it chugging up the channel when it was attacked by the four Japanese floatplanes.

"Kelly was an iron-minded man, all right," Richardson said. "He knew what he was doing. He didn't change course until the last possible splinter of a second so as to give the Jap no time at all to change aim. Then he flipped the boat over. The boat kicked to the right and the bomb hit the water nearby on the port side."

Shot up badly and taking on water, and with no operating weapons to fight with, Kelly had no alternative but to abandon the boat and try to save the crew, which had suffered two killed and three wounded.

Richardson raced to the scene just in time to help get the wounded ashore but not in time to shut off the one engine that was still working as the Japanese planes returned to finish the job. Kelly had abandoned the boat on a sandbar behind a native bamboo fish trap about twelve hundred yards offshore.

The planes swept in and set the boat afire.

"She was burning like a Christmas tree, hopelessly and beyond redemption," Richardson said. "I didn't realize fully at the time what that meant to me. We are all members of a rich, young, energetic country. When an American gets knocked off his perch in a fight and his perch is splintered up under him, the first thing he thinks of is, hell, I'll get me another perch, that's the least of it.

"But it isn't the least of it. No sir, it certainly is not."

Richardson had good reason to remember every detail. It was his twenty-fourth birthday.

Despite eyewitnesses and the testimony of those involved, historians seem to agree that no enemy ships were sunk the night of April 8–9. Kelly said he was "certain" that his last two torpedoes hit an enemy cruiser; Bulkeley, who thought it was a *Kuma*-class vessel, claimed that the cruiser was "sinking by the stern with her bow up in the air."

Japanese sources indicate that the *Kuma* itself was attacked by torpedo boats on this date but had taken only one hit—a torpedo that failed to explode. Whatever the damage, or lack of it, the *Kuma* remained afloat until January 11, 1944, when she was sunk off Penang by a British submarine. Historians agree, however, that the magnitude of the damage, or lack of it, neither increases nor diminishes the courage of the officers and men who pressed home a close-range attack on a dangerous enemy a hundred times their size.

Bulkeley nominated Lieutenant Kelly for the Medal of Honor for his "extraordinary heroism" during this action. The award was later downgraded to a Navy Cross. Bulkeley and Ensign Cox each received the army's Distinguished Service Cross (it was Bulkeley's second), and a total of eighteen Silver Stars were awarded to the two crews, two of them posthumously.

April 9 proved to be a historic day all around for the Americans. Later that day on the "Voice of Freedom," it was announced that the brave men of Bataan had surrendered after a long and brutal struggle.

Chapter Nineteen

Every Man for Himself

I even threw my dog tags away. . . . I don't mind telling you I was scared.
——Machinist's Mate First Class John Tuggle

Down to only two boats, the end of Squadron 3 was only a matter of days away.

Bulkeley had reported to General Sharp on Mindanao the morning of April 9 following the sea battle that he and Kelly's 34-boat had waged with Japanese cruisers and destroyers. Bulkeley asked for permission to return to Cebu to replace his boat's torpedoes and carry on the fight. General Sharp told him that the Japanese had landed and were marching on Cebu City. There were no torpedoes available anywhere.

A week earlier, while repairs were progressing on the 35-boat at Cebu City, Bulkeley had reassigned Ensigns Tony Akers and Bond Murray to Mindanao to form a gunboat team on Lake Lanao. The two young ensigns, with a crew of a dozen men, had managed to round up a "flotilla" of six vessels and armed them with machine guns, to be used to repel any aerial invasion of the lake.

Bulkeley called it his Lake Lanao Navy.

On April 9, the eleven-man crew of Bulkeley's 41-boat, to include Ensign Cox, officially joined that navy, which was put under the control of the army. In what had to be a bitter day, Bulkeley watched helplessly as the army took possession of the 41-boat and prepared to move it overland to Lake Lanao.

The boat was put on a trailer and towed over a mountainous trail with sharp turns and U bends, according to Machinist's Mate First Class John Tuggle.

"The boat never made it through. It got stuck in one of the bends and was blocking the road," Tuggle said. "We took everything usable off it. The Japanese eventually pushed the boat over the cliff to open the road. It was kind of sad to have the last of the boats destroyed. It was then we knew we'd be there for the duration."

Bulkeley was not only out of a boat, he was out of a job. No longer able to carry the fight to the enemy, Bulkeley was ordered out of Mindanao and was flown to Australia on the night of April 13.

Before he left, Bulkeley passed temporary command of Squadron 3 to the senior officer present, Ensign Cox, with instructions to carry on the fight at Lake Lanao. He also promised Cox that he would do all he could to get the rest of the squadron to Australia in the "very near future."

Bulkeley said he felt "rotten" leaving his men behind but consoled himself with the fact that General MacArthur was a big fan of the PT boats and would do all he could to get as many men out as possible. MacArthur had told him that the navy wanted to save as many of the officers as they could to help staff a new PT-boat school and training center that had opened on February 17 at Melville, Rhode Island, just north of Newport, on Narragansett Bay.

Bulkeley left for Australia believing that his executive officer, Lieutenant Kelly, was dead. He reported to MacArthur's headquarters that he had been told by a couple of unofficial sources, aviators who had left Cebu City at the time of the invasion, that Lieutenant Kelly and three enlisted men had been killed during a night action and were buried in a nearby cemetery.

In fact, two enlisted men (David Harris and Willard Reynolds) had been killed and were buried on the island and three others were wounded, but Kelly and his executive officer, Ensign Iliff Richardson, had escaped injury.

Bulkeley also had no word from Lieutenant Brantingham and the crew of the 35-boat. Bulkeley's initial report to higher headquarters declared both the 34 and 35 crews as missing.

As in much of his career, Bulkeley made his exit from Mindanao in an exciting fashion. Japanese gunners shot up his aircraft as it lifted off from Del Monte airfield, forcing the plane to make the long journey to Australia on three engines.

On the morning of April 12, three days after his 34-boat had been destroyed by enemy aircraft, Kelly awoke to the roar of guns and explosions. People were running everywhere, streaming out of Cebu City in all directions, one step ahead of the onrushing Japanese.

"Jap planes dropped leaflets"signed" by the Japanese commander Homma in English telling the Filipinos 'we are your friend' and offering a substantial reward for any American, dead or alive, and a handsome reward for any American officer. Nice guys," Kelly said. "Meanwhile, two Zero fighters were strafing the automobiles trying to get out on the road."

The Japanese struck so fast that Lieutenant Brantingham had only thirty minutes to destroy the 35-boat, which was still undergoing repairs at a marine railway just outside the city.

"While preparing the boat for demolition some fifteen minutes after the initial notice had been given, heavy explosions occurred in the oil compounds, throwing debris, oil, and heavy smoke over the shipyard," Brantingham wrote in an after-action report. "The destruction of the boat was accomplished under these conditions and I then went to Cebu City with my crew."

It is at this point that the remaining personnel of Squadron 3 went off in different directions seeking escape. Said Kelly:

> *People were streaming out—some Americans, and a few of our Navy. From them during the morning I heard that the Japs had come back and bombed what was left of our 34-boat on the beach. Well, that was over.*
>
> *Then I heard that Bulkeley wasn't dead—his boat escaped and was in Mindanao. That Brantingham had burned his 35-boat sitting there on "Dad" Cleland's marine railway—at least the Japs wouldn't get it. That Ensign Richardson had assembled what was left of our men, and joined up with our naval forces on Mactan Island, where they would all try to escape to the island of Leyte. It was the last I ever heard of them.*

Lieutenant Kelly appears to have headed south immediately; his exec, Ensign Richardson, hung around for a few days to help the army before joining up with some guerrilla forces. Brantingham was invited by some Filipino forces to escape to Leyte aboard a small launch. But because there wasn't room enough for his entire crew, he decided to stay a little longer to help in the defense of the city, directing his men to assist the army in the demolition of trucks and automobiles.

Brantingham's party, which included a warrant officer, nine enlisted men, and a civilian, traveled about twenty-five miles over mountain trails to the south, crossed over to Negros by native boats, and finally reached Mindanao and safety. The trip took almost two weeks.

Just before starting off on the trip, Brantingham ran into Ensign Richardson and attempted to persuade him to join forces with him. Richardson was actively assisting the Army Quartermaster Corps, personally directing the withdrawal of vital food and medical supplies and running the motor pool.

"Ensign Richardson insisted on continuing this work in spite of constantly being bombed and strafed by Japanese airplanes, refusing to join my party, believing his services were required here," Brantingham said.

Richardson would become one of the war's unsung heroes over the next three years as a key member of the Philippine guerrilla forces on Leyte. Rising to the rank of major, he became chief of staff to Colonel Ruperto Kangleon and ultimately became primarily responsible for the radio network that was General MacArthur's light back to Leyte in the late fall of 1944. Richardson was the subject of a book by Ira Wolfert, called *An American Guerrilla in the Philippines*, and a 1950 movie by the same name. The part of Richardson was played by Tyrone Power. Not bad for one PT boat. Richardson's boss aboard the 34-boat, Lieutenant Kelly, would be played by John Wayne in the movie *They Were Expendable*.

Richardson turned out to be quite a resourceful guy, one who seemed to thrive on living off the land and using his wits to outfox his Japanese pursuers.

"Young Iliff learned how to live alone without being lonely, and how to create his own environment out of himself," Wolfert wrote of Richardson.

Richardson was an only child; his father died when the young Richardson was four years old. In 1938, he dropped out of Compton College in California to see the world, spending eighteen months traveling in Europe and the Near and Far East. He enlisted in the navy in 1940 and later graduated from officer candidate school. He transferred to PT-boat service in the spring of 1941 after serving aboard a minesweeper in the Philippines.

When the Japanese moved into Cebu City on April 10, 1942, Richardson assisted the army in setting off many of the demolitions that turned the city into flames. Then he took off with the rest looking for safety. After several days of hiding out, Richardson and a few others decided to head for Leyte and then to Mindanao to catch a plane for Australia.

"I had a priority from MacArthur," Richardson said. "He had given it to all the PT people who had taken him out of Corregidor. We weren't supposed to use it until we had no more mosquito boats to fight off of."

Richardson made it to Mindanao, but he was told he was three days too late. The Japanese had taken Del Monte airfield. Rather than stay and run the risk of being taken prisoner, Richardson, along with ten Air Corps enlisted men and one navy enlisted man, joined forces and tried to sail a twenty-nine-foot boat to Australia. After it capsized in heavy surf, the crew headed back to Leyte.

"After a time getting organized we started out after the Japs," Richardson told the Associated Press after the Americans arrived in the fall of 1944. "When they were in the barrios [villages] we got out. When they got out we got back in. We made our own bullets and sniped at them continuously. When they went on troop patrols we ambushed them.

"The Japs never brought in anything. They foraged for food, and it was a strange sight to see a soldier in the great Japanese Army harvesting rice. Finally we became strong. And where the Japs first sent out one-man patrols, they had to send out 200-men patrols. The Jap controlled the sea but he couldn't control the islands."

Richardson wasn't the only guerrilla from Squadron 3.

Following the capitulation of Corregidor on May 6, General Wainwright sent emissaries to all the islands to order the American and Filipino forces to surrender. There were many who wanted no part of becoming a prisoner of war.

Said Machinist's Mate First Class John Tuggle, "We told the officer from Wainwright's staff that came to give us the order to get the hell out of our camp. We were not surrendering. It was an easy decision for me. We had given [the Japanese] a hard time with our boats and I didn't want to be captured by them after that. I even threw my dog tags away. . . . I don't mind telling you I was scared."

About a dozen enlisted members of Squadron 3, to include Ellwood

Offret, DeWitt Glover, William Konko, and Paul Owen, headed for the hills of Mindanao with other men from different branches of the service. Many of them made their way to a force controlled by army brigadier general Wendell Fertig and his colorful deputy, Colonel Charles Hedges. Fertig had spent five years in the Philippines running mining camps; Hedges, who was described as "the meanest man to ever get out of Oregon," was a lumberman in civilian life.

"Hedges was a mean old bastard," Tuggle said. "Everybody was scared to death of him because he would just as soon shoot you as talk to you. The natives called him 'Colonel Goddamn.'"

Fertig was equally dedicated to his job. He believed that there was nothing worse than surrendering. "It's one thing to take a beating," he said. "Every man has to take his beatings. But, damn it, no man has to surrender. It's the same thing as castration."

Fertig made many of these Americans second lieutenants, claiming that any man who had had the courage to refuse to surrender, or the guts to escape, and had proved able to stay alive thus far, was potentially able to help other people. That potential basically qualified him for a commission.

While operating as a guerrilla, Tuggle met a young Filipino woman who later became his wife. They had two children before the Americans arrived in late 1944. Tuggle credited his wife, who died in 1998, with giving him the ability to survive those three years as a guerrilla.

"I had a good wife that got me through the experience," he said. "Some people liked living in the jungle, some hated it. I never minded because I had her. She was the best."

Most of the American guerrillas from Squadron 3 stayed in the Philippines until the end of the war, but a few lucky ones managed to get themselves evacuated to Australia by submarine in the late summer of 1943. One of them was Chief Offret, who was evacuated because of a severe case of dysentery.

Offret had trouble saying good-bye, for he was plainly torn between his delight on being returned to the navy he loved, and his feeling of loyalty to the men with whom he had shared so much. Fertig hated to see Offret go, for, as sick and worn as he was, the chief had always done what he was asked, and had endured everything without complaint. Hedges did what he could to make Offret's leave-taking happier.

"Why any man would want to join the chickenshit Navy when he can live like a goddamned prince beats the hell out of me," Hedges said. "But I guess if you're born stupid, there's nothing else you can do. Anyway, after all I taught you, they'll make you an admiral."

Offret remained in the navy following the war and retired as a lieutenant commander.

Lieutenant Kelly was the first of the officers from Cebu City to reach Mindanao. He had a lot of help from the natives, who continued to wholeheartedly support the Americans.

"It took me days to get to Mindanao around through the islands begging rides in cars, hiring small boats to cross little island channels," Kelly said. "My objective was to join Bulkeley, who, they had said in Cebu, had escaped the destroyer and was in Mindanao. I wanted to make my report of my part of the battle to him as commander of our squadron."

Kelly was impressed with the natives, who couldn't do enough for the Americans.

"They were swell to us—ignorant guys, maybe, but nice and kind as they could be," he said. "I remember on the trail we overtook a ramshackle cart and a few natives, and an old native woman gave the cart driver hell for not putting the baggage in his cart—said we Americans were fighting for their people and they should help us.

"In those days in the jungle I learned more about how nice the simple Filipino people are than I'd learned in months in Manila; I also learned the more Americanized they are, the lousier they are."

Kelly reached Mindanao aboard a boat piloted by a Chinese smuggler. One of the first people he saw was Ensign Cox.

"Good God!" Cox said. "I heard you were dead!" Cox told him that Bulkeley had left for Australia and, thinking Kelly was dead, had made him (Cox) squadron commander. Kelly reported in to General Sharp, who sent him to the airfield, with a warning.

"There's not too much hope of getting out," General Sharp said. "There's almost no more gas to refuel the planes at this end, so I doubt they'll send any more."

Then, on April 23, when everything looked hopeless, Kelly was told to report to the airfield and bring everything he had with him. A priority list had been made up in Australia. Younger men with technical skills had first dibs on evacuation. The PT-boat captains had proved that their little ships could be useful in the war, and Washington wanted them back to help train new crews to carry on the fight.

There was room for thirty men on the plane, and there were more than a hundred waiting at the airfield to see whether their names were on the list.

Besides Kelly, Akers and Cox were also on the list, but they were up on Lake Lanao. The two young ensigns finally got the word and arrived just in time to bump a captain and a major. As it turned out, there would be several more flights out of Mindanao in the next few days. One of those seats went to Lieutenant Brantingham, who had reached Mindanao in late April.

Another officer from Squadron 3, Ensign Bond Murray, wasn't as fortunate. Murray was somehow overlooked on the last few manifests and took to the hills, where he joined some guerrilla forces. He was captured and died in a prison camp, the third officer of the squadron to suffer that fate; the other two were Edward DeLong and William Plant of PT-31. DeLong, who flew out of Corregidor just before the surrender, got as far as Lake Lanao before he was captured. He drowned while attempting an escape. Plant, who was captured on Bataan after the sinking of PT-31, died later in the war when a ship taking him to Japan was sunk by American bombers.

Just before Kelly, Akers, and Cox boarded their B-17, General Sharp called Kelly aside and gave him a message to relay to General MacArthur.

"Tell him that the end here is drawing near, and if help can't be sent, in a few days Mindanao will fall," Sharp said. "Of course probably he understands this and maybe nothing can be done. But if he asks what we need to hold out, tell him if we had a Navy task force—bringing up a tanker loaded with gasoline and a hundred thousand men; tell him to give me only that and we can hold here and start taking back the islands.

"I know probably he hasn't got them, but tell him that if he asks."

Before climbing aboard, Kelly, Akers, and Cox unstrapped their .45 pistols and gave them to those staying behind. They wouldn't be needing them where they were going.

Chapter Twenty

Welcome Home

We can't all be heroes. Some of us have
to stand on the curb and clap as they go by.
——Will Rogers

An exhausted Bulkeley arrived in Australia on April 14 wearing sneakers, pants, and a jacket. He had no shirt. He needed a shave, a haircut, and a long bath.

He slept for thirty-six hours. When he awoke, an Australian family provided him a uniform, shoes, socks, underwear, and $150 in cash.

MacArthur was clearly overjoyed to see him again and would say so in a glowing fitness report he arranged to have written on a proper navy form. Under "remarks," MacArthur wrote: "Lieutenant Bulkeley is an outstanding officer who has exhibited the highest qualities of courage, leadership and initiative. His operations in command of Motor Torpedo Boat Squadron Three during the Philippine Campaign were brilliant. He has demonstrated in action his fitness for promotion. I especially desire to have this officer assigned to this command."

MacArthur also showed his appreciation for taking him out of the "jaws of death" back on March 13 by nominating him for the nation's highest military award, the Medal of Honor. Predictably, the action ignited a firestorm of criticism from the navy.

"No way is MacArthur going to dictate a Medal of Honor for one of my officers," navy chief Ernest King fumed. "I will make the recommendation for the Navy."

And he did.

King also saw to it that MacArthur's "official" fitness report on Bulkeley was rewritten by Admiral Rockwell, who reluctantly gave him less than the highest evaluation in "military bearing and neatness of person and dress" category.

"It was a pleasure to write [the fitness report] out," Rockwell said in a letter to Bulkeley, "but I want to let you know that my personal admiration for you and all your brave boys is way stronger than I found myself capable of expressing—don't think I was trying to insult either your intelligence or very fine beard by working you over, for I only did that to strengthen the other words!"

Bulkeley spent the next two weeks in Australia compiling the obituary of his Squadron 3 and trying to get the rest of his officers and men out of the Philippines. They were scattered over several islands, and it wasn't known whether they were dead or alive.

Lieutenant Kelly and Ensigns Cox and Akers arrived in Australia at the end of April and joined Bulkeley in a brief homecoming celebration. The following day, all four received orders to proceed to the United States for assignment to a new motor torpedo boat school that began operation in February in Melville, Rhode Island.

Before they left, MacArthur called in Bulkeley for a little pep talk. Bulkeley was to carry a strong message back to Washington that the Philippines must be recaptured immediately with the help of large numbers of PT boats.

"When you get to Washington I want you to stress to the president and the secretary of war the crucial need to retake the Philippines at the earliest possible time," MacArthur said, cautioning Bulkeley not to put anything on paper, not even to make any notes of their discussion.

For nearly an hour MacArthur briefed Bulkeley on precisely what to say. He was to explain to the Washington bigwigs how stunned MacArthur and all fighting men had been on learning that the Philippines was being sacrificed on the altar of global strategy.

"And Johnny, don't add or subtract anything," MacArthur said to the impressionable young lieutenant.

Bulkeley would provide Admiral King with a confidential summary of MacArthur's verbal orders to him with regard to PT boats in the South Pacific war, including a proposal to grant these "unique" men special status and extra pay. Said MacArthur:

> *Motor torpedo boats should be the basis of a separate branch of the service for specialists who must have confidence in their own weapons. These boats can be used effectively for coastal defense 200 or 300 miles offshore, in the Philippine Islands, straits, narrows and potential blocks. There is no other location such as the Philippine Islands and the islands south of the Philippines where they can be so effectively used.*
>
> *With enough of this type of craft, hostile Japanese shipping could be kept from invading an island or continent, and kept 200 to 300 miles offshore.*
>
> *I want 100 or more MTBs here of your type (Elco) together with the improvements which have been developed since the outbreak of war. Two hundred boats if possible with the tenders, spare parts, and equipment necessary for them within eight months.*

This message was to be further delivered to the president, secretary of the navy, and secretary of war. Both proposals for special status and extra pay were denied.

The first leg of the four PT skippers' trip home took them to Canton Island, south of Hawaii, where they crossed paths with the advance party of the 1st Marine Division. They were heading in the other direction to New Zealand, where they would train for eventual action three months later on Guadalcanal.

"Far into the night the PT-boat commanders regaled us with the story of their breakout and perilous journey," Merrill Twining wrote. (Twining was assistant operations officer and operations officer of the 1st Marine Division during the Guadalcanal campaign and rose to four-star general before he retired in 1959.) "They spoke warmly of MacArthur but were more than a little critical of some of the staff officers who accompanied him and who had tried to force Bulkeley to abandon the crew of one of the two PT-boats when it became disabled. To his credit Bulkeley stoutly asserted his proper authority as commanding officer and determinedly enforced the law of the sea, which from time immemorial has denounced the abandonment of those exposed to its wanton cruelties. Bulkeley appeared modest and reserved. The other skipper—the one who would have been left behind—was far more outgoing and, understandably, somewhat more vehement."

The incident Twining wrote about apparently happened at Tagauayan Island on March 12 at the midway point of the journey to Mindanao. One of MacArthur's staff officers must have suggested reducing the number of crew members on the 34- and 41-boats to more comfortably accommodate the extra army passengers from the crippled 32-boat, which was remaining behind for repairs.

The foursome of Bulkeley, Kelly, Akers, and Cox flew on to Hawaii, then landed in San Francisco on May 7 for a short stopover, which included a long-awaited press conference.

Said the *New York Times* in its lead paragraph, "Lt. John D. Bulkeley of Long Island City, whose mosquito boat squadron, while harrying the Japanese Navy, wrote one of the most spectacular chapters in the history of the Philippines engagement, arrived today with three fellow officers. Their arrival was the first news that the seagoing "guerrillas" had been evacuated before the fall of Bataan and Corregidor."

The newspaper went on to describe an action where Bulkeley "leaped aboard" a sinking Japanese vessel, "pistol in hand," and took "captive the only two Japanese still in sight."

America had waited a long time to welcome home some of its live heroes. The American public finally had cause for a celebration.

Bulkeley told the press how his boats had taken MacArthur, his family, and staff off Corregidor. He paid a special tribute to the general's wife, saying that she endured the hazardous journey "in a heroic and brave manner."

Bulkeley barely had time to enjoy some American food before the plane was scheduled to fly overnight to New York. Sampling a couple of hamburgers, a smiling Bulkeley turned to Lieutenant Kelly and said, "Sure beats the hell out of boiled tomcat."

The plane landed at New York's La Guardia Field at 10:22 a.m. the next morning. Awaiting Bulkeley was his wife, Alice, nineteen-month-old daughter, Joan, and his father, Frederick. His mother, Elizabeth, waited at home with his five-week-old son, Johnny Jr.

Alice was just a couple of months pregnant when her husband had left China for the Philippines, and there were times when she didn't know whether he was dead or alive. She was overtaken by a flood of emotion when she saw him again, as a grateful nation welcomed him home as a national hero.

For his part, Bulkeley reveled in the media spotlight. Looking tanned and well rested in a fresh khaki uniform, Bulkeley told the newspapermen and newsreel cameras that "with a couple of hundred torpedo boats we could sweep the Japs from the sea" and that "man to man, we can run over them like a steamroller."

He regaled the media with what it was like to attack Japanese ships with his little PT boats.

"You feel like a clay pigeon on a shooting range," he said. "The feeling is suicidal."

Alice whispered to John that all was not right with their infant son, that he had been born with some physical and mental problems. She had hoped to have a private moment with John, but the crush of the crowd made it impossible.

With Ensign Akers remaining in California on a ten-day leave, the media blitz was just beginning for the other returning heroes, who were all from New York.

Bulkeley, proclaimed by the media the "No. 1 War Hero of Queens," went to church, then rode with his mother, Elizabeth, in a Mother's Day Parade on May 10 in the Sunnyside section of the borough.

Four days later, Bulkeley, along with Lieutenant Kelly and Ensign Cox, were honored guests at the Army and Navy Emergency Relief Parade in Manhattan.

Mayor La Guardia opened the speaking part of the occasion by saying, "We are here today for one purpose, to welcome three New York boys, who, though the war is only beginning, have already won fame and glory in the service—the courageous and valiant service they have rendered to their country. I want you to greet them."

Bulkeley told the crowd that he was overwhelmed by the response that he, Lieutenant Kelly, and Ensign Cox had received. He seconded the mayor's appeal for funds, but pointed out that he preferred to reverse the billing, calling it the "Navy and Army" relief fund.

"All I ask is that you think of those men on Bataan and how badly they needed your help," he said.

Two days later, Bulkeley turned a launching ceremony in Bayonne, New Jersey, for PT-103 into a rousing patriotic demonstration by the 2,000 workers of the yard. He told the crowd that the PT crews were ready to fight to the last man, but the boats must be built "faster, faster and ever faster."

Like a collegiate cheerleader, he put three questions to the yard employees.

"Are you going to give us the boats?" to which the 2,000 workers shouted, "Yes."

"Are you going to speed up production?" Again the group roared, "Yes!"

"Are you going to let them lick us?" This time the chorus was, "No!"

The next day, Sunday, May 17, the three officers were guests at the "I am an American Day" celebration, which included a parade and gathering at Central Park estimated at 1.25 million people. Songwriter Irving Berlin opened the festivities by singing "God Bless America." Private Joe Louis, the heavyweight boxing champion of the world, sat in the first row next to Ensign Akers, who had just flown in from California. Louis was later photographed shaking Bulkeley's hand.

According to the *New York Times*, Bulkeley was introduced by the mayor as one of the great heroes of the war. Then he modestly saluted as the huge crowd gave him an ovation. He told of the pride he had felt at being an American as he fought with "our hungry, sick and outnumbered troops" on Bataan.

"It was then that we proved once again that an American can lick anything near his weight in high explosives," he said, "and we also put an end to that story about Japs not surrendering. They did."

Bulkeley became so good at public speaking that the navy used him more and more at war-related functions. He became a magnet at countless rallies to sell war bonds, a role he grew very uncomfortable in.

"I feel like a darned fool asking folks to buy War Bonds," he remarked.

Still, his quips and one-liners generated a lot of publicity for the navy and the war effort.

One reporter asked Bulkeley which target he would prefer to bomb first, Berlin or Tokyo.

"Berlin," answered Bulkeley.

"Why Berlin?" the reporter asked.

"Business before pleasure," Bulkeley said with a grin.

The *Long Island Press* reported that Bulkeley was offered a two-week stage appearance at New York's Loew's State Theater, to which the navy hero responded: "The only theater I'd be interested in playing is Loew's Tokyo."

Bulkeley was a guest of Hollywood stars James Cagney and Robert Montgomery at the 21 Club in New York City. Little did Montgomery know that he would be playing Bulkeley three years later in the smash movie *They Were Expendable*.

Along with his war bond huckster duties, Bulkeley was assigned by the navy to recruit PT-boat skippers at universities throughout the country. After a recruiting speech at Northwestern University in Chicago, Bulkeley asked for fifty volunteers and got more than a thousand, virtually everyone in the room.

"That a young lieutenant, temporarily promoted to lieutenant commander, could be given the pick of more than a thousand commissioned officers, all of them college graduates, was in retrospect incredible," historian and author Nigel Hamilton wrote. "Fortunately for the U.S. Navy, Bulkeley could choose only a small number."

Bulkeley was as much an inspirational orator as he was an inspirational warrior, an extremely effective public speaker, and a national hero to boot. His name, face, and story were known throughout the country, and his fame grew even greater when the book *They Were Expendable* was published in late 1942. He was a genuine hero, one that many young men wanted to emulate.

One of his most famous recruits turned out to be John F. Kennedy, a future president of the United States.

Bulkeley's most significant appearance would come on August 4, 1942, when the newly promoted lieutenant commander visited President

Roosevelt in the Oval Office to receive his nation's highest decoration, the Medal of Honor.

Bulkeley wore his old washable khaki uniform that was used in wartime. Alice wore a dark suit she had purchased for the occasion. John, thin from a limited diet in the Philippines, and Alice walked up to the White House main gate and informed the guard that they had an appointment with the president. Bulkeley had no written invitation or anything to prove his identity.

The guard, extremely skeptical, called the Secret Service, which eventually placed a call to the White House presidential secretary for appointments. Two staff members appeared to greet the Bulkeleys. One of them told Alice that she was not invited and would have to wait outside.

"Stunned, Alice said goodbye to John as he rushed inside and turned away from the gates," her daughter, Joan, later wrote. "Her first thought was to go for a walk in Lafayette Park across the street. As she slowly sat down on a park bench, all she could conclude was that a background check by the president's staff must have revealed her ancestry. How could they allow a woman who was part Japanese and German to enter the Oval Office?"

Bulkeley walked up the pathway to the White House alone and from there was escorted to the Oval Office. Awaiting him was the chief of the navy, Admiral Ernest King, and President Roosevelt.

While Bulkeley was leaning over the desk for the medal to be put around his neck, Roosevelt whispered to him to "come back later this evening and have a chat." This Bulkeley did, with several very high-ranking officers also present. The questions were exactly what Bulkeley had been previously warned by FDR's assistants not to answer in detail. Their concern was to not upset the president by a story that relief for the Philippines had been expected by MacArthur and the other men in Bataan. But no one fooled Roosevelt, and Bulkeley's sense of honor recoiled at the assistants' advice. Roosevelt extracted the pitiful story, word by word. The message that MacArthur desired to be delivered to the president by Bulkeley was also passed. MacArthur's requirements to retake the Philippines were delineated, as well as MacArthur's bitter disappointment at finding on his arrival in Australia that no army or equipment to recapture the Philippines, let alone defend Australia, awaited him. All this the president absorbed], with no comment. "Mission accomplished," Bulkeley said to himself.

All eyes were on Bulkeley as he told of how stunned the fighting men were to learn no aid was on the way and how shocked MacArthur was to find upon reaching Australia that there was no Army for him to command. The looks turned to angry stares.

Bulkeley said he thought he could almost hear "the gnashing of teeth" by some of the senior officers as he left the room.

"At the time I thought it was sort of strange, the commander-in-chief of the armed forces having to whisper orders to me," Bulkeley said. "But after I had left the White House it struck me that some of his assistants had been trying to protect the president, that they wanted me to keep mum on the fact that we had taken a licking in the Philippines, that General MacArthur and every man on Corregidor and Bataan had thought big help was on the way.

"But I decided to hell with those namby-pamby people around Mr. Roosevelt. We weren't going to win the war by hiding the facts of life from the president of the United States. I have never believed in pussyfooting with facts. General MacArthur had ordered me to tell President Roosevelt the whole damned sordid story, and, by God, that's what I would do."

On behalf of MacArthur, Bulkeley pleaded for troops, weapons, airplanes, ammunition, and ships to be rushed to Australia in order to launch an offensive to recapture the Philippines. Chapter and verse, he relayed MacArthur's urgent request for two hundred PT boats within eight months. Despite MacArthur's warning to him, Bulkeley could not avoid the temptation to throw in some of his own views on how the war in the Pacific should be conducted.

Bulkeley's frank views didn't make the newly minted lieutenant commander a popular man around Washington, but there was little the military big shots could do to one of America's most celebrated fighting men.

Some Navy brass believed the quicker this "wild man" returned to his natural element and out of Washington was in the best interests of the country. In September, Bulkeley was given command of Motor Torpedo Boat Squadron 7, destination New Guinea. Also headed back to PT-boat service in the South Pacific were Kelly, Akers, Cox, and Brantingham. Kelly, promoted to lieutenant commander, was given command of Squadron 9, which became known as "Kelly's Kids." One of his boat commanders was Lieutenant Brantingham. Cox would later become commander of Squadron 40, just before the war ended in 1945.

When MacArthur returned to Corregidor on March 2, 1945, he did so with his typical grand sense of history. He arranged for four PT boats to take himself and his staff to that historic fortress island where they had fled the Philippines almost exactly three years earlier aboard four PT boats. One of the dignitaries invited as MacArthur's guest that day was George E. Cox, Jr., the same man who had piloted the 41-boat that personally carried the MacArthur family off the Rock back on March 11, 1942. Cox was now a lieutenant commander.

Epilogue

The book *They Were Expendable* became a runaway bestseller when it appeared in late 1942. It was condensed for *Reader's Digest* and featured in *Life* magazine, and it made the PT sailor the glamour boy of America's surface fleet.

It was an exaggerated reputation.

Because the book was written during the war, the author, W. L. White, had no way of verifying the squadron's claims of having destroyed or damaged two enemy light cruisers, two transports, an oil tanker, and several barges, landing craft, and planes. The eighty-three officers and men of Squadron 3 were widely scattered throughout the Philippines and Australia, and a few made it home to be reassigned. Casualties were reported at eighteen dead, including three officers—Lieutenant (j.g.) Edward DeLong and Ensigns William Plant and Bond Murray—who died as prisoners of war. A total of thirty-eight were captured. Nine died in prison camps and the other twenty-nine were liberated following the war. The rest headed for the hills and became guerrillas.

Postwar study of Japanese naval archives shows no evidence that any Japanese ships were torpedoed at the times and places that the Squadron 3 sailors claim to have hit them. Unfortunately, the most elaborately detailed claim of all, the sinking of a *Kuma*-class cruiser off Cebu Island by PT-34 and -41, most certainly is not valid, because the cruiser itself sent a full report of the battle to Japanese navy headquarters and admitted being struck by one dud torpedo (so at least much of the PT claim is true), but the cruiser, which happened to be the *Kuma* itself, was undamaged and survived to be sunk by a British submarine late in the war.

Although the fantastic and undeniably exaggerated claims of sinkings are regrettable, they in no way detract from the bravery of the sailors of Squadron 3. They were merely the victims of the nation's desperate need for victories.

The main accomplishments of PT boats were harassment of the enemy, torpedo attacks, assaulting enemy shore batteries and barges, reconnaissance patrols, rescue missions, landing scouts, and providing transportation for inspection tours. They were not designed for, and were not capable of, going toe to toe with cruisers, destroyers, or any other large warship.

Other myths were allowed to slip into the written and spoken word, such as the size of the armament aboard the boats and an exaggerated cruising speed of seventy knots or more.

In the fantasies spun by the nation's press, the PTs literally ran rings around enemy destroyers and, wrote historian Bern Keating, socked so many torpedoes into Japanese warships that you almost felt sorry for the outclassed and floundering enemy.

When Bulkeley returned to the States in May 1942, he beat the drums of his PT boats on recruiting trips around the country. Writer Nigel Hamilton, for one, said some of Bulkeley's claims were "absurd," nothing more than juvenile fantasies, but many of the inexperienced and innocent reserve officers and midshipmen ate it up. The more seasoned naval officers gritted their teeth and shook their heads.

One of Bulkeley's contemporaries, Alvin Cluster, later said:

> *I liked John. It was only in later years that I realized that his zeal in promoting himself was outsize to the man himself. The big thing was MacArthur. If MacArthur had traveled out of the Philippines by any other method, you probably would never have heard of John Bulkeley. And that would have been a blessing.*
>
> *America desperately needed heroes after Pearl Harbor, and they would seize on any exploit or any battle to show how great we were. The only reason PT-boats ever got the attention they did was that we had nothing else! They really didn't do a lot of damage. But Roosevelt had to point to somebody, and that's why Bulkeley and PT-boats got all that attention. . . . John Bulkeley was really a joke to a lot of officers.*

While the regular navy may have cringed at some of the outlandish and "lunatic" claims of Bulkeley, the public ate it up. The dash and audacity of the men aboard those doughty little cockleshells, hardly bigger than a stockbroker's cabin cruiser, appealed to the American mind. It was the story of David and Goliath again.

The navy brass, in a way, never completely forgave Bulkeley for his outspoken admiration of General MacArthur. It made him a minority of one. To his credit, Bulkeley remained ever loyal to MacArthur and never backed away from his position of respect.

In 1982, on the fortieth anniversary of the heroic escape to Mindanao, Bulkeley wrote a friend that he felt that MacArthur "was the greatest General as well as statesman since George Washington," adding that he felt that MacArthur's decision to use his boats was no less than an act of "genius."

One of the most fascinating, and bewildering, aspects of the fall of the Philippines was the political maneuvering by two of its biggest players, President Franklin D. Roosevelt and General Douglas MacArthur.

Looking back more than sixty years, it is incomprehensible that a president of the United States would ship men and supplies to Great Britain and the Soviet Union while at the same time ignoring the pleas of doomed Americans trapped on American soil in the Philippines. Roosevelt had promised Winston Churchill the previous August that the United States would deal with Germany first; then he reaffirmed that commitment in December after the Japanese attack despite overwhelming public opinion on the matter. He was vilified in the press, which accused him of deliberately and knowingly abandoning his own troops while diverting resources to other countries and other soldiers.

If an American president behaved in that manner today, he would no doubt be assailed for dereliction of duty and even treason. The public would rise up in righteous indignation and demand his impeachment.

In 1942, the animosity between the two men ran deep. Roosevelt lovers were MacArthur haters and vice versa. Roosevelt saw MacArthur as a potential political rival, and MacArthur regarded Roosevelt as a consummate "liar." It was a clash of two massive egos.

It was also common knowledge throughout the army that MacArthur and General George Marshall were not on good personal terms. MacArthur's career had skyrocketed after World War I. He rose to a four-star general and chief of staff, whereas Marshall, only a year younger, remained a lieutenant colonel. The fact that Marshall, who graduated from the Virginia Military Institute, was not a West Pointer definitely hurt him in the eyes of many career officers.

Eisenhower, who knew MacArthur as well as anyone after serving under him for seven years, was plainly skeptical of the general's value in winning the war in the Pacific.

"MacArthur is out of the Philippine Islands," Eisenhower wrote in his private diary on March 19, 1942. "Now Supreme Commander of 'Southwest Pacific Area.' The newspapers acclaim the move—the public has built itself a hero out of its own imagination."

When Corregidor fell on May 6, Eisenhower was moved to write in his diary: "Poor Wainwright! He did the fighting in the Philippine Islands, another got such glory as the public could find in the operation. General MacArthur's tirades, to which I so often listened in Manila, would now sound as silly to the public as they then did to us. But he's a hero! Yah."

The mercurial MacArthur was a handful, to be sure. A brilliant tactician, he was a genius at public relations. Of 142 communiqués released by his headquarters between December 1941 and March 1942, only one soldier—MacArthur—is mentioned in 109 of them. This, despite the fact that he set foot on Bataan only once.

"During his 77 days on Corregidor he visited Bataan only once," William Manchester wrote. "It was on Jan 10. He went because he was told it would help sagging morale. Visiting the men he proudly told them that 'help is definitely on the way. We must hold out until it comes.'"

Among those caught in the middle of this power struggle was the ever-loyal subordinate, Major General Jonathan Wainwright. He was left holding the bag when MacArthur left Corregidor and wound up spending almost three and a half years as a prisoner of war.

"It was well known that MacArthur had not been kind to the abandoned Wainwright after his own escape to Australia," historian and former navy secretary James Webb has written. "In truth, it had been Wainwright all along, rather than MacArthur, who had led the actual defense of Bataan and Corregidor. During the entire siege, MacArthur had left the relative safety of the dark, cool tunnels of Corregidor to visit his soldiers on the Bataan Peninsula only once. It was Wainwright who had directed the artillery, and walked the lines, and suffered the mosquitoes and pellagra and dysentery, and looked into the hopeless faces of dying American and Filipino solders as they withstood an unremitting Japanese advance. And it was Wainwright who in the end had been left behind to face the grim reality of defeat."

MacArthur had humiliated Wainwright several times, once radioing Washington shortly before the fall of Corregidor that "Wainwright has temporarily become unbalanced, and susceptible of enemy use." Having accepted the Medal of Honor for his flight from Corregidor, MacArthur refused to endorse the same medal for Wainwright, who had stayed and fought. He said that giving Wainwright the medal would be a "grave injustice" to others who "exhibited powers of leadership and inspiration to a degree greatly superior to his." MacArthur felt that Wainwright's surrender would have brought injustice to the hallowed medal.

Some believed that MacArthur considered himself the hero of Bataan and Corregidor, and giving Wainwright the same medal would make him a rival for popular acclaim.

General Marshall, who was surprised and distressed by MacArthur's refusal to endorse the Medal of Honor for Wainwright, asked Secretary of War Henry Stimson for an opinion. Both agreed that no purpose would be served by a public airing of the situation, and they were unwilling to risk exposing Wainwright or the army to the possibility of scandal or alienating MacArthur, who was idolized by the public and surely needed to spearhead the drive for victory over Japan.

When they next met, the day before the signing of the peace treaty in Tokyo Bay in September 1945, MacArthur was shocked at Wainwright's skeleton-like appearance. A white-haired shell of his former self, Wainwright broke down and wept, asking his former boss for forgiveness for having surrendered Corregidor. He had been haunted throughout his captivity by the belief that he would become the scapegoat for the loss of the Philippines. He was sure he would face a court-martial.

"Wainwright had carried the load, fought the impossible fight, suffered the insufferable, borne the unbearable. And here he was, begging for forgiveness from the very man who had left him and the others behind to suffer death, starvation and captivity," James Webb wrote.

MacArthur had gotten wind that Wainwright had agreed to have his memoirs published and was concerned what he might write.

"Well, Jonathan," MacArthur said to Wainwright after the surrender ceremony aboard the battleship *Missouri*, "I hear that you've been offered a lot of money for your memoirs."

Wainwright said that he was correct.

"Bully!" MacArthur said. "You write them, then send them to me and I'll check them and send them to the War Department."

A month later, when Wainwright recounted this exchange to his editor, Bob Considine, he grinned and said, "I didn't do any such thing." Wainwright, not surprisingly, had no intention of allowing MacArthur to alter his version of events.

Wainwright would get his Medal of Honor from President Truman a few days after returning from Japan. Truman, who despised MacArthur, wrote in his diary: "I don't see why in hell Roosevelt didn't order Wainwright to Australia and let MacArthur be a martyr. . . . We'd have had a real general and a fighting man if we had Wainwright and not a play actor and bunco man as we have now."

Unlike MacArthur, Wainwright was utterly guileless and, unlike MacArthur, he was loyal to a fault. In the few years he had left, Wainwright would never speak a word against his old commander.

Wainwright died on September 2, 1953. Noticeably absent at his funeral was MacArthur, who said he had "a previous engagement."

MacArthur was a controversial figure, to be sure, one who was seemingly wrapped in contradictions. Brilliant, articulate, and imaginative, he also displayed paranoia, arrogance, and such a sense of histrionics that one of his army commanders referred to him as "Sarah" behind his back, after the famous French actress Sarah Bernhardt. MacArthur inspired worship or revulsion, but not affection.

Dwight Eisenhower, asked late in his career what he did while serving as an aide to MacArthur in the 1930s, remarked: "I studied dramatics under him for five years in Washington and four years in the Philippines."

Part of MacArthur's difficulties in dealing with others in the U.S. military was his own chief of staff, Major General Richard Sutherland. As the gatekeeper to his boss, Sutherland was just as unapproachable as MacArthur.

"[Sutherland's] foul temper, large ego, and autocratic manner offended nearly every officer who crossed his path," General Walter Krueger said. "He was a brilliant loner and an indefatigable worker, often putting in sixteen-hour days. Sutherland's intensity complemented the perfectionist strain in MacArthur but his habit of running roughshod over other officers, treating them with contempt or condescension, left him without the respect of his peers." Learning of Sutherland's death in 1966, Krueger, himself seriously ill, remarked that "it was a good thing for mankind."

There is no doubt that MacArthur felt betrayed by Washington and its false promises of relief, and that he in turn had unknowingly deceived his soldiers in the Philippines. In the coming years, he became a lonely, angry man, suffering from countless bouts of paranoia where all but a select few were out to "get" him. His staff would always receive his undivided loyalty. Called the "Bataan Gang," though most of them had remained on Corregidor and hadn't set foot on the peninsula during the siege, they would form an insurmountable barrier between him and newcomers to the Pacific until late in the war.

MacArthur's seething dislike of Roosevelt lasted until the latter died in the spring of 1945. Told of his passing, MacArthur remarked: "So Roosevelt is dead. There's a man who could not tell the truth when a lie would serve just as well!"

The Philippines had become MacArthur's great obsession. He had a burning desire to erase this personal stain on his long and distinguished record. Not only had he been defeated in battle, in a most humiliating way, worse was that he had abandoned his men under fire in their most desperate moments. He would never get over this personal sense of failure.

MacArthur would be promoted to five-star general in late 1944 during the invasion of Leyte and would go on to become supreme commander of Allied occupation forces in Japan after the war. He was called one last time for duty as commander of United Nations forces in Korea in 1950. A few months later, he engineered a brilliant amphibious landing at Inchon to turn the tide and swing the momentum back to the Allies. He was summarily fired by President Truman for insubordination on April 11, 1951, returning to the United States for the first time since 1937 as a national hero.

MacArthur died on April 5, 1964, at the age of eighty-four.

"There is a tragedy that comes with MacArthur's kind of fame," historian James Webb wrote many years later. "When one measures a life by the enemies he has conquered rather than the friends he has made, it becomes important never to run out of battles. For what then is peace but a debilitating emptiness?"

Bulkeley would go on to command a force of torpedo boats and minesweepers charged with clearing the lanes to Utah Beach during the Normandy invasion of June 6, 1944. One of his most publicized assignments was commander of the Guantanamo Naval Base on Cuba during the mid 1960s. By now a rear admiral, Bulkeley engaged Fidel Castro in a public relations battle after the latter cut off the base's water supply, then accused the Marines of stealing water. While work proceeded to make the base water self-sufficient, Bulkeley decided he would prove to the world that he was not stealing any water. Before a large gathering of the press Bulkeley dug up a three-foot section of an underground pipe running into the base and hoisted it for all to see it was dry.

"Fidel was, and still is, a lying bastard," Bulkeley announced in typical fashion to the crowd of media.

Bulkeley would have an even longer career than MacArthur—fifty-nine years, in fact—and much of it was filled with danger and controversy. He was eighty-four when he passed away on April 6, 1996.

"He always had an uncanny propensity to stir things up," Bulkeley's son, Peter, said at his father's funeral service. "He fit the mold of Indiana Jones, hat, coat and all. Hard as leather on the outside . . . he wept over the decision that his men and our Army at Bataan were left behind to face an enemy of overwhelming strength."

In the summer of 2003, one of the last surviving members of Squadron 3, eighty-seven-year old John Tuggle, spoke lovingly of his old boss at the thirty-ninth annual PT Boat Convention in Lexington, Kentucky.

"I liked everything about him," Tuggle said in a cracking, tearful voice. "He was a nice guy. He never gave you a hard time. He was easy going and yet he was gung-ho about everything. He wanted everything done now. He was a man's man."

Appendix One

WALT DISNEY

June 18, 1942

Dear Lieutenant Buckley: [*sic*]

Your request for a painting of the mosquito riding the torpedo made us all very happy. We have followed your many exploits with great interest and, I might add, basked in reflected glory each time you sunk a Jap ship. Somehow, we all felt as though we had had a hand in it ourselves.

It is with great pride that we are forwarding to you, under separate cover, a replica of the insignia as best we remember it. The original design, which was made a long time ago, is lost so the picture we are sending you may vary somewhat.

My entire staff joins me in wishing you good luck and a continuation of the successes that have made your name a household word to the entire nation.

With deep admiration, I am

          Sincerely,

             Walt Disney [signed]

Appendix Two

Passenger List

PT-32—Crew officers: Lt. (j.g.) Vince Schumacher and Ensign Cone Johnson. Passengers: Brig. Gen. Spencer B. Akin, Brig. Gen. Hugh J. Casey, Brig. Gen. William F. Marquat, Brig. Gen. Harold H. George, and Lt. Col. Joe R. Sherr.

PT-34—Crew officers: Lt. Robert B. Kelly and Ensign Iliff Richardson. Passengers: Rear Adm. Francis W. Rockwell, Brig. Gen. Richard J. Marshall, Col. Charles P. Stivers, and Capt. Joseph McMicking.

PT-35—Crew officers: Lt. (j.g.) Henry Brantingham, Ensigns Anthony Akers and Bond Murray. Passengers: Col. Charles A. Willoughby, Lt. Col. LeGrande A. Diller, Lt. Col. Francis H. Wilson, and MSgt. Paul P. Rogers.

PT-41—Crew officers: Lt. John D. Bulkeley and Ensign George Cox. Passengers: General Douglas MacArthur, Jean and Arthur MacArthur, Ah Cheu, Maj. Gen. Richard K. Sutherland, Capt. Harold G. Ray, Lt. Col. Sidney L. Huff, and Maj. Charles H. Morhouse.

Source Notes

Preface

8 "strangest episodes": ibid., p. 206.

10 "Worse than beasts": Stephen E. Ambrose, *To America*, p. 112.

11 "For thirty years": Douglas MacArthur, *Reminiscences*, p. 138.

"Hitler was still the prime target": William Manchester, *American Caesar*, pp. 244–45.

13 "It was characteristic": ibid., p. 205.

14."This turn of events": W. G. Winslow, *The Fleet the Gods Forgot*, p. 26.

15 mutual irritability: Eric Morris, *Corregidor, The End of the Line*, p. 359.

Chapter One

24 "Back in through there": Bruce M. Bachman, *An Honorable Profession*, p. 189.

26 "one of my proudest moments": Breuer, *The Sea Wolf*, pp. 268–70.

Chapter Two

27 at Trafalgar: Breuer, *The Sea Wolf*, p. 4.

28 "Had this excellent craftsman": Bachman, *An Honorable Profession*, p. 6.

29 "Take your pick": ibid., p. 7.

 "Cruelest of the whole lot": Breuer, *The Sea Wolf*, p. 7.

31 "You couldn't say": Alden Hatch, *Heroes of Annapolis*, p. 233.

 "didn't have the best left jab": Bachman, *An Honorable Profession*, p. 11.

32 "cracked up an airplane": Breuer, *The Sea Wolf*, p. 9.

33 "I scrambled through the hatch": ibid., p. 2.

34 "I was mad as hell": ibid., p. 3.

Chapter Three

37 "I could not explain": Breuer, *The Sea Wolf*, p. 12.

37 "What a joyous sight": ibid., pp. 13–14.

39 "Mission accomplished": Bachman, *An Honorable Profession*, p. 154.

 "Catch myself smiling": ibid., p. 155.

40 "As I was the shore patrol officer": ibid., p. 158.

40 "She caught my eye": ibid., p. 159.

41 "On our first meeting": ibid., p. 158.

 "The Woods were just as fond": Joan Bulkeley Stade, *Twelve Handkerchiefs*, p. 52.

42 "not what Alice had expected": ibid., p. 55.

Chapter Four

47 Age of steam: Curtis L. Nelson, *Hunters in the Shallows*, p. 59.

47 Prototype boat arrived: ibid., p. 97.

48 Unexpected delays: ibid., p. 106.

50 "thought we were nuts": Breuer, *The Sea Wolf*, p. 20.

51 "To hell with that old bastard King": ibid., p. 21.

 "An exciting secret place": ibid., p. 23.

Chapter Five

57 opulent yet cheap: Eric Morris, *Corregidor, The End of the Line*, p. 3.

58 Exotic smell to the place: Duane Schultz, *Hero of Bataan*, p. 45.

59 "It was rumored": Edgar Whitcomb, *Escape from Corregidor*, p. 10.

"fighting a war and a hangover": Elizabeth M. Norman, *We Band of Angels*, pp. 4–5.

61 "sparkle went out of Manila": Schultz, *Hero of Bataan*, p. 52.

63 worn out his welcome: Robert H. Ferrell, *The Eisenhower Diaries*, p. 7.

64 "calm confidence of a Christian with four aces": John Hersey, *Men on Bataan*, p. 125.

excellent cuisine and music: Walter Karig, *Battle Report*, p. 127.

65 MacArthur's life in the Philippines: Ferrell, *The Eisenhower Diaries*, p. 37.

65 MacArthur had grown used to the bitterness: Frank Kelley, *MacArthur: Man of Action*, p. 104.

Chapter Six

69 "the highest priority": William Manchester, *American Caesar*, p. 192.

70 "practically useless": Nelson, *Hunters in the Shallows*, pp. 117–18.

"hoping they would be of some use": ibid., p. 119.

72 shiny pith helmets: Manchester, *American Caesar*, pp. 192–93.

73 "A flaming nut": Bachman, *An Honorable Profession*, pp. 162–63.

74 "at the risk of health": ibid., p. 163.

75 "We opened fire with our Very pistols": ibid., p. 163.

77 "with miraculous accuracy": Whitcomb, *Escape from Corregidor*, p. 13.

had never known defeat: Morris, *Corregidor, The End of the Line*, p. 4.

Chapter Seven

80 "more overt than that": Morris, *Corregidor, The End of the Line*, p. 78.

81 "looked like pepper": Donald Knox, *Death March*, p. 12.

82 "Go get me a bottle of beer": Jonathan Wainwright, *General Wainwright's Story*, p. 21.

"first decorations of the Pacific war": ibid., p. 22.

84 "powerless to do anything about it": Whitcomb, *Escape from Corregidor*, p. 20.

"limped back to our barracks": Knox, *Death March*, p. 17.

85 "shaking like a leaf": ibid., p. 16.

86. "how neat a job": ibid., p. 19.

"have them to remember": W. L. White, *They Were Expendable*, pp. 8–9.

89 "something was catching hell": ibid., p. 15.

"combat skill of the Japanese": Morris, *Corregidor, The End of the Line*, p. 116.

90 "flock of well-disciplined buzzards": White, *They Were Expendable*, p. 16.

91 "didn't know any better": Knox, *Death March*, p. 20.

92 "looked like butchers": White, *They Were Expendable*, p. 19.

93 wave of hysteria: John Toland, *But Not in Shame*, p. 56.

Chapter Eight

98 pineapple plantation airfield: ibid., p. 137.

99 "how completely impotent we were": White, *They Were Expendable*, p. 24.

"lived on our boats": ibid., p. 12.

100 "officers should lead": ibid., p. 13.

102 "I ought to shoot the bastards myself": Breuer, *The Sea Wolf*, p. 34.

104 melting into the hills: Manchester, *American Caesar*, p. 217.

They could have turned the beaches red: Morris, *Corregidor, The End of the Line*, p. 157.

106 to defend the Marne: Courtney Whitney, *MacArthur, Rendezvous With History*, p. 18.

107 headlong dash for Bataan: Ronald H. Spector, *Eagle Against the Sun*, pp. 110–11.

108 "greatest of sorrow": Wainwright, *General Wainwright's Story*, p. 46.

Chapter Nine

113 "they forgot the food": Knox, *Death March*, p. 43.
　bartered for some booze: ibid., p. 44.

114 and that was it: ibid., p. 45.

115 streets were deserted: White, *They Were Expendable*, p. 57.

118 danced to a portable: ibid., p. 49.
　"couldn't have tasted any better": ibid., p. 60.

Chapter Ten

120 "mansions of this jungle": Hersey, *Men on Bataan*, p. 78.

122 "thrown in the towel": Breuer, *The Sea Wolf*, pp. 35–36.
　"Do you get the picture, Barron?": ibid., p. 37.

123 fuzz remained fuzz: Stewart H. Holbrook, *None More Courageous*, pp. 56–57.

124 "neckties and smartly pressed pants": Schultz, *Hero of Bataan*, p. 137.
　only meeting on Bataan: Wainwright, *General Wainwright's Story*, pp. 49–50.

125 a stinging reminder: Morris, *Corregidor, The End of the Line*, p. 256.

126 "Not one rumor ever came to pass": Knox, *Death March*, p. 86.

127 "V for Vacate": ibid., p. 46.
　"That usually got a laugh out of them": ibid., p. 59.

128 "a test for the strongest teeth": Wainwright, *General Wainwright's Story*,

p. 49.

129 "cruelest deceptions of the war": Whitney, *MacArthur, Rendezvous With History*, pp. 33–34.

Chapter Eleven

132 "We tested everything": White, *They Were Expendable*, p. 67.

133 "we saw the red fire rising": ibid., p. 70.

134 "He jumped astride that wobbling, hissing torpedo": ibid., p. 71.

141 "I wasn't doing so well": Breuer, *The Sea Wolf*, pp. 47–48.

lobbed two hand grenades: Winslow, *The Fleet the Gods Forgot*, p. 69.

142 "had five holes in him": White, *They Were Expendable*, pp. 82–83.

143 "like a fly in a web": Robert J. Bulkley, *At Close Quarters*, p. 14.

144 "You've got to kill the enemy, a lot of them." Holbrook, *None More Courageous*, p. 56.

Chapter Twelve

149 "selfish and shortsighted": Steve Mellnik, *Philippine Diary, 1939–45*, pp. 92–93.

150 given up any hope of relief or rescue: Morris, *Corregidor, The End of the Line*, p. 357.

"fight to destruction": Douglas MacArthur, *Reminiscences*, p. 139.

151 Homma's brigades had been severely mauled: ibid., p. 331.

152 "a mess like this?": Schultz, *Hero of Bataan*, p. 142.

154 heavy stink of creosote: William B. Breuer, *The Sea Wolf*, p. 37.

153 "important for me to sit on sandbags": Toland, *But Not in Shame*, p. 177.

156 "you fought for my country": John Jacob Beck, *MacArthur and Wainwright*, p. 117.

157 using it for a paperweight: Clay Blair, Jr., *Silent Victory*, pp. 207–8.

reached the Rock: Manchester, *American Caesar*, p. 244.

159 knowing that they were expendable: White, *They Were Expendable*, p. 95.

159 "plenty of canned salmon": ibid., p. 93.

160 "let's do it again": Holbrook, *None More Courageous*, p. 57.

161 " 'Charlie Chan' in the Navy": Clark Lee, *They Call It Pacific*, p. 200.

"we would have a good chance": ibid., pp. 201–2.

162 "sentimental gesture": ibid., p. 202.

Chapter Thirteen

164 "on its last legs": White, *They Were Expendable*, p. 100.

"had second thoughts": Manchester, *American Caesar*, p. 250.

166 "no fuel is available here for a submarine": Beck, *MacArthur and Wainwright*, pp. 126–27.

167 "Jean was a bit queasy": Manchester, *American Caesar*, p. 254.

169 "a piece of cake": Breuer, *The Sea Wolf*, p. 54.

"touch of claustrophobia": (Sidney Huff's quotes are from two *Saturday Evening Post* articles: Sept. 22, 1951 and Sept. 29, 1951.)

171 "he elected to exercise": Beck, *MacArthur and Wainwright*, pp. 151–52.

thumb his nose at the enemy: Whitney, *MacArthur, Rendezvous With History*, p. 49.

172 would arrive too late: Manchester, *American Caesar*, p. 253.

"leave on the 14th": Bulkley, *At Close Quarters*, p. 16.

"PTs were ill-equipped": Nelson, *Hunters in the Shallows*, p. 40.

173 "inevitable destruction": ibid., p. 146.

"precious lace": White, *They Were Expendable*, p. 105.

175 "rather than leave with the rest of us": ibid., pp. 91–92.

"on such an occasion": Manchester, *American Caesar*, p. 255.

"general usefulness": MacArthur, *Reminiscences*, p. 141.

176 "near-panicked escape plan": Bachman, *An Honorable Profession*, p. 169.

177 "the requirements of war": ibid., p. 170.

"hoped to live there for months": White, *They Were Expendable*, p. 108.

Chapter Fourteen

179 "could be completed": Beck, *MacArthur and Wainwright*, p. 136.

182 "the morning of the twelfth": Wainwright, *General Wainwright's Story*, p. 2.

183 "We eat only twice a day over there": ibid., p. 3.

184 "all the determination the man has": ibid., pp. 3–4.

"a promise he could not keep": ibid., p. 5.

185 "leaving that very night": White, *They Were Expendable*, p. 113.

"not even a razor": Manchester, *American Caesar*, p. 257.

186 "kind of stunned silence": *Saturday Evening Post*, Sept. 22, 1951.

187 "We're coming back up here, Freddy": Beck, *MacArthur and Wainwright*, p. 144.

"You may cast off": Manchester, *American Caesar*, p. 257.

Chapter Fifteen

190 "entirely by compass and chart": White, *They Were Expendable*, pp. 119–20.

"riding with a madman": ibid., p. 122.

191 "I hope that we get there": ibid., pp. 122–23.

192 "in a concrete mixer": MacArthur, *Reminiscences*, pp. 143–44.

"chafed his hands hour after hour": Manchester, *American Caesar*, p. 259.

193 "gone over the side": White, *They Were Expendable*, p. 126.

194 "The ship's superstructure": Beck, *MacArthur and Wainwright*, p. 147.

195 "leaving even the lookout behind": Beck, *MacArthur and Wainwright*,

p. 129.

196 "[Arthur] was most unhappy": Manchester, *American Caesar*, p. 261.

"seasickness may be a joke": White, *They Were Expendable*, p. 131.

197 "I'll boil you in oil": Toland, *But Not in Shame*, p. 272.

Chapter Sixteen

200 "no one to wait on them": White, *They Were Expendable*, p. 135.

"probably lucky at that": Bulkley, *At Close Quarters*, p. 18.

201 "you can have them": White, *They Were Expendable*, p. 137.

202 "happy as a baby": ibid., pp. 140–41.

205 "I wouldn't have believed it possible": ibid., p. 141.

"crossing the Delaware": Manchester, *American Caesar*, p. 262.

207 "Brand-new bombers": Toland, *But Not in Shame*, p. 274.

"We would gladly have removed our clothes": Beck, *MacArthur and Wainwright*, p. 269.

208 the pilot scrambled aboard: Morris, *Corregidor, The End of the Line*, p. 362.

209 "That won't sit well with a lot of people": Beck, *MacArthur and Wainwright*, p. 167.

Chapter Seventeen

214 "one way or the other": Breuer, *The Sea Wolf*, p. 68.

"whatever means is necessary": ibid., p. 157.

215 "play poker with them": White, *They Were Expendable*, pp. 146–47.

217 "ready to come with us?": Bulkley, *At Close Quarters*, p. 21.

"forget the damn suitcases": Bachman, *An Honorable Profession*, p. 173.

218 "fifteen million dollars": Breuer, *The Sea Wolf*, p. 71.

"not nice things to crawl around on": White, *They Were Expendable*, pp. 152–53.

219 "walk on water": Breuer, *The Sea Wolf*, p. 72.

220 "bottom of our hearts": Bachman, *An Honorable Profession*, p. 173.

Chapter Eighteen

224 "great gourmet, too": White, *They Were Expendable*, p. 156.

"You fight 'em and I'll fix 'em": ibid., p. 157.

225 observed no explosion: Bulkley, *At Close Quarters*, p. 21.

226 cruiser's searchlight dimmed: Winslow, *The Fleet the Gods Forgot*, p. 79.

227 "stone cold and black": Ira Wolfert, *American Guerilla in the Philippines*, pp. 13–14.

"thought he was a goner": White, *They Were Expendable*, p. 167.

228 searching the water back of us: ibid., p. 169.

229 "save our wounded men": Breuer, *The Sea Wolf*, p. 81.

"give him a decent burial": White, *They Were Expendable*, pp. 175–76.

230 "flipped the boat over": Wolfert, *An American Guerilla in the Philippines*, p. 19.

"isn't the least of it": ibid., p. 24.

Chapter Nineteen

235 "strafing the automobiles": White, *They Were Expendable*, pp. 183–84.

236 "last I ever heard of them": ibid., p. 182.

237 "learned how to live alone": Wolfert, *An American Guerilla in the Philippines*, p. VII.

238 "I had a priority": ibid., p. 42.

239 "same thing as castration": John Keats, *They Fought Alone*, p. 10.

240 "they'll make you an admiral": ibid., pp. 293–94.

"it took me days": White, *They Were Expendable*, pp. 191–92.

"In those days in the jungle": ibid., p. 188.

242 "I doubt they'll send any more": ibid., pp. 196–97.

"he hasn't got them": ibid., p. 203.

Chapter Twenty

243 Slept for thirty-six hours: Breuer, *The Sea Wolf*, p. 85.

244 "No way is MacArthur": ibid., p. 85.

"very fine beard": Bachman, *An Honorable Profession*, pp. 203–4.

245 "don't add or subtract anything": Breuer, *The Sea Wolf*, p. 88.

250 "Business before pleasure": ibid., p. 97.

"could choose only a small number": Nigel Hamilton, *Reckless Youth*, p. 503.

251 "turned away from the gates": Stade, *Twelve Handkerchiefs*, p. 88.

252 "Mission accomplished": Bachman, *An Honorable Profession*, p. 43–44.

"that's what I would do": Breuer, *The Sea Wolf*, p. 102.

"Despite MacArthur's warning to him": ibid., p. 102.

Epilogue

255 exaggerated reputation: Bern Keating, *Mosquito Fleet*, pp. 16–17.

256 desperate need for victories: ibid., pp. 17–18.

almost felt sorry: ibid., p. 19.

257 "Bulkeley was really a joke": Hamilton, *Reckless Youth*, p. 501.

an act of genius: Nelson, *Hunters in the Shallows*, p. 149.

259 "help sagging morale": Manchester, *American Caesar*, p. 235.

260 "grim reality of defeat": James Webb, *The Emperor's General*, pp. 104–5.

Marshall was surprised and distressed: Schultz, *Hero of Bataan*, p. 335.

Wainwright had carried the load: Webb, *The Emperor's General*, p. 106.

261 "You write them, then send them to me": Schultz, *Hero of Bataan*, p. 404.

261 "play actor and bunco man": ibid., p. 418.
262 "good thing for mankind": Edward J. Drea, *MacArthur's Ultra*, p. 16.
  Lonely, angry man: Manchester, *American Caesar*, p. 275.
263 "a debilitating emptiness?": Webb, *The Emperor's General*, p. 36.
  "in the Philippines": Manchester, *American Caesar*, p. 166.
  "a lying bastard!": Bachman, *An Honorable Profession*, p. 92.

Selected Bibliography

Ambrose, Stephen E. *To America*. New York: Simon & Schuster, 2002.

Bachman, Bruce M. *An Honorable Profession*. New York: Vantage Press, 1985.

Beck, John J. *MacArthur and Wainwright*. Albuquerque, NM: Desert Press, 1974.

Blair, Clay, Jr. *Silent Victory*. New York: J. P. Lippincott Co., 1975.

Breuer, William B. *Sea Wolf*. Novato, CA: Presidio Press, 1989.

Buckley, Robert J., Jr. *At Close Quarters*. Annapolis, MD: U.S. Government Printing Office, 1962.

Bulkeley, John D. Personal papers. Abilene, KS: Dwight Eisenhower Library, 1970.

Daws, Gavan. *Prisoners of the Japanese*. New York: William Morrow & Co., 1994.

Drea, Edward J. *MacArthur's Ultra*. Lawrence, KS: University Press of Kansas 1952.

Ferrell, Robert H. *The Eisenhower Diaries*. New York: W.W. Norton & Co., 1981.

Goodwin, Doris Kearns. *No Ordinary Time*. New York: Simon and Schuster, 1994.

Gunther, John. *Riddle of MacArthur*. New York: Harper & Brothers, 1950.

Hamilton, Nigel. *Reckless Youth*. New York: Random House, 1992.

Hatch, Alden. *Heros of Annapolis*. New York: Julian Messner Inc., 1943.

Hersey, John. *Men on Bataan*. New York: Alfred A. Knopf, 1942.

Hoagland, Edgar D. *The Sea Hawks*. Novato, CA: Presidio Press, 1999.

Holbrook, Stewart H. *None More Courageous*. New York: MacMillan Co., 1942.

Huff, Sidney L. *My Fifteen Years With MacArthur*. New York: Lippincott Co., 1964.

Karig, Walter, and Welbourn Kelley. *Battle Report*. New York: Rinehart and Co., 1944.

Keating, Bern. *Mosquito Fleet*. New York: G. P. Putnam's Sons, 1963.

Keats, John. *They Fought Alone*. Philadelphia: J. B. Lippincott Co., 1963.

Kelley, Frank, and Cornelius Ryan. *MacArthur: Man of Action*. Garden City, NY: Doubleday, 1950.

Knox, Donald. *Death March*. New York: Harcourt Brace, 1981.

Leckie, Robert. *Delivered From Evil*. New York: Harper & Row, 1987.

Lee, Clark. *They Call It Pacific*. New York: Viking Press, 1943.

Lee, Clark, and Richard Henschel. *Douglas MacArthur*. New York: Henry Holt & Co., 1952.

MacArthur, Douglas. *Reminiscences*. New York: McGraw-Hill Book Co., 1964.

Manchester, William. *American Caesar*. New York: Little Brown & Co., 1978.

Mellnik, Steve. *Philippine Diary 1939–1945*. New York: Van Nostrand Reinhold Co., 1969.

Morrill, John. *South From Corregidor*. New York: Simon and Schuster, 1943.

Morris, Eric. *Corregidor, The End of the Line*. New York: Stein and Day, 1981.

Nelson, Curtis L. *Hunters in the Shallows*. Washington, DC: Brassey's, 1998.

Norman, Elizabeth M. *We Band of Angels*. New York: Random House, 1999.

Romulo, Carlos P., *I Saw the Fall of the Philippines*. Garden City, NY: Doubleday, 1946.

Schultz, Duane. *Hero of Bataan*. New York: St. Martin's Press, 1981.

Spector, Ronald H. *Eagle Against the Sun*. New York: The Free Press, 1985.

Stade, Joan Bulkeley. *Twelve Handkerchiefs*. Tucson, AZ: Patrice Press, 2001.

Toland, John. *But Not in Shame*. New York: Random House, 1961.

————. *The Rising Sun*. New York: Random House, 1970.

Twining, Merrill. *No Bended Knee*. Novato, CA: Presidio Press, 1996.

Wainwright, Jonathan. *General Wainwright's Story*. Garden City, NY: Doubleday, 1945.

Webb, James. *The Emperor's General*, New York: Broadway Books, 1999.

Whitcomb, Edgar. *Escape From Corregidor*. Chicago: Henry Regnery Co., 1958.

White, W. L. *They Were Expendable*. New York: Harcourt Brace & Co., 1942.

Whitney, Courtney. *MacArthur, His Rendezvous With History*. New York: Knopf, 1956.

Winslow, W. G. *The Fleet the Gods Forgot*. Annapolis, MD: Naval Institute Press, 1982.

Wolfert, Ira. *An American Guerrilla in the Philippines*. New York: Simon and Schuster, 1945.

Index